Charles Bukowski

Twayne's United States Authors Series

Frank Day, Editor

Clemson University

TUSAS 684

CHARLES BUKOWSKI
Michael Montfort

Charles Bukowski

Gay Brewer

Middle Tennessee State University

Twayne Publishers
An Imprint of Simon & Schuster Macmillan
New York

Prentice Hall International
London • Mexico City • New Delhi • Singapore • Sydney • Toronto

Twayne's United States Authors Series No. 684

Charles Bukowski
Gay Brewer

Twayne Publishers
An Imprint of Simon & Schuster Macmillan
1633 Broadway
New York, New York 10019

Library of Congress Cataloging-in-Publication Data

Brewer, Gay, 1965–
    Charles Bukowski / Gay Brewer.
        p.   cm. — (Twayne's United States authors series ; no. 684)
    Includes bibliographical references and index.
    ISBN 0-8057-4558-0 (hardcover)
    1. Bukowski, Charles—Criticism and interpretation.   I. Title.
    II. Series: Twayne's United States authors series ; TUSAS 684.
PS3552.U4Z56   1997
811'.54—dc21   97-5880
                                                               CIP

10 9 8 7 6 5 4

Printed in the United States of America

*For Daniel R. Barnes
and Francis R. Ginanni*

Contents

Preface

Charles Bukowski's popularity in America reached a peak in 1987–88 with the release of the Barbet Schroeder film *Barfly* and in recent years since his death in 1994 has continued to increase dramatically.[1] *Barfly*'s attendant media attention found Bukowski interviewed in film magazines and even the grocery-aisle weekly *People*, while the poet reportedly turned down offers to appear on *The Tonight Show* and *60 Minutes*. Eyes squinted, grinning, amused but vaguely disgusted by the fanfare, Bukowski told the reporters how it had been, how it was, and, as always, stylishly embellished history with fiction. During the 1990s, his Hollywood flirtation ended, Bukowski continued to productively and quietly work in his San Pedro home. As it had been for nearly 40 years, his focus was on the poem, his lifeline to sanity, to immediate reclamation of daily events, and to the transformation of the mundane into the extraordinary. The reputation that he had cultivated for so long, of a gruff and durable old lion, continued to solidify. A one-man theatrical show, *Buk: The Life and Times of Charles Bukowski*, was composed from his writings. The biography *Hank* was released by Random House. Inevitably, graduate-school scholarship focused on the author.[2] The small-press fanzine *Sure, the Charles Bukowski Newsletter*, a journal of pastiches and brief essays, began publication. Perhaps most significant, *Run with the Hunted: A Charles Bukowski Reader* was released in 1993 by HarperCollins, Bukowski's first publication from a major New York commercial press. Edited by his longtime publisher and editor, John Martin, the 500-page volume, chronologically arranged according to events in Bukowski's life, testifies to the writer's achievement.

Predictably, Bukowski's death in 1994 from leukemia initiated a flurry of small-press tribute issues and memoirs from acquaintances and friends. A poem was published in *Poetry*, arguably the most prestigious poetry magazine in America, and another on the cover of *Prairie Schooner*, accompanied by one of Bukowski's trademark doodles.[3] A lengthy obituary was featured on page 1 of the *Los Angeles Times*, and the *Village Voice* noted that "at the Grammys recently, Bono quoted Bukowski to Frank Sinatra, which is almost as bleak and funny as any-

thing Bukowski ever wrote."[4] Still, despite such apparent cultural inte-
gration and gradual signs of weakening in academe's hostility, it is difficult to predict the fate of Bukowski's popular and especially critical reputation, as well as how long the mythos of Bukowski, which he actively
perpetuated, will mingle with the reception of his work. Most of the
scant criticism written during the author's life was either adoring or
damning, with little middle ground, and both approaches tend to
embrace myopic readings of his voluminous oeuvre. Russell Harrison's
Against the American Dream: Essays on Charles Bukowski, published by
Black Sparrow in 1994, is remarkable not only for being the first truly
full-length critical study of its subject but also for attempting balanced
scholarship and historical context. I hope that the present volume,
Charles Bukowski, also assists in a fair and full assessment of Bukowski's
literary significance.

The greatest challenge in writing this book was thoroughly and
coherently accounting for Bukowski's prodigious body of published
work, and I have opted for the expedient of concentrating on the standard and available Black Sparrow and City Lights editions. Most of the
biographical information contained in the brief first chapter is reiterated
later in relation to appropriate texts. Bukowski wrote from experience,
although the extent of his craft has generally been underacknowledged
by both supporters and detractors. At its best, his work earns its under-
standings, its truths, and its discoveries through a direct and honest
apprehension of experience, without outside ideas imposed. Charles
Bukowski's writing continued to evolve as he grew older, and the poetry
in particular strives toward increasing simplicity, directness, and, most
radically, a rejection of metaphor. Many of his later short stories are
remarkable for their control, economy, and subtlety. In the opinion of
many, including the author himself, his best writing was done in his sixties, long after some readers had noted a supposed slippage in ability.
Throughout, his allegiance to the creative act as a redemptive and reju-
venating ritual remained paramount.

No attempt has been made to include a primary bibliography of
Bukowski's periodical publications. He published thousands of poems
and stories beginning primarily in the late 1950s, in the hundreds of
small-press magazines that were the cornerstone of his career. Many,
even most, of these magazines were small and poorly distributed and by
nature disappeared quickly. The secondary bibliography includes the
most significant articles and reviews of Bukowski's work and everything
concerning the author that is cited in this volume. Again, the number of

obscure small-press essays written on Bukowski, especially during his truly underground notoriety during the 1960s and 1970s, makes compiling an exhaustive secondary bibliography virtually impossible.

Luckily for Bukowski's many readers, collections of posthumous poetry will continue to appear into the next century. The author exaggerated that Black Sparrow has "a whole drawer full. . . . I'll be dead and there'll be a book coming out every year for 15 years."[5] Self-effacing humor, anticipation of death, and skepticism toward any rarefied conceit for art are typically Bukowskian. Once dead, he would have no choice but to consign his work and reputation to the hands of the living, and he warned in advance of trusting the unavoidable revisionism of literary history:

> one thing I do
> know: when a man is
> living
> many claim relationships
> that are hardly
> so
> and after he dies, well,
> then it's everybody's
> party.[6]

I am indebted to the Faculty Research Committee, Middle Tennessee State University, for the grant that allowed me time to write two chapters of this text. Several generous individuals were instrumental in the collection of materials and in the preparation of the volume: I would like to thank Betty McFall, MTSU Interlibrary Loan, whose continual helpfulness and detective work in the location of secondary sources was invaluable; Charley Durham, for encouraging me to undertake the project; Kevin Griffith, for copying relevant material from Ohio State and elsewhere; John Martin, of Black Sparrow Press, for helpfulness with information regarding Bukowski's life, easiness to work with regarding permissions, and generous commitment of time in reading proofs; Michael Montfort, for his willing offer of photographs and general encouragement; Gundolf Freyermuth, for the manuscript of his *Notes of a Dirty Old Man Dying*; Impressions Book and Journal Services, Inc., for their very valuable contributions in editing and production; Martin Hester, of Avisson Press, for sending an advance copy of material regarding Bukowski from *Miller, Bukowski, and Their Enemies*; Edward L. Smith, for back issues of *Sure, the Charles Bukowski Newsletter*; Jeffrey Weinberg, proprietor of Water Row Books; Claudia Barnett, for her support, enthusiasm, and loan of a computer to revise this manuscript; and Jasper, for his vigilance and unfaltering companionship. I don't think the book could have been written without him.

Grateful acknowledgment goes to Black Sparrow Press for permission to quote from its many volumes of poetry and prose by Charles Bukowski, and to City Lights Books for permission to quote from its three volumes of Bukowski short prose.

Chronology

1958   Divorce finalized 18 March. Henry Bukowski Sr. dies 4
       December. After two decades of short-term labor jobs,
       begins a position with the postal service. Jane Cooney
       Baker dies at age 49 of excessive drinking.

1960   *Flower, Fist and Bestial Wail*, a pamphlet of poems in an
       edition of 200, is published by Hearse Press in October.

1962   Meets Frances Smith. *Longshot Pomes for Broke Players*
       and *Run with the Hunted*.

1963   *The Outsider* 3, published by Jon Webb, names
       Bukowski "Outsider of the Year." Webb's Loujon Press
       elaborately hand prints *It Catches My Heart in Its Hands:
       New and Selected Poems 1955–1963*.

1964   Marina Louise Bukowski born to Charles Bukowski
       and Frances Smith 7 September. Meets John Martin.

1965   Returns to New Orleans in March. Writes many of the
       poems that appear in *Crucifix in a Deathhand*, pub-
       lished that year by Loujon Press in an elaborate edition
       of 3,100. *Cold Dogs in the Courtyard* and *Confessions of a
       Man Insane Enough to Live with Beasts*.

1966   Begins corresponding with Carl Weissner, his later
       German translator and European agent. John Martin
       forms Black Sparrow Press and publishes broadsides of
       Bukowski's poems in the spring and summer. *The
       Genius of the Crowd* and *All the Assholes in the World and
       Mine*.

1967   Begins writing "Notes of a Dirty Old Man" column for
       Open City, a Los Angeles alternative newspaper.

1968   *At Terror Street and Agony Way* published by Black Spar-
       row. *Poems Written before Jumping out of an 8 Story Window*.

1969   With Neeli Cherry (Cherkovski), begins the literary
       review *Laugh Literary and Man the Humping Guns*,
       which publishes three issues from 1969 to 1972. Pub-
       lished with Harold Norse and Philip Lamantia in Pen-
       guin Modern Poets Series, no. 13. *Notes of a Dirty Old
       Man* and *The Days Run Away like Wild Horses over the
       Hills*. At age 49, resigns from post office to pursue
       career as professional writer, with a promise of $100
       per month support from John Martin.

1970   Completes *Post Office* in three weeks.

1971   *Post Office.*

1972   *Mockingbird Wish Me Luck* and *Erections, Exhibitions and General Tales of Ordinary Madness.*

1973   Taylor Hackford documentary *Bukowski* debuts on KCET-TV, Los Angeles, 25 November; viewers file protests with the FCC, but the film wins best cultural program of the year from the Corporation for Public Broadcasting. *South of No North.*

1974   *Poems Written before Jumping out of an 8 Story Window*, translated by Carl Weissner, sells 50,000 copies in Germany. *Burning in Water, Drowning in Flame: Selected Poems 1955–1973.*

1975   *Factotum.*

1976   Meets Linda Lee Beighle at a reading in September.

1977   *Love Is a Dog from Hell.*

1978   Visits Germany; on 17 May, Bukowski's reading in Hamburg draws over 1,200 people. In October, appears on the French television talk show *Apostrophes* and walks off set. *Women.*

1979   Signs contract with Barbet Schroeder to write a screenplay. Buys a house and moves to San Pedro. *Play the Piano Drunk like a Percussion Instrument Until the Fingers Begin to Bleed a Bit* and *Shakespeare Never Did This.*

1981   *Dangling in the Tournefortia.*

1982   *Ham on Rye.*

1983   *Hot Water Music.*

1984   *War All the Time.*

1985   Marries Linda Lee Beighle 18 August.

1986   *You Get So Alone at Times That It Just Makes Sense.*

1987   In February, filming begins on *Barfly*, directed by Barbet Schroeder from a screenplay by Charles Bukowski, starring Mickey Rourke and Faye Dunaway. The film premieres in the fall. *The Movie: "Barfly."*

1988   *The Roominghouse Madrigals: Early Selected Poems 1946–1966.*

Chapter One

Introductions

Biography

Henry Charles Bukowski was born on 16 August 1920 in Andernach, Germany. His father, Henry Bukowski Sr., an American GI serving in World War I, had met and married Katherine Fett while stationed in Andernach. The Bukowski family lived for a while in Germany, but then, homesick for America, Henry Bukowski Sr. returned with his family to the United States in 1923. They soon settled in Los Angeles.

Two events during the 1930s appear to have been especially central in Charles Bukowski's adolescence and subsequently in his development as a man and a writer. Henry Bukowski Sr., who lost his job as a milk deliveryman during the depression, grew increasingly abusive toward his son, frequently taking the boy into the bathroom and beating him with a razor strop. Bukowski documents this abuse by his father in horrible detail in the novel *Ham on Rye,* and throughout Bukowski's work the figure of the menacing, mean-spirited father, misshapen and made cruel by a failed American dream of wealth and progress, is predominant.

The second central event in young Charles Bukowski's life seems to have begun in 1934, between his graduation from Mount Vernon Junior High and the beginning of his sophomore year at Los Angeles High School. An acute case of *acne vulgaris,* manifesting itself as large, disfiguring boils, appeared on the boy's face, shoulders, and back. In 1935 he underwent lengthy and painful treatments of drilling and radiation at Los Angeles County Hospital, during that period missing a semester of school. Isolated and self-conscious about his physical appearance, Bukowski apparently wrote his first short story later that year, featuring the exploits of the World War I flying ace Baron Manfred Von Richthofen.

In 1939 Bukowski enrolled at Los Angeles City College and took classes in journalism and English. By this time, his father's beatings had culminated in a violent response from the son. Bukowski was living on his own and had discovered alcohol. For more than 40 years, he would drink for escape, for release, and without apology. He often wrote of his

1

discovery of wine—which took place in the basement of a friend's house, with the friend's father's wine casks—as a magical turning point in his life, one that allowed him to survive an abusive father, a disfiguring skin condition, and a turbulent life of poverty and obscurity. Bukowski commented decades later, "I have a feeling that drinking is a form of suicide where you're allowed to return to life and begin all over the next day. It's like killing yourself, and then you're reborn. I guess I've lived about ten or fifteen thousand lives by now."[1] In 1941, disenchanted with academics and formal education, the young man left Los Angeles City College without graduating.

During the 1940s, Bukowski attempted to remain uninvolved in America's renewed war interests. Probably in 1942 he took a bus to New Orleans, then joined a railroad crew to work his way back to Los Angeles. This trip was the beginning of several peripatetic years in which Bukowski crossed and recrossed the country, spending time in Philadelphia, New York City, St. Louis, Atlanta, and many other cities, periodically returning to Los Angeles. In late 1942, he was arrested in a Philadelphia rooming house by FBI agents. The charge of draft evasion was partly a mistake due to Bukowski's failure to register his frequent changes of address. He spent 17 days in Moyamensing Prison and then, after psychiatric examination, was exempted from service in World War II, perhaps for antisocial tendencies.

In 1944, while working as a warehouse packer in St. Louis, Bukowski had a short story, "Aftermath of a Lengthy Rejection Slip," accepted by Whit Burnett's prestigious *Story* magazine, and in 1946 his "Twenty Tanks from Kasseldown" appeared in *Portfolio: An International Review*. Despite these early rumblings of success, Bukowski, worn down by several years of traveling, drinking, menial jobs, and literary obscurity, returned to Los Angeles in 1946. Apparently by choice, he quit writing and dedicated the subsequent decade to drinking and physical survival. These years of alcoholic bingeing, shared with Jane Cooney Baker, whom he met in 1946, constitute a large portion of the infamous "barfly" years upon which much of the Bukowski myth was built.

This part of the author's life culminated in 1955 when he was taken by ambulance to Los Angeles County Hospital with a bleeding ulcer caused by alcoholism. Bukowski claimed to have received 11 pints of blood and was expected to die. Days later, miraculously alive, he left the charity ward with strict orders never to take another drink. He soon began drinking again, and, more importantly, he began writing. This time the genre was poetry.

Bukowski was soon publishing in the small presses. He traded correspondence with Barbara Frye, editor of the Texas magazine *Harlequin*,
and partly as a joke proposed to her in a letter. Charles Bukowski and
Barbara Frye were married in Las Vegas in the fall, and during 1955 and
1956 the couple spent several months in Wheeler, Texas, where Frye's
wealthy family lived. The couple then returned to Los Angeles, and on
18 March 1958, following a struggle of incompatible lifestyles, their
divorce was finalized. Henry Bukowski Sr. died on 4 December of the
same year. Following two decades of short-term labor positions and
unemployment, Bukowski began work with the postal service, where he
would remain for nearly 12 years. Also during this period, Jane Cooney
Baker, with whom Bukowski had become reacquainted, died at the age
of 49 of excessive drinking. The author would lament her death and celebrate her life for decades in his writing.

Beginning in the late 1950s, Bukowski published increasing amounts
in the "little" magazines. Pamphlets of his poems, beginning with
Flower, Fist and Bestial Wail in 1960, started to appear. Aided by, and
instrumental in, the so-called mimeograph revolution, which enabled
literary reviews to be printed easily and inexpensively, the author's
stature as an underground poet, perhaps "the" underground poet, flour-
ished. In 1963, *The Outsider* 3, published by Jon Webb, named
Bukowski "Outsider of the Year," with an accompanying cover photo
and special section in the issue. Meanwhile, Bukowski's daughter,
Marina, was born to Frances Smith in 1964. During these years he continued to work full-time at the post office, a job he felt to be increasingly draining and physically, mentally, and spiritually debilitating.

Bukowski's underground career in part climaxed with the appearance
of two elaborate and lovingly printed volumes from Jon and Louise
Webb's Loujon Press, *It Catches My Heart in Its Hands* in 1963 and *Crucifix in a Deathhand* in 1965. Despite the writer's renegade reputation
during this time as a boozing, volatile, and womanizing rogue, a recollection by Steve Richmond of his first meeting with Bukowski, in 1965,
suggests that the older poet's public persona was already obscuring the
dedication and serious intent of Bukowski the writer: "Papers and pens
and paper clips, etc., are also on top of Hank's desk. It's all very neatly
organized. Immediately I can see Hank's extreme focus and self discipline, just by the way his working papers are so neat, so organized, perfect order. Hank is waging a campaign and his supplies and how he
keeps them will definitely not be his undoing. He is taking over modern
literature, that's all, he's taking over."[2] In 1967, Bukowski's weekly col-

umn "Notes of a Dirty Old Man" began appearing in the alternative newspaper *Open City*, giving Bukowski a wider and more immediate audience and further spreading his underground fame in Los Angeles. In early 1969, Bukowski and coeditor Neeli Cherkovski founded the literary review *Laugh Literary and Man the Humping Guns*. Three issues appeared.

Perhaps the single most important decision in the author's career came at the end of 1969. In November, at the age of 49, Bukowski resigned from the postal service in the hopes of becoming a professional writer. He was bolstered by an offer of $100 per month in perpetuity by John Martin, who in 1964 had met Bukowski and subsequently founded Black Sparrow Press to publish him. The importance of Bukowski's relationship with Martin, and the stability and freedom allowed him by his long relationship with Black Sparrow, can hardly be overstated. "Black Sparrow promised me $100 a month for life if I quit my job and tried to be a writer. Nobody else even knew I was alive. Why shouldn't I be loyal forever."[3]

Bukowski wrote *Post Office*, his first novel, in three weeks in early 1970, and the book was published the following year. Yet another phase of his life and career had begun. "At the age of 50," recalled the author, "I quit my job and decided to become a professional writer, that is, one who gets paid for his scribblings. I figured either that or skidrow. I got lucky" (Ring, 36). For the rest of his explosive career, Bukowski was appreciative of his relatively late start and late success. "And it's a lucky thing to have been a working man until I was fifty. It kept me grounded in realities—dull, stupid realities, but they were there and it's part of everything" (Andrews, 166). Early literary acclaim, by contrast, had historically demonstrated its destructive allure, as Bukowski noted late in life to a discouraged younger writer: "You know what happens to those who get early success, the edge leaves and they fall away, they soften and vanish."[4]

Throughout the 1970s, Bukowski's literary stock continued to rise, particularly in Germany, where his work was translated and marketed by his European agent, Carl Weissner. In 1974, *Poems Written before Jumping out of an 8 Story Window* sold a staggering 50,000 copies in Germany, unprecedented for a collection of poems. By 1978, when Bukowski visited his native country and drew more than 1,200 for a poetry reading in Hamburg, his popularity there equaled a rock star's. This overseas success was particularly important for its financial advantages, which, along with the increasingly successful Black Sparrow editions, ensured the author's independence and artistic freedom. To Gerald Locklin, Bukowski's almost unrivaled freedom as a writer, "with plenty of money and permanently alienated from the literary establishment," accounts for much of his success: "Bukowski has no reason to compromise what may be the greatest freedom enjoyed by any published writer in American history."[5]

Further success, and the pinnacle of Bukowski's public recognition in America, was initiated when he signed a contract with Barbet Schroeder in 1979 to write a screenplay. The resulting script finally appeared as the film *Barfly* in 1987. Bukowski had during the interim moved from a Los Angeles apartment to a house in San Pedro in 1979, married Linda Lee Beighle in 1985, and begun to write with characteristic candor and humor about his fame, the BMW and expensive wines considered no less absurd than the decades of hunger and poverty. One critic noted that Bukowski wrote about his new life "with the same romanticized, even nonchalant sense of loss used in his earlier work."[6] The last 15 years of his life, until his death from leukemia on 9 March 1994, were productive years of monogamy, financial stability, and relative calm.

Bukowski's work evolved until the end, including his last novel, *Pulp*, published only weeks after his death, where "the weariness with the banal, the meaningless, the cruelty, just as before . . . [is] confused with the days he knew were his dying ones, his last time."[7] He claimed that he continually strove to make his later poetry "more and more bare, essential" in contrast to academic poetry "playing secret and staid games, snob and inbred games which are finally anti-life and anti-truth."[8] On another occasion, he elaborated that "there is nothing wrong with a poetry that is entertaining and easy to understand. Genius could be the ability to say a profound thing in a simple way."[9] The writer never retreated from his often-stated disappointment with the literary canon and with the tradition of poetry and its tendency toward preciousness. "The basic realities of the everyman existence . . . [are] something seldom mentioned in the poetry of the centuries. Just put me down as saying that the poetry of the centuries is shit. It's shameful."[10] And central to Bukowski's work, always, was his dedication to the process of creation and his belief in it as a regenerative necessity, a compulsive antidote to the tedium and disappointment of daily life and fellow humans. "If I stop writing I am dead. And that's the only way I'll stop: dead" (Ring, 37).

Contexts

Charles Bukowski's writings, like the man himself, resist classifications and categories. The influence of Ernest Hemingway has been well documented and was a debt that Bukowski frequently recognized, albeit often with tongue in cheek. Although he shares with Hemingway the central subject of the male psyche, a preoccupation with death, a heavy reliance on dialogue, and, at his best, a marvelous and evocative linguistic economy, Bukowski sets himself apart by his consistent use of humor. Hemingway's tragic fatalism is recast as absurd black comedy, and the implications of this recasting are far-reaching. Bukowski commented, "You know, we're monstrosities. If we could really see this, we could love ourselves . . . realize how ridiculous we are, with our intestines wound around, shit slowly running through as we look each other in the eyes and say 'I love you,' our stuff is carbonizing, turning into shit, and we never fart near each other. It all has a comic edge . . . And then we die. But, death has not earned us" (Penn, 96). His work also anticipated, and doubtlessly influenced, the "dirty realism" prominent in the 1970s and 1980s, particularly the stories of Raymond Carver.[11] But Bukowski's persistent focus on the lower class and his unrepentant use of drink and scatological idiom, in the context of his assault on academe and his ribald and insouciant humor, contribute to setting him apart stylistically and ideologically. These elements also account in part for the sometimes harsh critical reception of his work.

Bukowski remained faithful to poetry throughout his career. Verse seemed to remain his primary love, an allegiance that in itself conspicuously separates him from Hemingway and another writer to whom Bukowski is frequently compared, Henry Miller. Both Miller and Bukowski were brilliantly intuitive in turning biographical material into art with both exuberance and seeming ease. Doren Robbins, speaking also of Céline and Cendrars, notes that for Bukowski and Miller the "idea of being canonized is incomprehensible . . . what is indestructibly iconoclastic in literary tradition is implicit in their work; they exist with eminence whether they are integrated or not. . . . There is in each writer a kind of reckless liberty."[12] The reader senses an inimitable freedom in Bukowski and Miller, an immediacy, a sensuality, and a celebration of the exigencies of the body. Any reader of both authors, however, is struck not only by their dedication to different genres but by their radical dissimilarity, ultimately, in temperament. Miller's stance is typically one of aggressive embrace, Bukowski's generally one of self-imposed separation. Most telling, the lengthy philosophical and intellectual asides of Miller are clearly anathema to Bukowski, who increasingly in his writing avoids explanation, connections, even metaphor.

Yet despite their differences, Miller is perhaps more similar to Bukowski than any of their contemporaries, largely due to the spontaneity of the authors, the biographical component in their work, and the mythic personae surrounding them. In the essay "Hemingway and Miller," the distinctions Norman Mailer offers between his subjects demonstrate, in the context of Hemingway, Miller's comparability to Bukowski:

> With the exception of Hemingway, he has had perhaps the largest stylis-tic influence of them all. Yet there is still that critical space. Miller has only been written about in terms of adulation or dismissal. . . . The dif-ference between Hemingway and Miller is that Hemingway set out to grow into Jake Barnes and locked himself for better or worse, for enor-mous fame and eventual destruction, into that character who embodied the spirit of an age. . . . Without stoicism or good taste, or even a nose for the nicety of good guts under terrible pressure, Miller is still living closer to death than Hemingway, certainly he is closer if the sewer is nearer to our end than the wound.[13]

For both Miller and Bukowski, fictional and public personae were cru-cial to their art: "The real Henry Miller . . . is not very different from his work, but more like a transparency laid over a drawing, copied, and then skewed a degree. He is just a little different from his work. But in that difference is all the mystery of his own personality, and the para-doxes of a great artist" (Mailer, 86–87). For Bukowski, the shifting of experience into fiction, particularly in the novels, is a skillful method of selection and reorganization that is frequently overlooked by both admirers and detractors. Clearly, however, Bukowski's Henry Chinaski is a constructed persona, often behaving at a determinable distance from the writer Bukowski. This distance is particularly evident in the novel *Women*.

In an excellent essay on Bukowski's letters, Russell Harrison suggests that two personae emerge in the author's work, the more distanced and ironized Chinaski and the "more subtly differentiated" character who appears in poems, some short fiction, and implicitly in many first-person accounts and seems to more closely and directly represent the sentiment of Charles Bukowski the writer.[14] Such a distinction is as fully evident when one begins to separate Bukowski from his public persona of poseur, abusive performer, and violent curmudgeon whose writing is offhand and casual. For example, although he downplayed revision, Bukowski in interviews frequently mentioned retyping, changing words, and deleting lines. He clearly differentiated between himself and a public character constructed early and intentionally. "To get somebody to read your poems you have to be noticed, so I got my act up. . . . Actually, I am not a tough person and sexually, I am almost a prude, but I am a nasty drunk and many strange things happen to me when I am drunk. . . . I am ninety-three percent the person I present in my poems; the other seven percent is where art improves upon life" (*NYQ*, 322). The Bukowski image, like Hemingway's, was finally a self-aggrandizing burden perpetuated as much by his readers as by the author. The recent appearance of the author's extensive letters has been revelatory in demonstrating the difference between man and myth. His early letters, in particular, are far less mediated than work intended for publication. The man revealed is self-doubtful, pained, and above all dedicated to the trade of writing.

Bukowski is equally unclassifiable among his poetic contemporaries. In earlier decades, he was linked with the loose, poorly defined "Meat School" poets, who, according to one critic, "write in a tough, direct masculine manner about the concerns of the *lumpenproletariat*, as opposed to the anguished middle-class poets with precious or ambiguous styles."[15] The merits of such a classification are outweighed by its self-serving tone, and such a "school," in retrospect, appears to have comprised little more than Bukowski and a handful of slavish and largely forgotten followers. On a different note, although Robert Lowell is often credited with an influential insertion of idiomatic language into academic verse, this revolution was already well under way with Bukowski and other underground poets. Jack Grapes notes this incongruity in literary history according to the canon: "Robert Lowell's *Life Studies* is often cited as the work that changed the idiom of American poetry. The natural, spoken, confessional lyric. Whenever I read that, I'm always a bit surprised. This Orwellian rewriting of history, as if what goes on in the academic world is all that goes on in the world."[16] Harrison makes a crucial distinction between Bukowski's tone and Lowell's "privileging of the experiential content by virtue of a privileging of the poetic *persona* by some quality (status or unusual sensitivity). This is absent in Bukowski's poetry. . . . Indeed, Bukowski explicitly rejects the idea of his experience as critical, or culturally symbolic."[17]

A similar difference also separates Bukowski from the Beats, with whom he is often wrongly paired. "In Bukowski we now have the experience made significant by virtue of its proletarian quality, the opposite of its status under the Beats and the Confessionals. By removing the aura of privilege from this experience and revealing what Lowell (and the Beats) had in a way mystified and idealized, as ordinary proletarian pleasure(s), Bukowski registers a more significant change than the earlier poets" (Harrison, 43). The lack of an explicit political agenda in Bukowski's poems and his internalized focus on private and lower-class labor experience distinguish him from the more ideologically public, expansive, and reductively politicized Beats. Despite a qualified admiration for Ginsberg's poems, Bukowski's attitude toward the Beats remained consistent. The following late letter was reproduced in a memorial issue of *Beat Scene* dedicated fully to Bukowski: "The Beats somehow make me sad. It's like they just didn't come through. They hung together too much. And talked too much—about themselves. And they went for the media, the limelight. They slacked off on their work, their creation. It weakened. It's like they had no carry-through. Fame mattered more than just doing it."[18]

Bukowski's comments and work nearly always lead back to the writing act itself, a preemptive, conciliatory, and regenerative ritual that renders life livable. He expressed no interest in schools, movements, or explicit ideologies, instead attempting to write directly, with honesty and humor, of his experiences. "The old man speaks against a world that has failed, but a failure he refuses to accept. The way out is not through the dark hall where the landlady, the priest, the matador beckon. It is through pen and paper, in creating the poem, the artifact, the fossil emerged from living skin" (Grapes, 23). Once he resumed writing at the age of 35, Bukowski did not stop for nearly 40 years, not until his body failed him. The attempt of the romantic, experiential poet is, through the formulation and organization of that experience, to learn and prepare. Bukowski was obscene, resilient, and sui generis. His work is surprisingly resistant to defeat, to the destruction of talent by either the physical debilitation of poverty or the spiritual seductions of fame. "I've always been worried about my damn soul—maybe I worry too much. But you carry in one hand a bundle of darkness that accumulates each day. And when death finally comes, you say right away, 'Hey, buddy, glad to see ya!' "[19]

Chapter Two
The First Four Novels

Post Office

Charles Bukowski ended nearly 12 years of employment with the U.S. Postal Service in 1969 and at the age of 49 courageously began his first novel. Although he had been publishing poetry regularly in the small and underground presses, he was still an obscure author, and with the support of John Martin and the Black Sparrow Press, Bukowski immersed himself in the challenge of transforming his recent years of exploited and alienated labor into novelistic form. Neeli Cherkovski, Bukowski's biographer, recalls that the author "plunged into writing *Post Office* the day after he quit his job. . . . [H]e completed the manuscript in less than three weeks."[1]

Not only is *Post Office* a jarring criticism of bureaucratized labor in America, but it is also imbued with the typical Bukowski humor, usually self-deflating to his persona Henry Chinaski, almost always satirical. The position of postman is itself weighted not only with the tradition of an American institution but also with folkloristic humor. Jack Byrne notes that "even before Dagwood Bumstead, the postman was a source of neighborhood fun and hilarity captured over and over in the popular culture of the times."[2] Bukowski does not hesitate to display himself, through Chinaski, as society's fool. This tendency is established early in the novel, in a Chaplinesque dance between dog and mail carrier: "[T]here was a German Shepherd, full-grown, with his nose halfway up my ass. . . . I put the mail back into the leather pouch, and then very slowly, very, I took a half step forward. The nose followed. I took another half step with the other foot. The nose followed."[3] This slapstick physical comedy, with Chinaski as clown, segues into *Post Office*'s motif of performance: the protagonist alternately appears as con man, Billy-the-Kid tough guy, mail boss, humble employee, and Louisiana trapper. Sometimes these roles amount to little more than allowing a misconception by a second party; sometimes they are the exaggerated play of a prankster amusing himself by the exposure of public conceits.

Section 2 of the novel is an interlude between postal jobs that places Chinaski in an unlikely rural setting. Finding himself in a small Texas town and married into a millionaire's fortune, the protagonist mines the section for all its tall-tale, country-bumpkin possibilities. This is epitomized in the scene in which Chinaski knowingly submits himself to a family joke, an invitation to see buffalo:

> "The wind's right," said Wally. "Just climb in there and walk a ways. You've got to walk a ways to see them."
> There was nothing in the field. They thought they were being very funny, conning a city-slicker. I climbed the fence and walked on in. (*Post*, 59)

This scene exemplifies Bukowski's self-deprecating humor. Chinaski, who willingly submits himself to the amusement of the crowd, still doesn't expect the charging buffalo he barely escapes. The joke is on him, yes, but not quite the one he anticipated. His willing gullibility is replaced by the exigency of physical safety. Still, he expected to look foolish, and despite Chinaski's claims of loving the small town, he seems trapped in a prolonged farmer's-daughter routine in which he is the victim.[4]

The motif of Chinaski as clown is also developed in a religious context. Particularly early in the novel, when the character is a substitute postal carrier, several allusions are offered for Chinaski as a comic Christ to supervisor Jonstone's arbitrary deity. Being called back to Jonstone's Oakford Station is going "back on the cross again" (*Post*, 18). The supervisor, referred to simply as "Stone" by Chinaski, wields an omnipotence that appears to include even weather and time. "It was one of those continuous rains, not hard, but it *never* stopped. . . . Jonstone in the Sky, have Mercy! I was lost in the dark and the rain. *Was* I some kind of idiot, actually? Did I make things happen to myself?" (*Post*, 27). Having struggled back to the station through the flood, Chinaski and colleague Tom Moto discuss their ontological position and Jonstone's influence:

> I walked over, punched out, then stripped to my shorts and stood in front of a heater. I hung my clothes over the heater. Then I looked across the room and there by another heater stood Tom Moto in *his* shorts.
> We both laughed.
> "It's hell, isn't it?" he asked.
> "Unbelievable."

"Do you think The Stone planned it?"
"Hell yes! He even made it rain!" (*Post,* 30)

The exchange is typical of Bukowski. Both men are stripped and once again reduced to clown or fool. Both refer to the hell of life and answer their damnation with laughter. Chinaski is shown not to be alone in his belief of Jonstone's treatment of the forsaken workers; it is Tom Moto who first suggests their boss's engineering of disaster.

References in *Post Office* to organized religion show that institution clearly inadequate in meeting the needs of the lost and the damned. Chinaski is confused by an empty church and unsure of its delivery address; ultimately, its only uses for him are a swig of communion wine and a private "service" on the church commode, in the dark. Chinaski unwillingly accepts his role as substitute savior, employing colloquial uses of "hell," "Jesus," and "Christ" frequently. "For Christ's sake, I thought, who in hell but me would ever get caught in a scene like this? I picked up the wine, had a good drag, left the letters on the robes, and walked back to the showers and toilets. I turned off the lights and took a shit in the dark and smoked a cigarette" (*Post,* 22). Bukowski establishes the satirical connection between an absent redeemer and his own humble protagonist, a drunken prophet of nothing languishing under the burden of his failed message. "The whiskey and beer ran out of me, fountained from the armpits, and I drove along with this load on my back like a cross, pulling out magazines, delivering thousands of letters, staggering, welded to the side of the sun" (*Post,* 39). The wording of this passage, with another direct mention of crucifixion and oblique references to communion, stigmata, and the sun/son, is conspicuous.

Throughout the early chapters of *Post Office,* Chinaski is besieged by the lost and the lonely, the grotesque, the abandoned, and the forlorn, all of whom are dependent on him for salvation. "Lady, I don't have a letter for you" (*Post,* 39). Are bills all he can bring? inquire the disinherited. "Yes, ma'am, that's all I can bring you" (*Post,* 40). Chinaski is a failed savior who, barely distinguishable from those he walks among, also refuses to assume the full burden of their mutual drama. "I turned and walked on. It wasn't my fault that they used telephones and gas and light and bought all their things on credit" (*Post,* 40). Appropriately, the novel begins during the Christmas season, but Chinaski warns that the post office would "hire damned near anybody" (*Post,* 13) to put a leather sack on his back and trudge along the cheerless streets. The job of

Santa/clown, the responsibility of saint without gifts or message, is a "trick" (*Post*, 13) any drunk can undertake.

The culmination of the Jonstone/God and Chinaski/Christ plot ends section 1. After another silly and arbitrary passing down of law from "god" to man, this one involving where workers may place their caps, Chinaski denies Jonstone three times, discarding unread each of three consecutive memos. The law of the father is revoked. "I looked at him, and then dropped the write-up into the wastebasket without reading it. . . . The Stone went back to his chair and sat down. He didn't type anymore. He just sat looking at me" (*Post*, 49–50). Immediately afterward, thematically consistent with Chinaski's rejection, he resigns as carrier. He has nothing to deliver to the people. Indeed, throughout *Post Office*, Chinaski stringently avoids the company of others; their voices assault him. His separation from the post office, however, is short-lived. He quits his job at an art store and returns in the new position as clerk/sorter (a rejection of the rarefied "art" space for a return to the source of the writer's true material, the crippling world of men working) primarily because the art manager Freddy whistles all day. At the post office, the unpublished novelist Janko sits next to Chinaski to "complain and rant, night after long night, about the misery buried deep in his twisted and pissed soul," sending the protagonist "home each night dizzy and sick. He was murdering me with the sound of his voice" (*Post*, 127). Chinaski wants no confessions, no soul sharing with the lost who gravitate toward him throughout Bukowski's oeuvre. Working in the world of men, with its exploitative demands for physical labor, exacts both physical and mental costs: "When the tub was full I was afraid to get into it. My sore body had, by then, stiffened to such an extent that I was afraid I might drown in there. . . . I couldn't get settled. Every time I moved, it cost me. The only time you are alone, Chinaski, I thought, is when you are driving to work or driving back" (*Post*, 144).

The representations of orthodox religion that appear in *Post Office* have little efficacy for Chinaski. Shortly after he is burned by a falling Christmas tree, "the pointed star coming down like a dagger" (*Post*, 108), his renewed relationship with Betty ends with her death by alcohol poisoning. These scenes are the most poignant in the novel. Chinaski sees Betty's coming death in her eyes, eyes showing a lifetime of disappointment and betrayal, and he is unable to stop it. One of the rare occasions Bukowski shows Chinaski losing his blasé composure is at Betty's deathbed. "I'll bet if that were the president or governor or

mayor or some rich son of a bitch, there would be doctors all over that
room doing *something!* Why do you just let them die? What's the sin in
being poor?" (*Post*, 111). The slip into the plural pronoun betrays Chinaski as social critic; he too is impotent to do more, he too is a victim. It
is an uncustomary moment of tenderness and vulnerability, a bit embar-
rassing, and therein lies the scene's power. After Betty is dead, her
estranged son arrives in a new Mercedes-Benz. "That's when he stopped
seeing his mother, when he got that good job" (*Post*, 112).

Post Office presents an American class system in which the ethical
base, the god, is unmistakably money. The funeral ritual, intended to
solace the living and release the dead, is meaningless but is carried out
for want of anything better. Even the difficulty of hiring a priest seems
class based. "There was some doubt that Betty was a true Catholic. The
priest didn't want to do the service. Finally it was decided that he would
be half a service" (*Post*, 113). The implication is that Betty's poverty and
alcoholism cast doubt on her identity as a "true" Catholic. Bukowski
writes the brief funeral scene in flat, staccato sentences emphasizing
Chinaski's jagged isolation and the moment's lack of spiritual solace.
"The priest read his thing. I didn't listen. There was the coffin. What
had been Betty was in there. It was very hot" (*Post*, 114).

Christ appears in the novel only as exclamation and ineffective exple-
tive, as when Chinaski notes the name's imposition into orgasm. "It
seemed to last and last. Then I rolled off. 'Oh Jesus Christ,' I said, 'Oh
Jesus Christ!' I don't know how Jesus Christ always got into such
things" (*Post*, 141). This wry comment nevertheless achieves its dual
meaning, the unavoidable imposition of Christianity that pervades even
common speech, and yet the act and location where Chinaski may find a
rare moment of release almost akin to worship: "I finally worked her
clothing off and I was in. It was hard getting in. Then she gave way. It
was one of the best. I heard the water, I heard the tide going in and out.
It was as if I were coming with the whole ocean" (*Post*, 141). This is as
close to a communion as Chinaski experiences, and following the pattern of the novel, it too is soon undercut.

One critic noted that Bukowski in his writing "approached a level of
immediate experience that was almost religious in nature."[5] The
author's insistence on immediacy, particularly in *Post Office*, implies
much of the truth of Chinaski's "doctrine." The novel comprises a series
of risings and fallings in fortune. Each time Chinaski feels better about
his life or himself, or indulges in the fantasy of a rich or comfortably
domestic life, those conceits are deflated by the next attack of work,

women, or authority. A consideration of individual submission underlies it all. "And it's clear that this world—of bondage—was made possible only through one utterly ironic condition: man's acceptance of tyranny" and "the process of *Post Office* is one that continually strips Bukowski down; yet each time this occurs, he pulls himself up with purified vision" (Glazier, 40). Although on the one hand Chinaski accepts, demurs, and drops out, his elasticity is central to his indefatigability. "What is important throughout *Post Office*," writes Harrison, "is that Chinaski refuses to accept the alienated situation as normal" (139). Glazier adds that "Chinaski's value as antihero is his resiliency, his ascension from the 'death' of blind obedience. He speaks no language but the real. There is no swaying, no circumnavigating the issues" (41). This courage to face always forward, to deny nothing that is true or real— synonymous terms in Bukowski—is Chinaski's strength.

The comic Christ (or perhaps more accurately, comic Antichrist) motif that Bukowski establishes in the novel's first section is suggested again in the sixth and final section. Chinaski accuses a counselor of wanting to "hang" (*Post*, 180) him as a scapegoat for the imperfection of the work system. Shortly afterward, Chinaski inadvertently sets a room of mail on fire with his cigar, a harrowing of postal hell. "The flames were burning my hands. I *had* to save the United States mail, third-class junkmail!" The injury to the hands is telling and achieves another culminating moment in which Chinaski silences his god/boss. "The supervisor walked up to say something to me. I stood there with the burned catalogue in my hand and waited. He looked at me and walked off" (*Post*, 182). This scene anticipates Chinaski's final rejection of "the wisdom of the slave" (*Post*, 189). He quits the post office for the last time.

Bukowski argues in *Post Office* that only the crucial ingredient of money separates the low class from the high, those damned to a life of labor from those enjoying an existence of leisure. In his many years as a postal clerk, Chinaski never grows accustomed to the tedious and crippling work: "But the pay was better than at the art store. And, I thought, I might get used to it. I never got used to it" (*Post*, 68). The syntax of this passage is echoed later in the novel, during Chinaski's lucky phase at the racetrack and a leave of absence at the post office. "It was clean sheets, a hot shower, luxury. It was a magic life. And I did not tire of it" (*Post*, 138). At another point, when Fay thanks him for being kind during her birth labor, Chinaski responds, "I'd like to *be* nice. It's that god damned post office" (*Post*, 153). The connection here is clear: vitiating labor transforms men into grotesque parodies and battered, broken monsters. When the luck—that is, the money—holds, Chinaski is as willing and able as anyone to enjoy the luxuries of life, both in personal consumption and in generosity toward others. As the money goes, however, so goes the luck, and this grace period at the track ends with the intrusion of a woman. As long as Chinaski indulges in the hard-fought silence and privacy that he worships, his life is like a dream.

Bukowski does suggest that the common man, the laborer, may not only endure his existence but begin to instigate a modest salvation. One of the author's chief responses to the burden of life, found throughout his work, is laughter. Two things are bullishly consistent about Chinaski: his maintenance of a second life, a "real" life outside of the job (and usually to the disapproval of the bureaucratized system of labor), and his desire to laugh. "It was gung ho for a new man, especially one who drank all night, went to bed at 2 a.m., rose at 4:30 a.m. after screwing and singing all night long, and, almost, getting away with it" (*Post*, 21). Chinaski is conscious of the disparity between his work and nonwork hours and summarizes this antagonism after the post office sends a nurse to his apartment to corroborate a reported illness. "Damn, they won't let a man live at all, will they? They always want him at the wheel" (*Post*, 96). Laughter is frequent in Bukowski and necessary for the preservation of sanity, but often even the purest laughter of release is melancholy:

I tossed and turned, cursing, screaming a little, and laughing a little too, at the ridiculousness of it.

I laughed. It was a rather sad laugh, I'll admit. But it came out.

I sat across from Betty. She crossed her legs, kicked her heels, laughed a little. It was like old times. Almost. Something was missing. (*Post*, 81, 88, 93–94)

Chinaski's recalcitrance involves never fully submitting to the "moral" requirement of behavior delineated in the post office code of ethics and littering the novel in the jargon of official memos. Despite the fact that the post office is a permeating presence in his life for more than 11 years, he never fully submits and never relinquishes. "Chinaski does not simply *express* this philosophy: his life embodies it. Taking your fate into your own hands, despite the outcome, initiates the process of restoring man's humanity" (Glazier, 41).

Chinaski, at the conclusion of *Post Office*, can engineer only the beginnings of his own restoration. He equates his severance from the post office shackles with parakeets set free earlier in the novel. "After living in a cage I had taken the opening and flown out—like a shot into the heavens. Heavens?" (*Post,* 192). Despite these overtures of Christlike ascension, the truth remains that a domestic bird released into the wild has little chance of surviving in the "heaven" of freedom. The last pages of the novel follow Chinaski submerging himself in an odd ritual of self-purgation. " 'More to drink! More to drink! More to drink!' I was flying up to heaven; they were just talking—and fingering each other" (*Post,* 193). This peculiar and harrowing rite of passage—an inversion of alcoholic descent—is necessary and distinguishes the protagonist from those around him. In the stories of the adult Chinaski, the novel is unique in that it barely mentions the craft of writing. All of art is relegated to a derogatory backdrop—self-indulgent writing workshops, a hackneyed novel by a lunatic, an art store with corrupt workers. What is absent is the Chinaski of legend, the wine-drinking late-night raconteur. Although Bukowski was writing and publishing poems throughout the period recounted in *Post Office,* this information is oddly omitted.

Finally, it becomes apparent that in the novel's conclusion Bukowski is forging the persona present in his subsequent fiction. Through a denial of self-abnegating labor and a subsequent flight through hell, Chinaski the artist is formed, his habits of creation fomented as we watch. "When I came to I was in the front room of my apartment, spitting into the rug, putting cigarettes out against my wrists, laughing. Mad as a March Hare. I looked up and there sat this pre-med student. A human heart sat in a homey fat jar between us on the coffeetable" (*Post,* 193). Chinaski the writer has been painfully born. He awakes from the madness of routine into the creative madness of a new life. His adamant refusal of the pickled heart further hints at a denial of his previous role: no more life of the dead. Earlier in the novel, Chinaski had already tipped his hand: "I wanted the whole world or nothing" (*Post,* 63). This sentiment contains the arrogance and impossibility of both the gambling man and the artist. For Bukowski these are the same, and at the end of *Post Office* the character at last has the courage of his long-shot convictions. "In the morning it was morning and I was still alive. Maybe I'll write a novel, I thought. And then I did" (*Post,* 196).

Factotum

Bukowski's second novel, *Factotum,* took the author nearly four years to complete (Harrison, 294), a radical commitment in comparison to *Post*

Office's brisk composition in three weeks. Cherkovski notes that despite personal distractions and a demanding public reading schedule, Bukowski worked on the novel intermittently throughout 1973, 1974, and 1975 (Cherkovski, *Hank,* 245). To Harrison, *Factotum* is "the single most important book in Bukowski's career" (231); the critic cites the control and tightness of tone, the subtle distancing and objective handling of the Chinaski persona, and, in a lengthy and cogent analysis, the novel's historically important treatment of changing labor relations in post–World War II America. *Factotum,* although written several years after *Post Office,* fictionalizes the period of Bukowski's life prior to the earlier novel and thereby increases the authorial distance from the material, a distance Bukowski exploits for a smooth and ironized treatment of his rootless twenties. Using Los Angeles as a rough nucleus, the young Chinaski travels by bus back and forth across the country—to New Orleans, New York City, Philadelphia, St. Louis, and Miami—in the process finding and losing over 20 jobs against a sketchy backdrop of a country in and out of war.

Bukowski's immediate influences in writing *Factotum,* both in sensibility and in approach, were Knut Hamsun's *Hunger* and John Fante's *Ask the Dust,* both for which he acknowledged admiration. Harrison elucidates some of the attraction: "The solitary man alone in his room, a recurring image in Bukowski's writings, appears in Fante as well. The isolation and the first-person narrative produce [*Ask the Dust's*] extreme subjectivity, and connects it with Hamsun's *Hunger* as well as *Factotum*" (224). All three novels concern socially isolated young men wandering large, uncaring cities, exploring their stunted sexuality and striving for literary prominence. The novels are tied by the poverty of their protagonists and by a nearly ahistorical attention to the unique individual crisis of starvation (whether physical or spiritual). Hamsun's character contends that "the poor man has to look carefully around him every time he takes a step, he wisely mistrusts every word he hears from others; for him the simplest acts involve obstacles and problems. His senses are sharp, he is a man of feeling, he has experienced painful things, his soul has been burned and scarred."[6] In the twisted souls populating Hamsun's Christiania, one clearly sees the antecedents of those inhabiting Bukowski's damned and dying Los Angeles. Admirers' comments on Hamsun can often seem equally applicable to Bukowski. Robert Bly speaks of the Norwegian's "insolent wit," his characteristic distrust of the bourgeoisie, and his "impulsive and exuberant life."[7] Isaac Bashevis Singer adds that Hamsun's protagonist "is lonely, not because he cannot make friends, but because he has no patience for others. He suffers the shame of those who must rise above their fellow creatures or perish."[8]

John Fante's *Ask the Dust* lacks Bukowski's sophisticated uses of distancing and irony and is burdened with a Catholic guilt missing in the later novel's rejection of conventional beliefs. Still, the development of Henry Chinaski was undoubtedly influenced by Fante's persona Arturo Bandini, as Bukowski testifies in his preface to the rereleased *Ask the Dust*: "Yes, Fante had a mighty effect upon me."[9] He recalls screaming at the woman he was living with, "Don't call me a son of a bitch! *I am Bandini, Arturo Bandini!*" In *Ask the Dust*, notes Bukowski, "the humour and pain were intermixed with a superb simplicity" ("Preface," 6). Fante wrote in his novel, "What the hell, I used to say, take your time, Bandini. You got ten years to write a book, so take it easy, get out and learn about life, walk the streets."[10] The balm of these words for the obscure and isolated young Bukowski must have been considerable; in fact, the passage seems to anticipate—and perhaps encouraged—the decade from his mid-twenties to mid-thirties when he quit writing almost entirely.

The three novels share similar plots, particularly in the protagonists' struggle to write successfully. Virtually identical scenes appear approximately one third into each novel. The struggling writer receives a short letter from the editor he worships, who accepts a piece of writing. To Hamsun's narrator, "the letter shot through me like a stream of light" and "I laughed and cried, leaped in the air and ran down the street, stopped and beat my legs, swore wholesale at no one about nothing" (Hamsun, 61). For Fante's Bandini, "The letter slipped from my fingers and zigzagged to the floor. I stood up and looked in the mirror. . . . I picked the letter up and read it again. I opened the window, climbed out, and lay in the bright hillside grass. My fingers clawed the earth. . . . Then I started to cry" (*Fante,* 57). Chinaski's response, although contained to his room, is very similar: "Never had the world looked so good, so full of promise. I walked over to the bed, sat down, read it again. I studied each curve in the handwriting of Gladmore's signature. I got up, walked the acceptance slip over to the dresser, propped it there. . . . I couldn't sleep. I got up, turned on the light, walked over to the dresser and read it again."[11] These scenes occur in contrast to the disappointing and labored lives the men are leading, a burst of light, hope, and luck, capricious though that luck may be.

The previous scenes share another important aspect: a young man's vivacity. *Hunger*, Hamsun's first novel, was published when the author was 31; *Ask the Dust,* Fante's second novel, was published when its author was 30. These are novels written not only about but by young men. For obvious reasons—their directness toward sexuality, their first-person consciousness, their wit, the isolation of their writer protagonists—the stories appealed to and moved the young, struggling Bukowski. *Factotum,* however, is markedly different from its predecessors, in large part due to the maturity of its author and his distance from the experience used. Bukowski was 55 when *Factotum* appeared in print in 1975. The novel deals with material roughly 30 years earlier, working-class America during World War II and the subsequent, supposed boom years. Harrison contends that Bukowski successfully "rewrites" and improves both his influences, and the distance of age plays a huge part in this accomplishment. The author's rejection of conventional social values and labor relations is radically advanced from Fante's conventional burden of guilt and shame, and "while the dynamics of the two writers are similar, depicting the male protagonists' social and sexual anxieties, Bukowski, more aware of the source of the conflict, has achieved an ironic and humorous depiction of this protagonist" (Harrison, 230). The perverse psychosexual power struggle throughout *Ask the Dust* never fully convinces of the author's control over his material, and the novel, for all its considerable force, is ultimately a partly realistic and partly romanticized treatment of the young artist, one lacking Bukowski's subversive humor.

Although Knut Hamsun employs considerable irony, *Hunger* is intentionally a highly individualized account of a self-conscious "hunger" artist "detached from his social condition" (Harrison, 235). Bukowski, despite his frequent label as an aberrational malcontent, achieves something more universal in *Factotum.* For Harrison, this chiefly involves the work's preoccupation with labor, a theme obviously absent from *Hunger.* "Bukowski's genius was to take over Hamsun's 'disinterested subject,' strip him of his idealism and make him—however tenuously and unwillingly—a member of the working class. In *Factotum,* Bukowski materialized Hamsun's spiritual marginality of the 1890s into a material refusal of the 1970s" (Harrison, 235). This difference argues for *Factotum's* deeper social significance: "The despair of *Hunger's* protagonist is remediable by a job while Chinaski's is not" (Harrison, 234). Chinaski summarizes an opinion common in Bukowski's writing: "But starvation, unfortunately, didn't improve art. It only hindered it. A man's soul was rooted in his stomach. A man could write much better after eating a porterhouse steak and drinking a pint of whiskey than he could ever write after eating a nickel candy bar" (*Factotum,* 63). Once again, the elements of success, achievement, and luck—even those surrounding the artistic muse—are put into a socioeconomic context. Starving does not improve art, and neither, posits *Factotum,* does debilitating menial labor. What is efficacious is leisure time and accumulated wealth, both difficult to acquire in *Factotum*'s circumscribed world.

A common bond between *Post Office* and *Factotum* is their focus on work, a focus even more acute in the second novel. "What is different about these novels is their relentlessly negative depiction of all aspects of work and a fundamental questioning of its usefulness. While previous authors did not glorify work, it was seen as necessary" (Harrison, 125). Moreover, "in *Factotum* Bukowski offers a radical, generalized critique of work and its function in U.S. society and, for the first time, a strategy of resistance. In *Factotum* the refusal to work has become systematic and programmatic" (Harrison, 145). The novel charts the terribly deadening effect of repetitive, unskilled labor. Chinaski is tortured not by a particular job but by every job. Often the short chapters begin with the protagonist abruptly in a new workplace, with no transition from the old except the tired, sardonic, bemused tone of the narrator's voice. Almost all of the jobs, however, share the salient characteristic of tedium. Their banality and monotony cripple the soul and leave the body stiffened, the mind exhausted:

> The work was easy and dull but the clerks were in a constant state of turmoil. They were worried about their jobs.

> For each poster you took out there was a new poster to replace it. Each one took forever. It was endless.

> I'd had dull stupid jobs but this appeared to be the dullest and most stupid one of them all.

> He never sent you home after six hours, for example. You might have time to think. (*Factotum,* 16, 43, 147–48, 57)

A typically stultifying job is Chinaski's tenure at a dog biscuit factory, where a sequence of powerful, Dantesque images is undercut by the triviality of the product. The narrator, overseen by "a toothless elf with a film over his left eye," bakes the biscuits. "The flames of the oven leaped fifteen feet high. The inside of the oven was like a ferris wheel. Each ledge held twelve screens" (*Factotum,* 45). The surreal suggestion of the

setting is not lost on the workers suffering there. "On such jobs men
become tired. They experience a weariness beyond fatigue. They say
mad, brilliant things. Out of my head, I cussed and talked and cracked
jokes and sang. Hell boils with laughter. Even the Elf laughed at me"
(*Factotum*, 46). This scene recalls a previous moment when Chinaski, just
arrived in New York City, finds that the "El ran level with the window"
(*Factotum*, 40) of his boarding room. The willful outsider is haunted by
visages of the ghosts of the earth. He will not be left alone as he desires.
"Then the room filled again with light. Again I looked into the faces. It
was like a vision of hell repeated again and again. Each new trainload of
faces was more ugly, demented and cruel than the last. . . . The arrival
and departure of the faces continued; I felt I was having a vision. I was
being visited by hundreds of devils that the Devil Himself couldn't tol-
erate. I drank more wine" (*Factotum*, 40). The moment's effectiveness is
largely due to its humorous subtext. Chinaski calmly watches the faces,
goes out for wine, and returns to watch some more. He is disgusted and
compelled, yet vaguely indifferent. The ironic tone of his lofty rhetoric
dramatizes this vision of the damned too horrible for hell. The mundane, comic reality of an apartment rocked by passing trains, a commonplace in situation comedy, undercuts the tone. To end the scene,
Chinaski as clown performs a slapstick routine of putting on his new
suit, which is too small, and ripping through the jacket and pants: "As I
tried to fasten them, the seam split in the seat. I reached in from behind
and felt my shorts" (*Factotum*, 41). The routine of the world is grotesque,
demented, and also absurd.

For a few days or weeks, Chinaski endures each deadening job as it
appears, but *Factotum* is remarkable for the frequency and nonchalance
with which the protagonist leaves these positions. He continually and
arbitrarily quits, the cause being neither money nor the particular circumstances or environment per se, but more a kind of general, disinterested rejection. When he does not quit, he is fired, and the novel implies
that Chinaski goes to great lengths to ensure that no job will last long.
If he cannot effectively engineer his termination, then he will fabricate
an imaginary issue to necessitate departure. Such a program empowers
him. "I always started a job with the feeling that I'd soon quit or be
fired, and this gave me a relaxed manner that was mistaken for intelli-
gence or some secret power" (*Factotum*, 130). This "secret power,"
through its very indifference, often allows Chinaski to intimidate superi-
ors. Of course, he fails anyway sooner or later, usually and preferably
sooner. And why not? Another city waits. "Packing was always a good

time" (*Factotum,* 66). Harrison sees such behavior as integral to Bukowski/Chinaski's subversive resistance to American labor relations: "Because the causal relationship between human labor and wealth has in fact ceased to exist, distributing wealth on the basis of one's work no longer makes sense. . . . The absenteeism, the lateness, the malingering, the pilferage, all the minor forms of resistance, must be seen in the context of changes that were taking place in the relationship between labor and capital in the 1960s and 1970s, as part of a broader movement reflecting objective social change, rather than mere subjective maladaptation" (150).

One interesting aspect of Harrison's thesis that Bukowski is revolutionary in his fictional depiction of the working class is the importance again placed on the distance between Bukowski and the biographical and historical contexts of his material. In other words, if the author is reflecting changing labor relations during the years of the novel's composition, he is then overlaying the 1940s setting of *Factotum* with these notions. "The idea that the worker would prefer not to work goes against the grain of the traditional socialist ideology, where work, and the worker, were glorified" (Harrison, 149). One can detect such a subversion subtly enacted in *Factotum*'s World War II setting. "At some point during our hellish nights World War II ended. The war had always at best been a vague reality to me, but now it was over" (*Factotum,* 100). The novel often has a timeless quality, evidenced, for example, by the broken clock Chinaski "fixes" to suit his own surreal notion of time. Still, more so than in *Hunger* or *Ask the Dust,* historical reference points—of America during and after World War II—are important. *Factotum*'s mentions of patriotism and national pride provide an intriguing contrast to Chinaski's denial of such ideologies.

America's tradition of military service and nationalist machismo represent just the sort of obviousness and unwarranted pride that Henry Chinaski opposes by his very existence. A patron in a bar announces that he hasn't "had a hard-on since Teddy Roosevelt took his last hill" (*Factotum,* 48). Chinaski's father is portrayed as cruel, self-loathing, and violent, the demonic archetype of the first-generation immigrant. His love of country is indistinguishable from a demented love of self and personal conceits. The character appears briefly in *Factotum* and is associated with World War I, and the narrator is revealed as a product of that conflict, a war baby. "My son, if it wasn't for the First World War I never would have met your mother and you never would have been born" (*Factotum,* 33). Chinaski is noncommittal to such a comment. His father accuses him of not wanting "to serve his country in time of War"; the son, in turn, recasts the older man's wartime rhetoric, eliminating the suggestion of choice: "The shrink said I was unfit" (*Factotum,* 33). Although Chinaski himself seems indifferent to the war and to the appeals of demagogues, Bukowski inserts periodic reminders that the national landscape during the novel is one depleted of its most robust young men. "You're not in the army?" (*Factotum,* 53). Chinaski looks suspicious by his presence. "Are you 4-F?" (*Factotum,* 56). *Factotum* makes clear that when the soldiers return, the protagonist's problems will merely increase in severity: available women and available jobs will become even scarcer. "Tens of thousands of young men were fighting in Europe and China, in the Pacific Islands. When they came back she'd find one" (*Factotum,* 65). In this regard, the ongoing war is to the protagonist's advantage.

On the few occasions when the war enters Chinaski's thoughts, it is abstract, distant, and usually treated with irony. In the novel, the sole job that the narrator regrets losing is "during World War II," when he was "working for the Red Cross in San Francisco" (*Factotum,* 161). He enjoys the position not for patriotic reasons but due to its ease and proximity to the nurses. In a wonderful war parody, Chinaski recalls getting the blood collection truck lost behind enemy lines, where the "skid row guys were aching to rape the lot of us." He delivers the nurses to the appropriate church two hours late. "Across the Atlantic, Hitler was gaining with every step. I lost that job right then and there, unfortunately" (*Factotum,* 162). He is comically unfit for combat. In another scene, Chinaski burns himself with ointment trying to eliminate crabs, and his girlfriend Jan wraps his testicles in gauze in a raucous ironizing of the nurse-and-wounded-soldier story. "Around and around and around. Poor little balls. Poor big balls. What have they done to you? Around and around and around we go" (*Factotum,* 147). When a supervisor inquires about Chinaski's limp, he responds:

> "I was frying some chicken in the pan and the grease exploded, it burned my legs."
> "I thought maybe you had war wounds."
> "No, the chicken did it." (*Factotum,* 150)

This ridiculous fabrication hints at his being "chicken," or cowardly. The character's noninvolvement with the war and his indifference to its resolution remain his strongest implied criticism.

Chinaski's prophecy that the war's conclusion will be detrimental to him is fulfilled during the final third of the novel. After the soldiers return, he undergoes a steady and seemingly irremediable decline. The World War II truck that carries a load of workers—from which only Chinaski is rejected—to pick tomatoes is a sharp contrast to any typical portrait of postwar prosperity. Even the narrator's praise of a Japanese woman seems an implicit criticism of the popular paranoia of "them and us," of enemy, of "other": "Japanese women instinctively understood yesterday and today and tomorrow. Call it wisdom. And they had staying power. American women only knew today and tended to come to pieces when just one day went wrong" (*Factotum,* 183). This observation contains historical and political implications, and perhaps a warning—there is wisdom in defeat. Victory is represented by flash, superficiality, and ignorant youth.

Factotum depicts a humorous but devastating version of the eviscerated lower-class laborer. Bukowski's own working-class background adds authority to this stance and is the foundation of its author's political content: Chinaski's refusal to work "is positive in its implicit demand for something more than material affluence. Consumption and accumulation as ends in themselves were never a part of the Chinaskian project" (Harrison, 13). The character searches for a "delicate balance . . . between what we endure and what little ground we need to claim for ourselves" (Glazier, 42). He seems to maintain this balance through artistic isolation. Although Chinaski's concern with writing is less the focus of *Factotum* than in the comparable novels by Hamsun or Fante, the theme of creative expression is far more present than in *Post Office*. In Bukowski's earlier novel, it is not until the final pages that Chinaski metamorphosed into a writer. Although *Factotum* recycles earlier biographical material, the second novel deals more extensively with the writer's dilemma, perhaps due to Bukowski's own growing reputation by 1975.[12]

Nevertheless, it is not until page 55 of *Factotum* that Chinaski identifies himself as a writer, "temporarily down on my inspirations," and then the mention is derisive. Afterward, Chinaski periodically daydreams about the editor Gladmore and admits both his productivity and his self-doubts: "I wrote three or four stories a week. I kept things in the mail. I imagined the editors of *The Atlantic Monthly* and *Harper's* saying: 'Hey, here's another one of those things by that nut . . .' " (*Factotum,* 59). He then pretends to be writing a libretto for Wilbur Oxnard's opera *The Emperor of San Francisco,* work for patronage and booze that makes Chinaski "realize how disgusting my life has become" (*Factotum,* 78). He later denies his profession altogether. "Hell, I can't write. That's just conversation. It makes the landlady feel better. What I need is a job, any kind of job" (*Factotum,* 126). Repeatedly he mocks his college journalism courses, and, after applying for a job at a newspaper, he is hired as a janitor. The writing ideal, which to an extent individualizes Chinaski's experience, ultimately conflates with *Factotum*'s more universal theme of working-class frustration. "And I wanted to be a writer. Almost everybody was a writer. . . . Of those fifty guys in the room, probably fifteen of them thought they were writers" (*Factotum,* 166). His humility is tinged with pride, his denial of talent with the resignation that it is not his time yet and for most men it never is.

Factotum's power derives from its unique blend of humor and hopelessness. It is a funny novel, but a bleak one, recreating a depleted country overrun by indigents. The body is wracked, and the mind necessarily follows. Sexual liaisons are temporary and more sad than joyful. Hope, for the have-nots, is rare and often delusional. On an odd occasion when Chinaski wields the power to hire others, he recognizes the impossibility of equitable distribution of labor and decides according to an arbitrary toss of coins: "The four who bring me back a penny get to wash dishes today!" (*Factotum,* 193). The jobs go to the lucky and the strong. The prize itself is dubious but preferable to hunger. "The other bums retreated slowly down the loading dock ramp, jumped off, and walked down the alley into the wasteland of downtown Los Angeles on a Sunday" (*Factotum,* 193). Chinaski soon rejoins the shuffle of the lost. "I walked along the loading dock, then I jumped into the alley. Coming toward me was another bum. 'Got a smoke, buddy?' he asked. 'Yeah.' I took two out, gave him one, took one myself. I lit him up, then I lit myself up. He moved east and I moved west" (*Factotum,* 196). Despite Chinaski's antisocial proclivities, his disdain for social stratification, and a passion for art that further separates him from others, *Factotum* demonstrates that men's lives are linked, even if only in the solidarity of defeat. At the Farm Labor Market, "any man's chance was our chance, but when [the window] closed, hope evaporated. Then we had each other to look at" (*Factotum,* 197–98).

Women

Bukowski's third novel, *Women* (1978), is his longest and demonstrates the distance between author and persona more clearly than any of his other novels. The subject of the work is sexual relationships, and analogous to *Factotum*'s stream of menial jobs, *Women* inundates the reader with continual, overlapping female characters. Most of the 20 women whom Chinaski has, or attempts to have, sex with are not present for long, a few chapters or sometimes a few pages. A swirl of sexual frenzy overtakes the novel as it does the protagonist, and the women maintain separate identities only through the reader's concentrated effort. Although the loose, manic episodes of *Women* were criticized for lacking novelistic structure, Bukowski's approach is appropriate to his material. Moreover, the author hints at the method and artistic discernment behind the madness. Chinaski criticizes a woman's novel-in-progress because its author "presumed that the reader was as fascinated by her life as she was—which was a deadly mistake."[13] He defends the hard life captured in his fiction to a skeptical fan as being "partly true" (*Women,* 31) and later defines fiction to an interviewer as "an improvement on life" (*Women,* 197).

Women takes place roughly from 1970 to 1977, the years following *Post Office* during which Bukowski/Chinaski, although still living in the same poor neighborhood, is enjoying minor fame as a poet. Like *Post Office, Women* was written shortly after the conclusion of the period the novel chronicles, but the later work is much longer and more ambitious. During the years between the novels' compositions, Bukowski greatly improved as a prose writer. *Women* deftly uses physical details to reveal character and lacks the redundancy of the earlier novel, suggesting more confident editing by its author. Most important, a definite and ironic separation between the author and his protagonist has been established. The methods of fictionalizing that Bukowski hints at are predominantly exaggeration and compression. Exaggeration allows the humorous treatment of painful experience and the alteration and completion of thematic concerns. Compression, meanwhile, accounts for an overwhelming onslaught of women in what feels like a brief period.

Even more than in *Factotum,* events beyond the focused concern of the novel are eliminated. Harrison notes that although *Women* coincides with a particularly turbulent period of American history, it contains no mention of Vietnam, Cambodia, Kent State, or even Watergate (161). In addition, the compressed events initiate a confused sense of time in the book, indicating Chinaski's own befuddlement. The protagonist reveals in his first sentence that "I was fifty years old and hadn't been to bed with a woman for four years" and states in the second paragraph that he met Lydia Vance "about 6 years ago and I had just quit a twelve year job as a postal clerk and was trying to be a writer" (*Women,* 7). Although the syntax of the second paragraph indicates a flashback in time from the first, apparently this is not the case; the story then proceeds with the introduction of Lydia Vance. This confused catalog of years that begins the novel is never quite clarified. Several references to the post office in the novel remind one of Chinaski's recent escape. At the same time, in the hands of the now more accomplished novelist Bukowski, the narrator seems older and more complex than his *Post Office* counterpart.

Chinaski's age becomes a curious motif in *Women.* Approximately one-third into the novel, two women appear at the writer's door and announce their ages as 32 and 23. "Add your ages together," he responds, "and you've got me" (*Women,* 108). Although Chinaski is 50 at the story's opening, he now identifies himself as 55. Eighty pages later he is "almost 60 years old" (*Women,* 188) and near the end of the novel announces to "Death" that he has lived "almost 6 decades" (*Women,* 277). This rapid aging is telling in two ways. First, it again demonstrates Bukowski's intentional use of compression. In "real" time, Chinaski ages from 50 to nearly 60, although the novel feels as if it covers a period of little more than a few months. Hence, the themes of sexuality, women, and self-examination are isolated and intensified. Twenty women over seven years is obviously less impressive for Chinaski than, for example, over seven months, and the compressed events create the added pressure necessary for the character's revelations. Second, continual references to age clarify Bukowski's awareness of his protagonist's anachronistic beliefs: "It is evident in . . . *Women,* we have the phenomenon of a man whose deepest attitudes to women were shaped almost a half-century earlier than the era in which they were being given artistic expression" (Harrison, 19).

The novel explosively juxtaposes ingrained chauvinistic traits with the rising consciousness of the 1970s. Bukowski exploits these contrasts. "How odd that everybody was younger than I" (*Women,* 179), Chinaski notes with deceptive simplicity before confiding that "there's nothing worse than an old chauv pig" (*Women,* 182). In the context of *Women's* primary concern—the protagonist's reconciliation between a contemporary world and an antiquated burden of destructive chauvinism—the preoccupation with his advanced age becomes important. Sara, one of the few "good" women depicted in the novel, ironically asks, "Are you prejudiced against old age?" Chinaski's response is predictable: "Yes, everybody's old age but mine" (*Women,* 262). The predicament of the novel is such that Bukowski's editor John Martin reportedly saw it "as the great black humor book of the women's movement" (Cherkovski, *Hank,* 262). Critic Jimmie Cain contends that the first three novels "coalesce in a trilogy," charting the "chronology of the author's physical, psychological, and, to a greater degree, aesthetic development."[14]

"It was easy to write about whores, but to write about a good woman was much more difficult" (*Women,* 101). This quote summarizes Bukowski's ambition in *Women,* a challenge due in part to his own history and attitudes. A recurring glibness on Chinaski's part involves the attitude that his infidelities and late-blooming sexual romps are part of the writer's work. "I pumped and I pumped. One more fuck. Research" (*Women,* 260). He explains to a woman, without allowing her to recognize the irony, that he is "working on a novel" (*Women,* 257) and rationalizes that "women, for me, were almost impossible to fictionalize without first knowing them" (*Women,* 227). In reality, little writing is shown to be accomplished during the novel despite the protagonist's literary reputation. Chinaski scribbles a poem when time permits, often a love poem that is a response to his increased sexual activity, then frequently hides or loses the poem. He seems full of self-doubt, confused by his fame, and unable to reintegrate his diffused personality. "I had imagined myself special because I had come out of the factories at the age of 50 and become a poet. Hot shit. So I pissed on everybody just like those bosses and managers had pissed on me when *I* was helpless. It came to the same thing. I was a drunken spoiled rotten fucker with a very minor *minor* fame" (*Women,* 240). A lacerating self-recrimination that begins to appear late in the novel often seems disingenuous. The hyperbole of the final sentence, undercut by the subsequent act of betrayal that inevitably follows such a passage, renders Chinaski's words more as further justification than as sincere regret. In short, the reader's sympathetic identification with Chinaski deconstructs in *Women.* Bukowski intentionally represents the worst characteristics of male posturing in "that tradition as we have come to associate it with Hemingway, Miller and Mailer" (Harrison, 203).

Chinaski does not present himself as either a great lover or a great fighter, but his language is saturated with the macho fervor of an earlier age. He equates poetry readings, which sicken and diminish him, with being "in the ring alone with the bull" and "like climbing into the prize ring" (*Women,* 149, 202). There is more than a hint of mockery in such analogies, a facetiousness akin to his charge that Hemingway was "too serious" and considered life "always total war." Following this criticism, Chinaski speaks of his own small, feminine hands and his amazement that earlier in his life he "had managed to win 30 percent of [his] fights" (*Women*, 201). This is hardly an impressive average, but the reference locates him in an incriminating masculine setting. Chinaski's inconsistent comments about his own vulnerability are linked to his overall skepticism toward success as a writer. "To work like a mule until you were fifty at meaningless, low jobs, and then suddenly to be flitting about the country, a gadfly with drink in hand" (*Women*, 231). Nevertheless, he takes to the prestige of his new role, suggests its relation to sexual prowess, and demonstrates his talent for it. "Performance is performance" (*Women*, 202).

The narrator's sentiment about performance is double-edged: he "plays" the poet-lover throughout *Women*, resulting in a dazed, vertiginous uncertainty about himself. He comments that events seem "like a movie" (*Women*, 67), and he moves through a kind of detached fantasy as his life unreels. The novel continues this motif with its mentions of film stars, including references to two celebrity graveyards. The implications for Chinaski are not promising. Moreover, even for Bukowski, *Women* seems to have an inordinate emphasis, page after page, on vomiting and drink. The vomiting is obviously symptomatic of an unsettled and unhealthy lifestyle. Chinaski is unreconciled with himself—early and late scenes find him staring into mirrors—and something inside is not right. The drinking, too, serves its traditional roles of crutch, induced courage, and excess. Chinaski confesses, "If I had to choose between drinking and fucking I think I'd have to stop fucking" (*Women*, 176). The statement of this opposition anticipates his girlfriend Lydia's advice: "If you want to drink, drink; if you want to fuck, throw the bottle away" (*Women*, 203). Generally, alcohol abuse in *Women* seems less celebratory than in the earlier novels. Rather than an after-hours entrance to a better world, the consumption is more personally protective. "The drinking can be viewed as a means of allaying Chinaski's underlying anxiety, or a hostile, sadistic way of hurting women by denying them the full pleasure, and intimacy, of successful lovemaking" (Harrison, 210). A common occurrence in the novel is an inability to ejaculate, to consummate the sexual activity often initiated by the woman. This failure is consistently linked to alcoholism and allows the narrator's seeming passivity as he maintains a last refuge of sexual control through failure. The novel makes clear that women have a greater sex drive and a greater sexual interest than Chinaski, who often cannot consummate the act regardless. The notion of the hard-drinking, hard-fucking male writer is subverted on several levels, consciously by Bukowski, perhaps subconsciously by his fictional persona.

"Be kind to me, Joanna, sucking and fucking aren't everything" (*Women*, 126), pleads Chinaski; nevertheless, how long he may stay with her will be determined by his "performance" (*Women*, 128). Not only is this portrayal an inversion of the traditional male conqueror, but traditional roles of male and female, of domination and submission, are also inverted. The protagonist is a mess of confused feeling, fragility, and spiteful violence. One of the novel's most interesting and consistent reversals casts the "tough guy" in a hackneyed role of repressed female. Besides his small hands and sexual ambivalence, Chinaski is vain about his attractive legs, showing them off to women at any opportunity. (He also claims to be a leg man, and his appreciation clearly extends to his own.) He is "kept" by one woman after another, letting the female typically set the schedule and the rules. *Women* also discusses Chinaski's peculiar innocence. He arrives at his first poetry reading "about to bust [his] cherry" (*Women*, 8). Near the end of the novel, he professes a latent puritan streak, which he equates with the following admission: "In a sense I've always been a virgin" (*Women*, 287). He is sentimental, emotionally needful, teary-eyed, and twice feels as if he is being raped by a female aggressor. Such behavior is hardly prototypical for the virile he-man.

Several of the novel's women are emotionally, financially, and psychologically more stable than Chinaski. Even Lydia, portrayed during their long relationship as progressively frenetic and hostile, early on engineers a switching of roles. She wants "to sculpt his head" (*Women*, 11), a double entendre signifying her role as both artist and sexual mentor (she teaches him to perform cunnilingus). Chinaski readily accepts the two parts assigned him: subject and student. In a touching moment, he buys a new shirt for their meeting, exposing a boylike vulnerability and attention to appearance unprecedented in earlier self-representations. "I had bought the shirt because I was thinking about her, about seeing her. I knew that she knew that, and was making fun of me, yet I didn't mind" (*Women*, 13). One of the most comical examples of the Chinaski-Lydia reversal is during an unlikely Utah camping expedition. "What the hell would Jack London do? What would Hemingway do? Jean Genet?" (*Women*, 86). The narrator, panicked and lost during a short hike, is rescued by the confident and nonchalant outdoorswoman. He doesn't bother to be embarrassed. "Lydia, I *love* you!" (*Women*, 87).

Chinaski often seems as overwrought as the worst stereotype of the emotionally dependent woman:

> At last I slept. When I awakened in the morning Katherine was sitting on the edge of the bed brushing those yards of red-brown hair. Her large dark eyes looked at me as I awakened. "Hello, Katherine," I said, "will you marry me?"
> "Please don't," she said, "I don't like it."
> . . . She said, "It's just *sex*, Hank, it's *just sex!*" Then she laughed. It wasn't a sardonic laugh, it was really joyful. She brushed her hair and I put my arm around her waist and rested my head against her leg. I wasn't quite sure of anything. (*Women*, 99–100)

Lean writing and terse dialogue, hallmarks of what could be perceived as a male tradition of writing, are present, and yet the accompanying sensibilities are nonexistent. Harrison notes that "whenever, in *Women*, Chinaski attempts . . . to act 'in character,' he is unsuccessful" (212). Expectations of the persona are continually subverted. On nearly every page, macho behavior is twisted, deflated, analyzed, and dissected. Sometimes Chinaski is conscious of his limited, prescribed behavior, but often he is not. This older, more hesitant character would rather avoid a fight than seek one out.

Several words and sensibilities are repeated in *Women*: boredom, madness equated with love, and most tellingly fear. Chinaski consistently claims to be afraid—of readings, and most of all of women. When he is caught surreptitiously drinking, this exchange follows:

> "I was afraid, I guess."
> "You? Afraid? I thought you were the big, tough, drinking, woman-fucker?"
> "Did I let you down?"
> "No."
> "I was afraid. My art is my fear. I rocket off from it." (*Women*, 189)

The male's comments seem to begin honestly, but something troubling, a suggestion of posing and contrivance, emerges in the linking of fear and art. He obviously realizes during his most lucid moments that he is not his old self. "I couldn't understand what had happened to my life. I had lost my sophistication, I had lost my worldliness, I had lost my hard protective shell. I had lost my sense of humor in the face of other people's problems. I wanted them all back. I wanted things to go easily for me. But somehow I knew they wouldn't come back, at least not right away" (*Women*, 238–39). Still, each evidently sincere moment is undercut by either another infidelity (his addiction) or another hyperbolic blast of self-recrimination. "A murderer was more straightforward and honest than I was. Or a rapist. . . . I was truly no good. I could feel it as I walked up and down on the rug. *No good*." The indulgent tone of Chinaski's lamentations qualifies their honesty. "I was writing *The Love Tale of the Hyena*" (*Women*, 236). His stance is confession tinged with braggadocio.

Women is finally not a fun book to read, despite its humor. Inspired by Boccaccio's *The Decameron,* Bukowski undertook a novel that confronts the immobilizing ennui of American society and the impermanence of love in all human relations. "It was not so much love with Boccaccio. It was sex. Love is funnier, more ridiculous. That guy! He could really laugh at it" (quoted in Cherkovski, *Hank,* 263). The reader's sympathy for Chinaski is limited and grows more strained as the novel progresses. Indeed, hateful and violent scenes of sexual animosity supply the novel's most troubling aspect.[15] Almost as often as love is equated with madness, sex—as penetration, splitting, "fucking"—is associated with hatred. Some of this feeling is related to childhood repression and, again, a theme of puritan release: "When I came I felt it was in the face of everything decent, white sperm dripping down over the heads and souls of my dead parents" (*Women*, 77). The penetration of the female is often explained in terms of spiritual as well as physical domination. "It was like raping the Virgin Mary. I came. I came inside of her, agonizing, feeling my sperm enter her body, she was helpless, and I shot my come deep into her ultimate core—body and soul—again and again" (*Women*, 99). In a later scene, Chinaski grabs "Tanya's head and forced [his] cock into the center of her skull" (*Women*, 286). More than once, he attempts to split and separate the woman beneath him. "I tried to rip her apart, I tried to split her in half" (*Women*, 249).

In the best light, such scenes epitomize Chinaski's research—the attempt to explore the woman as a metaphor for the mystery he cannot solve—and demonstrate his psychological pain. Nevertheless, little sympathy is intended for the desperate violence in such scenes, and Bukowski regularly undercuts his protagonist's existential aggression. "When Iris came out of the bathroom smiling, my cock went down" (*Women*, 249). The woman remains whole, even satisfied. Tanya's skull, too, remains intact. "I hadn't split that 90 pounds in half. She could handle me and much much more" (*Women*, 282). Even the apotheosis of male domination, sexual penetration, is ironized. It simply does not accomplish much. The woman is unchanged, and the male is left puzzled. "I leaned over and gave her a long kiss. Her tongue darted in and out of my mouth. I hated her. My cock began to rise" (*Women*, 259). This is a problematic scene, crafted without humor by Bukowski. How far does Chinaski progress by the novel's end? A furious, nearly hysterical round of whores and failed fellatio culminates his frustration.

The novel ends with a renewed vow to Sara, the "good woman" (*Women*, 290) whom the protagonist has alternately avoided and abused. He then rebuffs the telephone advance of "a cute chick," Rochelle, which represents virtually the only moment in *Women* when he rejects a sexual overture. "I hung up. There I had done it—that time" (*Women*, 291). Finally, Chinaski greets a tomcat, similar to one he encountered earlier. The new cat "wasn't frightened" (*Women*, 291) of him, a telling omission in a novel based primarily on fear. Has an irrevocable change occurred in the character? Bukowski is familiar with compulsion, obsession, and addiction, and he avoids a tidy fictional solution. Chinaski's recovery must be undertaken anew each day.

Ham on Rye

Bukowski's fourth novel, *Ham on Rye* (1982), follows the pattern of *Factotum*—a novel that treats Chinaski's more distant recollections following a novel of the immediate past (*Post Office*, *Women*). In this case, the subject matter is Chinaski's youth and upbringing, and again, as in *Factotum*, his sure handling of the material is noticeably more objective than the "immediate" novels. In *Ham on Rye*, a prequel to Bukowski's previous work, one witnesses the gradual and inevitable formation of the adult Chinaski. Each feature of the persona is by turn introduced: drinking, classical music, rooming houses, attitudes toward sex, writing habits, and tastes in literature. These are explained through an extended examination of family, a topic seldom explored earlier. *Ham on Rye* considers especially three issues "in a serious and extended fashion" that were previously untapped in Bukowski: "relations with and between his parents, relations to the social world of his peers, and . . . politics" (Harrison, 162). The adult Chinaski's behavior, rather than postulated as the idiosyncratic response of one individual, is given cogent social and psychological motivations.

Chinaski's earliest recollection, as an infant in Germany, begins to stress his isolation from family. "I felt good under the table. Nobody seemed to know that I was there. . . . Two people: one larger with curly hair, a big nose, a big mouth, much eyebrow; the larger person always seeming to be angry, often screaming; the smaller person quiet, round of face, paler, with large eyes. I was afraid of both of them."[16] The tone is detached, lonely, and fearful; Bukowski's objectified descriptions stress distance, an omnipresent lack of love and nurturing. "I never spoke to them by name. I was 'Henry, Jr.' These people spoke German most of the time and in the beginning I did too" (*Ham*, 10). This early separation is obviously linked to Chinaski's subsequent need and preference for solitude, a need in turn connected with a love of silence and a mistrust of spoken language: "I liked the sound of the keys best up at one end of the piano where there was hardly any sound at all—the sound the keys made was like chips of ice striking against one another" (*Ham*, 10). This last image is exceptional, capturing at once the desolation of the family and the infant's withdrawal, meanwhile foreshadowing the drinking that the protagonist credits as his salvation from routine. A palpable sense of displacement and wrongness permeates the early chapters: "When I went back in my bedroom I thought, these people are not my parents, they must have adopted me and now they are unhappy with what I have become" (*Ham*, 42).

As the narrator approaches adulthood, this sense of otherness does not diminish, but the boy's guilt and confusion slowly, painfully, become the young man's dismissive disgust:

> I looked at my father, at his hands, his face, his eyebrows, and I knew that this man had nothing to do with me. He was a stranger. My mother was non-existent. I was cursed. Looking at my father I saw nothing but indecent dullness. . . . Centuries of peasant blood and peasant training. The Chinaski bloodline had been thinned by a series of peasant-servants who had surrendered their real lives for fractional and illusionary gains. Not a man in the line who said, 'I don't want a house, I want a *thousand* houses, *now!*' " (*Ham*, 192–93)

He rejects the traditional family structure and its attendant labor values, embracing instead a radical politics of individual achievement. This anticipates (and recalls) the brazen claim in *Post Office*: "I wanted the whole world or nothing" (*Post*, 63). Such desire is paradoxical; its impossibility for the working-class speaker, the very illogic of the demand, achieves a spiritual victory.

Chinaski's discovery of the library and literature grants him the language to begin articulating his animosity. "I remembered what Ivan had

said in *The Brothers Karamazov*, 'Who doesn't want to kill the father?' "
(*Ham*, 217). Such a statement renders the dedication of *Ham on Rye*, "for
all the fathers," acerbic irony. Although *Ham on Rye* is a remarkably
objective and distanced account of his difficult childhood, this bil-
dungsroman is also Bukowski's least humorous novel. Several amusing
scenes involve the author's jabs at the ignorance and conceit of youth,
yet the result is solemn. The rejection of the father is total and nonnego-
tiable. Henry Chinaski Sr. is perhaps the most fully drawn character,
besides his protagonists, of any character in Bukowski's fiction. The
roundness of the characterization leaves little room for laughter. The
elder Chinaski is physically abusive, loud, seething with failure, and sustained primarily by hatred as he suffers "that most horrible of all American fates, downward social mobility. . . . Bukowski's rendering of his
father is an extremely effective rendering of an individual shaped—
warped, really—by social class. Though a member of the working class
by virtue of his jobs . . . his is clearly the class consciousness of a petty
bourgeois" (Harrison, 168). It is this false class alignment—peasant
blood confused with a rich man's delusions—that Chinaski Jr. recognizes and refuses. Chinaski Sr. is a powerless monster at the end of a
failed American dream of avarice.

Ham on Rye exposes the fraudulent myth of social advancement
through merit or hard work. "My mother went to her low-paying job
each morning and my father, who didn't have a job, left each morning
too. Although most of the neighbors were unemployed he didn't want
them to think he was jobless" (*Ham*, 113). The father's frustration, van-
ity, and defeat repeatedly erupt as domestic violence. Stranded in the
depression and a country devoid of any sustaining belief except the
unreachable one of wealth and status, the Chinaski household fractures.
The son soon rejects the lies of ownership, of merit, and of disciplined
labor. "My father liked the slogan, 'Early to bed and early to rise, makes
a man healthy, wealthy and wise.' But it hadn't done any of that for
him. I decided that I might try to reverse the process. . . . I wallowed
there in the dark, waiting for something" (*Ham*, 208–9).

The young Chinaski's withdrawal anticipates the behavior of the isolated adult artist. In a stultifying environment, misunderstood, mistreated,
and misguided, the boy and his physical and psychological withdrawals
are inextricable. "I liked to stay in bed for hours, even during the day
with the covers pulled up to my chin" (*Ham*, 38). Later, the need for
aloneness and silence is necessitated by deforming boils on the body. "I
was still tough but it wasn't the same. I had to withdraw. I watched

people from afar, it was like a stage play. Only they were on stage and I was an audience of one" (*Ham*, 122). The mere opportunity to walk and speak with one of the girls "would have made me feel very good" (*Ham*, 122). This distance, fully internalized, remains in the adult as a defining habit. Chinaski's pose of toughness is undercut by his obvious inexperience and vulnerability. "I looked at my virgin cock. 'I'm a man,' I said. 'I can whip anybody's ass' " (*Ham*, 188). Already, the adolescent hopes that his isolation may have an ultimate reward. "I watched them come out of the water, glistening, smooth-skinned and young, undefeated. I wanted them to want me. But never out of pity. Yet, despite their smooth untouched bodies and minds they still were missing something because they were as yet basically untested. When adversity finally arrived in their lives it might come too late or too hard. I was ready. Maybe" (*Ham*, 168).

In part, Bukowski's subject is the training of the hard, critical eye of the writer, and yet his recollection of the suffering boy is unmistakably poignant. The youth's wishful thinking about survival contains a truth that the reader recognizes, but it is a costly truth that makes the moment no easier. Chinaski's boils force him to watch "the frolics of California adolescence from the estranged point of view of monster-outsider."[17] In a pattern present throughout Bukowski's work, other misfits and outsiders flock to the narrator as their reluctant leader. Often he resists these overtures of friendship, longing instead for the beautiful upper-class life denied him. "Then I caught a glimpse of my reflection staring in at them—boils and scars on my face, my ragged shirt. I was like some jungle animal drawn to the light and looking in. Why had I come?" (*Ham*, 193). Ernest Fontana's contention that Chinaski descends from "both Frankenstein's monster and Kafka's Gregor" (6) seems accurate in the harsh light of the protagonist's self-condemnations. As a metaphor of disease, the boy's affliction is "of the surface, of the skin," beneath which he develops "notable powers of incorruptible skepticism, candor, independence, endurance, and self-assertion" (Fontana, 7). His disfigurement teaches hard lessons of humiliation and social ostracism. The beautiful people, Chinaski/Bukowski counters, are soft and sick inside.

Harrison notes that "Bukowski's own views are substantially more nuanced and moderate than Chinaski's" (160), and, in interviews, Bukowski's depiction of his upbringing was thoughtful, considered, and relatively free of resentment: "Very good discipline all the way through, but very little love going in either direction. Good training for the world, though, they made me ready. Today, watching the children, I'd say one thing they taught me was not to weep too much when something goes wrong. In other words, they hardened me to what I was going to go through: the bum, the road, all the bad jobs and the adversity. Since my early life hadn't been soft, the rest didn't come as such a shock" (Wennersten, 36). Nevertheless, the father's beatings of young Chinaski are brutal and made more so by their arbitrariness. After the first whipping, the boy asks his mother why she had not helped him, to which she ominously responds, "The father is always right" (*Ham*, 39). A simple domestic tableau of the father shaving, rather than eliciting admiration or mimicry in the son, is nightmarish. "There was only father and the razor strop and the bathroom and me. He used that strop to sharpen his razor, and early in the mornings I used to hate him with his face white with lather, standing before the mirror shaving himself. Then the first blow of the strop hit me" (*Ham*, 70). The father—mad, demented, foaming—is sadist and torturer, releasing the fury of a failed life on the only human seemingly in his control. Finally, the beatings end as abruptly as they began. "He hit me again. But the tears weren't coming. My eyes were strangely dry. I thought about killing him. . . . He hit me again. The pain was still there but the fear of it was gone. . . . Something had happened. The bath towels knew it, the shower knew it, the mirror knew it, the bathtub and the toilet knew it. My father turned and walked out the door. He knew it. It was my last beating. From him" (*Ham*, 121). The encounter is a lengthy, terrible, harrowing finale, and yet it represents a Pyrrhic victory for the son. A regrettable lesson has been learned, tied to the toughness Chinaski cherishes. Fear has been beaten away.

The father's attacks relate to the frequent fistfights in *Ham on Rye* and elsewhere in Bukowski's writings. Physical punishment, often recreational and undertaken with indifference, is linked to an endurance necessary for survival. The fights represent a test and a purgation. "But I wasn't frightened, for a change, and that felt good" (*Ham*, 159), explains Chinaski, although he is almost always outmatched. Toughness is presented as his greatest ability. He can take it, and he even gets in a few shots of his own, a rare opportunity to offer any counterattack. A symbolic fight with Jimmy Newhall, a football halfback, concludes the high-school recollections of the novel. The protagonist has the dubious benefit of his previous beatings. "But as he continued to punch, my fear vanished" (*Ham*, 214). Chinaski's theory that a soft life of popularity and beauty is inferior training for the adult world seems vindicated. "He was terrified. Terrified because he didn't know how to handle defeat. I decided to finish him slowly" (*Ham*, 215). Although it demonstrates some of the sadistic impulses of the father, this scene too is a victory for Chinaski. The crucial difference between father and son lies in the son's hatred of the manipulation of the weak and outcast. Nothing disturbs or angers the protagonist more than the abuse of power. When a cat is cornered by a bulldog, probably set up by other boys, Chinaski agonizes. *Ham on Rye* is full of references to flies and spiders. The narrator detests spiders and often destroys their webs. He explicitly compares the spider's leisurely, murderous behavior and his father's threatening sadism. "The King Spider was after me. I strode forward to meet it." As if on cue, his mother appears from behind a bush. "*Henry, Henry,* don't go home, don't go home, your father will kill you!" (*Ham*, 245).

Humanity in *Ham on Rye* is typically depicted as brutal, cowardly, and obsessed with appearance. Chinaski is likely not the only boy being beaten. Others in his grammar and junior high schools are unusually big and tough, and paradoxically these qualities are attributed to their difficult lives. "We all came from Depression families and most of us were ill-fed, yet we had grown up to be huge and strong. Most of us, I think, got little love from our families, and we didn't ask for love or kindness from anybody. We were a joke but people were careful not to laugh in front of us" (*Ham*, 91). For them, fighting is both symptomatic and therapeutic. The country's promise of success is a sham based on unbreachable class distinctions, and the boys recognize this. High-school graduation day epitomizes the charade of educational benefits:

> Jimmy Hatcher sat next to me. The principal was giving his address and really scraping the bottom of the old shit barrel. "America is the great land of Opportunity and any man or woman with a desire to do so will succeed . . ."
> "Dishwasher," I said.
> "Dog catcher," said Jimmy.
> "Burglar," I said.
> "Garbage collector," said Jimmy.
> "Madhouse attendant," I said.
> "America is brave, America was built by the brave . . . Ours is a just society."
> "Just so much for the few," said Jimmy.
> ". . . a fair society and all those who search for that dream at the end of the rainbow will find . . ."
> "A hairy crawling turd," I suggested. (*Ham*, 196)

For America's disenfranchised youth, the falsity of achievement based on merit is so self-evident that they respond with open derision. "At the age of 25 most people were finished. A whole god-damned nation of ass-holes driving automobiles, eating, having babies, doing everything in the worst possible way, like voting for the presidential candidate who reminded them most of themselves" (*Ham*, 174). *Ham on Rye* depicts a cruel and mendacious nation, as false and hollow at its center as the shining youths on its beaches.

Chinaski rejects the traditional values he witnesses and is unmoved by the country's entrance into World War II. He feels he has nothing to protect. All brokers of power are ultimately corrupt, all are mad bullies. Throughout the novel, in small and insidious ways, the boy is made to feel humiliated by his German background. He has not come to America by choice, and neither has he mixed homogeneously into the great melting pot: "for Bukowski-Chinaski, Los Angeles is not the chosen territory of exile" (Fontana, 4), and the racial and class determinations of his life are clear. "I made practice runs down to skid row to get ready for my future. . . . What were doctors, lawyers, scientists? They were just men who allowed themselves to be deprived of their freedom to think and act as individuals." He presents his alternative: "I went back to my shack and drank" (*Ham*, 274). *Ham on Rye* clarifies, however, that Chinaski is not alone in isolation; the disinherited and disenchanted number many.

At least five suicides occur in the novel, secondary characters whose self-destructions are reported in an offhand manner. These acts, both obvious and senseless, are unsurprising to the protagonist. Chinaski, too, considers the possibility of escape. "Sitting there drinking, I considered suicide, but I felt a strange fondness for my body, my life. Scarred as they were, they were mine." Toughness demands that one endure life, preferably with the mythical aplomb of the outlaw or gangster. "I would look into the dresser mirror and grin: if you're going to go, you might as well take eight, or ten or twenty of them with you" (*Ham*, 274). The criminal fringe is individual and self-empowered and therefore admirable. "That summer, July 1934, they gunned down John Dillinger outside the movie house in Chicago. He never had a chance. . . . A lot of people admired Dillinger and it made everybody feel terrible. Roosevelt was president" (*Ham*, 125). The "they" of Roosevelt and government, instead of serving as an inspiration or even as a balm to the working classes, are the murdering agents of freedom and independence. The public gangster, a romanticized and anachronistic figure, represents the individual fighting the system, almost miraculously transcending class restrictions and the inequitable distribution of wealth.

Alcohol and literature are the two methods that Chinaski discovers for escaping the arbitrary restrictions and limited possibilities his society offers. Both transport him to an imaginative place of improved experience, a place of altered consciousness relatively without bounds. His reaction to his discovery of wine is more than a boy's bluster: "I wasn't worried about anything. We sat on a park bench and chewed gum and I thought, well, now I have found something, I have found something that is going to help me, for a long time to come. The park grass looked greener, the park benches looked better and the flowers were trying harder" (*Ham*, 96). The infant Chinaski notes the "brilliant" (*Ham*, 11) eyes and gentleness of his alcoholic relatives; his grandfather and uncle are virtually angelic in contrast to Chinaski Sr., who despises them. Moreover, young Chinaski is hit—that is, marked—by a drunk driver. His future has found him.

The protagonist's other outlet is the imaginative escape of literature, both through reading books in the library and by writing his own early stories. His fantasies begin with elaborate sports fictions; although these may be typical of the young, Chinaski's are elaborate, the precursors of escapades he will soon begin to write.[18] The initial written "story" in the novel is a fifth-grade essay on a speech by Herbert Hoover that Chinaski didn't attend. The essay is purely imaginative, a satire of political jargon. The historically disregarded president is quoted as announcing: "Soon we would all sleep peacefully, our stomachs and our hearts full" (*Ham*, 83). The boy enjoys having his essay read and has an early sensation of the authority that language can impart. "My words filled the room. . . . Some of the prettiest girls in the class began to sneak glances at me. All the tough guys were pissed. Their essays hadn't been worth shit. I drank in my words like a thirsty man" (*Ham*, 83). Bukowski's metaphor of thirst again associates drink with spiritual nourishment and the writing act.

The novel's other early fiction is the adolescent war adventure of "a German aviator in World War I. Baron Von Himmlen. He flew a red Fokker" (*Ham*, 146). The Himmlen adventures, though raucous, sadly highlight Chinaski's isolation and desire for acceptance, both as an individual and as a native German. The Baron is superhuman in combat, rarely speaks, drinks alone, and disdains women. "He was an ugly man with scars on his face, but he was beautiful if you looked long enough— it was in the eyes, his style, his courage, his fierce aloneness" (*Ham*, 146).

As Chinaski ages, he continues to spend his time alone, writing stories, yet dismissing notions of a special talent. "I had written ten or twelve stories. Give a man a typewriter and he becomes a writer" (*Ham*, 246). Despite his disavowal of literary aspirations, the stories are clearly important to the young man; his father's violation of them initiates a final split with the son. Both respond vehemently to the typed pages, and the boy leaves home. "I went after my manuscripts first. That was the lowest of the blows, doing that to me. They were the one thing he had no right to touch. As I picked up each page from the gutter, from the lawn and the street, I began to feel better" (*Ham*, 247).

Concurrent with Chinaski's early writing efforts, and just as crucial to his growth and survival, is his discovery of the library. "Words weren't dull, words were things that could make your mind hum. If you read them and let yourself feel the magic, you could live without pain, with hope, no matter what happened to you. . . . To me, these men who had come into my life from nowhere were my only chance. They were the only voices that spoke to me. 'All right,' I would say" (*Ham*, 152). Between the impossibility of school and the brutality of home, Chinaski finds a place where he belongs, and he answers the call of literature with "yes." In several passages, he dissects and criticizes specific major authors, yet the exuberant tone even of his disappointments indicates a young man in the throes of discovery. He begins to speculate on the behavior of authors placed in his own situation, a practice the adult Chinaski would continue. "What would Maxim Gorky have done under such circumstances?" (*Ham*, 219). Voices from other times and places become his mentors. Several authors, noted or unnoted in the library, influence both the style and substance of Bukowski's novel. Chinaski's move to Bunker Hill foreshadows a debt to John Fante. The candor and unintentional wisdom of Chinaski as a boy remind the reader of Huck Finn, and the novel's title, *Ham on Rye*, is a reference to J. D. Salinger's famous story of adolescence, *The Catcher in the Rye*. Bukowski's flat, satirical language and sharp juxtapositions sometimes recall Kurt Vonnegut.[19]

The influence of Hemingway on Bukowski is obvious. Superficially, the authors share an emphasis on sports competition, its codified rules and definitive actions. "Finally they had to let it go. Then it was yours to destroy and the harder they threw it in the harder you could hit it out of there" (*Ham*, 182). More significantly, Bukowski learns and employs the clear, declarative sentence that his predecessor mastered. "And then along came Hemingway. What a thrill! He knew how to lay down a line" (*Ham*, 152). Several scenes in *Ham on Rye* also remind one of Hemingway. When Chinaski's mother asks him whether he loves her, he responds, "I really didn't but she looked so sad that I said, 'Yes' " (*Ham*, 52). This is reminscent of the conclusion of "Soldier's Home." The incompetent doctors who examine Chinaski's boils (*Ham*, 132) mimic the bumbling hesitance of a similar committee considering Frederick Henry's wounds in *A Farewell to Arms*.[20] Last, Bukowski, although a humorist, like Hemingway typically injects his characters with an emotional remoteness, an ethic of detachment and survival.

Another literary influence evident in *Ham on Rye* is James Thurber. When a friend objects that Thurber is "upper-class folderol," Chinaski counters that the former humorist knew "that everyone is crazy" (*Ham*, 258). Although the influence seems on the surface unlikely due to the authors' dramatically different class preoccupations, the high jinks, physical humor, and satirical wit contained in Thurber obviously appealed to Bukowski. Even the crude cartoons—of drunks, dogs, birds, and women—that became a Bukowski trademark are reminiscent of Thurber's illustrations, as if drawn by a primitive cousin. A generation older than Bukowski, Thurber could also be emulated and admired at a less-threatening distance than contemporaries. Thurber tellingly defines the life of the humorist writer:

> To call such persons "humorists," a loose-fitting and ugly word, is to miss the nature of their dilemma and the dilemma of their nature. The little wheels of their invention are set in motion by the damp hand of melancholy.
>
> Such a writer moves about restlessly wherever he goes, ready to get the hell out at the drop of a pie-pan or the lift of a skirt. His gestures are the ludicrous reflexes of the maladjusted; his repose is the momentary inertia of the nonplussed. He pulls the blinds against the morning and creeps into smoky corners at night. He talks largely about small matters and smally about great affairs.
>
> . . . It is his own personal time, circumscribed by the short boundaries of his pain and his embarrassment, in which what happens to his digestion, the rear axle of his car, and the confused flow of his relationships with six or eight persons and two or three buildings is of greater importance than what goes on in the nation or in the universe. He knows vaguely that the nation is not much good any more; he has read that the crust of the earth is shrinking alarmingly and that the universe is growing steadily colder, but he does not believe that any of the three is in half as bad shape as he is.[21]

This extract represents an extraordinarily apt description of the Chinaski persona, including his clownishness, restlessness, and general indifference to history and politics.[22]

Bukowski meticulously fashions his fictional self to respond to an absurd and dangerous world. Humor, even at one's own expense, is perhaps the wisest, most necessary, and most durable response. Hans Mayer wrote that "laughter is always tied to inappropriate behavior, to an offense against social conventions" (quoted in Harrison, 174). The young Chinaski, offended against, becomes the adult offender. He "oscillates between the two poles of proletarian *Weltanschauung:* that of pure self-interest . . . and that of a utopian change in social relations" (Harrison, 178). *Ham on Rye* offers compelling social, physical, and psychological possibilities for Chinaski's dysfunctional behavior, just as the novel begins to delineate the protagonist's virtues—courage, toughness, creativity, and individuality. Despite both imposed and self-created limitations, Chinaski remains a romantic and an idealist. He cannot have the world, but neither can the world entirely have him.

Chapter Three
Short Prose

Notes of a Dirty Old Man

During 1967 and 1968 Bukowski contributed a regular column, "Notes of a Dirty Old Man," to the Los Angeles independent newspaper *Open City*. His writings were a combination of autobiographical reporting and recollection, stories containing an element of the fantastic, and, peculiar for the author, explicit political musings generated by the turbulent period in American history. Julian Smith notes that the column "took its place alongside coverage of student unrest, the New Left, black power, civic and police corruption, the draft resistance, drug information, and adverts for sexual contacts and services."[1] Finally, Bukowski had accumulated "about 70 columns" in as many weeks, according to their author "a gathering of filthy stories and inane ravings."[2] More than half of these were collected in book form under the column's title and published in January 1969 by Essex House, "a North Hollywood press specializing in pornographic books," according to Bukowski's biographer. He continues that it "didn't take long for the twenty thousand copies printed to completely disappear from bookstore racks. This success resulted from Hank's exposure in the L.A. underground newspapers and helped enhance his status as a cult figure" (Cherkovski, *Hank*, 206).

Despite the book's continued popularity among Bukowski's works, *Notes of a Dirty Old Man* is an uneven collection. The writing, while loose, energetic, and entertaining, is also prolix and at times self-indulgent. The author, in fact, luxuriates in the excessiveness of the writing. Without question, the weekly commitment to a column, and the unbridled latitude offered by his editors, had an efficacious effect. "He was permitted not only to let it all hang out, he was encouraged in his explicitness, vulgarity, antiacademicism, fearlessness, and abuse of all orthodoxies, the liberal not excluded" (Locklin, "Setting Free the Buk," 28). Bukowski's stature as an underground poet had been growing for over a decade, but *Notes of a Dirty Old Man* marked his sustained return to prose and guaranteed a wider audience than he had previously known. He writes in the foreword to the columns that "for action, it has poetry beat all to hell. . . . But with *NOTES*, sit down with a beer and hit the typer on a Friday or a Saturday or a Sunday and by Wednesday the thing is all over the city. I get letters from people who have never read poetry, mine or anybody else's."[3]

The columns had an inestimable influence on the creation of the Bukowski mystique: the violent and abusive loner, bard of the L.A. streets. He cultivates such a persona in the columns, with varying degrees of intentional irony. One can imagine the interest in, and anticipation of, the weekly installments as they appeared; yet in retrospect, the whole seems less impressive than its parts. Nevertheless, *Notes of a Dirty Old Man* is pivotal in Bukowski's development as a prose writer. In his late forties, with his early stories two decades behind him, he had yet to write a novel. Certainly the confidence and attention the author acquired from the *Open City* columns were an impetus in his dedication to full-time writing. The speed and workmanlike skills of the journalist could only have helped in the rapid composition of *Post Office*.

The collection's historical importance in Bukowski's oeuvre notwithstanding, it is difficult to fully share its enthusiasts' excitement. One critic cited the columns' "deliberately disordered syntax, a 'spontaneous' typewriterese that creates its effect by a radical difference from smoother, more literary writing" (Smith, 57). The text is doggedly ungrammatical, redundant, and dedicated to its supposed artlessness. These effects may represent an attempt "to align writing with *spoken* rather than *written* conventions" (Smith, 57). A large portion of the biographical material in *Notes of a Dirty Old Man* is recycled in *Post Office*, *Factotum*, *Barfly*, and several short stories. In nearly all cases, the subsequent use of experiences is more distanced, nuanced, and sophisticated. Readers devoted to Bukowski's poetry were apparently a bit baffled, in the late 1960s and early 1970s, by the emergence of their hero as a prose writer. As early as 1974, Steve Richmond shared this ironic and overblown prophecy: "A major literary figure whose days of poetry are basically over and whose days of momentous prose are now occurring." He argued that Bukowski had more *"followers* each day" and that "His truth is as real as Christ's."[4] Such hyperbole does a disservice to Bukowski as a dedicated artist, a man whose ability as a prose writer, particularly with short fiction, improved dramatically over the two following decades. One need only compare the masterful, controlled storytelling of the 1983 collection *Hot Water Music* with the 1960s columns to prove the writer's growth. Earlier themes are readdressed. "Decline and Fall," "The Upward Bird," and "The Death of the Father I," each quite a different story, each haunting, recall materials and themes from *Notes of a Dirty Old Man* but are far superior treatments.

Notes of a Dirty Old Man has its merits, and readers' allegiance to the book is understandable. The columns are often comic, the satiric edge sometimes sharp, and already the author's dialogue crackles. The stories, told mostly in the first-person voice and often in the present tense, achieve an engaging immediacy. Despite the prose's tendency to ramble and a lack of clearly determined ironic distance in the voice, the collection is energetic. Unfortunately, the writing is too conscious of its hip unconventionality, which often distracts from the powerful content. For example, the eccentric use of lowercase letters to begin sentences seems little more than an unnecessary gimmick. Harrison argues that the writing is ultimately "as mannered as consciously literary prose. . . . Such writing calls attention to itself as much as the writing it reacts to, 'loaded' in Roland Barthes' words 'with the most spectacular signs of fabrication' " (256). As Bukowski's career progressed and he handled material with increasing authority, stylized and typographical distractions disappeared.

Whatever the arguable success of the author's attempt at "an impression of artless spontaneity" (Smith, 57), the contents of *Notes of a Dirty Old Man* are violent and fantastic; the effect is sometimes shocking and the reading always interesting. In one story, a man who has wings and is known by the conspicuous initials "J.C. for short" (*Notes*, 17), salvages the season of a losing baseball team. The night before the deciding pennant game, mobsters cut off J.C.'s wings. Maddened by the mutilation of his "savior," the team manager, Bailey, shoots Bugsy Malone in the back of the head during the game. Predictably, the Blues win the game anyway, and the story ends with Bailey reflecting on God and man from his prison cell. Another story ends with a similarly ironic flourish. One morning, Henry Beckett, in Kafkaesque fashion, awakens to find that his face and body have turned "gold-colored with green polka dots" (*Notes*, 109). Frustrated by medicine's lack of answers and by what he determines is an unlivable future, he takes a rifle to the top of a knoll and begins shooting drivers on the highway. Shortly before he is killed by the police, after they refuse his surrender, he notices that the spots have disappeared. "Henry ripped at his shirt, looked at his chest: WHITE" (*Notes*, 116). Such stories—the two described loosely represent, of course, religious and racial allegories—stress the randomness of disaster and the impossibility of the individual's control. Definitive action is inevitably destructive and pointless. If circumstances right themselves, this happens too late. The oddest element of these stories is their casual, almost lighthearted tone. Even the damned seem resigned to the absurdity of their demise.

At other moments, murder is presented with a terrible banality. A tailor continues to sew amid an apartment stinking with corpses, and a visiting friend reacts routinely to the bodies and makes a decision. "well, man, I can't call the police on you. you're my friend. you'll have to settle it yourself. but do you mind telling my why you killed those people?" The tailor's response, that he "disliked them" (*Notes*, 95), is as much explanation as the story offers. We infer that such characters, disenfranchised and isolated, enact events that match the random impossibility of their own lives. It seems significant that the tailor apparently surrenders, and he does so before he eats the lobster that would signify his own association with upper-class delicacies.[5] "the sun was gone and it was getting dark, and then he thought about Becky and then he thought about killing himself and then he didn't think about anything. . . . he never got to eat that lobster" (*Notes*, 98).

One of the collection's most effective stories involves a father and daughter playing together as they wait for the mother and the mother's lover to pick up the girl. The reader anticipates that this is a fictionalized reminiscence of Bukowski with his daughter, until the father suddenly, with a kind of "still magic," slices a butcher knife "four or five times across Marty's throat" (*Notes*, 74). Marty, the other man, falls backward down the steps. The father calmly sits again with his daughter to finish their game as the mother runs through the streets with news of the murder. The story ends on an enigmatic note: "and the sky was blue and the bread was in wrappers, and for the first time in years her eyes were live and beautiful. but death was really boredom, death was really boredom, and even the tigers and ants would never know how and the peach would someday scream" (*Notes*, 75–76). The mother is enlivened by murderous violence, but the finally unanswerable ennui encompassed in the repetition of the penultimate clause undermines the beauty of mad, desperate acts. When Bukowski and his daughter appear later in the book, in a relatively peaceful and nurturing scene, the earlier story of family mutilation still resonates. *Notes of a Dirty Old Man* generates much of its peculiar power through such jarring juxtapositions of material and tone.

The violence in the book is suitable to what Bukowski sees as a turbulent age on the brink of a revolution of which he is equally skeptical. "that's what this decade is: the Decade of the Experts and the Decade of the Assassins" (*Notes*, 56). The author is suspicious of assassins and experts alike: that is, those who enact violence for oblique social gains or for a minor personal notoriety, and the so-called experts who explain, cajole, and always maintain a status quo that validates their authority. Bukowski's political diatribes are not particularly original, but they are fascinating to hear from a man who seldom wrote about such matters explicitly, a writer who, as his career progressed, became increasingly adept at presenting his sociopolitical ideologies through art, by illustration rather than exposition.

Notes of a Dirty Old Man repeatedly returns to one subject that its author feels will offer a salve to society's wounds—literature. Several stories begin by establishing, directly or ironically, that Bukowski is a writer. The narrative will then turn in a radically different direction, leaving any reader who recalls the earlier information wondering about its inclusion. Still, a self-orientation toward literature and the writing life seems, finally, important to the book's agenda. Bukowski writes about meeting Neal Cassady and later visiting the famous writer L——. Direct references to himself and to his audience continually play up the "writerly" component of the columns. Last, the book suggests that even if writing does not save the writer, it may constitute the last best hope for a spiritually starving country: "so here we are mixing Revolution and Literature and they both fit. somehow everything fits, but I grow tired and wait for tomorrow" (*Notes*, 86). Once again, the tedious impossibility of days and nights and more days truncate insight. In *Notes of a Dirty Old Man,* Bukowski struggles to discover his message. The thoughts contain a markedly low level of abstraction and often trail off or are left undeveloped. What the author does know, intuitively, is that literature can bring something necessary and healing to difficult lives. These early columns are handmade and sometimes crooked road signs by an author finding his own way and inviting us to follow.

Erections, Ejaculations, Exhibitions and General Tales of Ordinary Madness

In 1972 City Lights Books released Bukowski's mammoth collection of short fiction, *Erections, Ejaculations, Exhibitions and General Tales of Ordinary Madness*. The lengthy title suited the book, which included 64 stories and ran nearly 500 pages. Subsequently, these stories were divided into two volumes, *Tales of Ordinary Madness* and *The Most Beautiful Woman in Town*, and these popular editions have remained in print.

Bukowski's followers greeted the original collection with excitement, and one exuberant fan wrote: "They can be called the most honest, straightforward, enlightening, and important stories published in this country in the last couple of decades. . . . Beside Charles Bukowski's mindbombs, most other short stories are effete puffballs, collegeboy finger exercises that have little to do with reality or the world outside."[6] Harrison, however, recently offered a more qualified assessment of stories that suffer from some of the same indulgences as *Notes of a Dirty Old Man*: "The sex scenes in the early stories were repetitious and simplistic. . . . This is all too close to, if it is not actually, the language of pulp fiction. . . . The repetitive, sometimes sloppy, writing is a result of an aesthetic credo that marred a fair amount of Bukowski's early work, especially the prose" (253, 255). This "credo" includes the importance of apparent spontaneity and the avoidance of the seemingly literary.

Yet taken as a whole, these stories are an amazing and various assemblage. Some were published in *Open City*, some in the men's magazines *Knight* and *Adam*. With the latter associations, Bukowski, no doubt intentionally, severed any possibility of his stories receiving serious consideration by academia. The pieces collected in the *Tales of Ordinary Madness* volume are an eclectic combination of essays on literature, horse racing, and drug culture disguised as Platonic dialogues with friends and younger writers; scenes of prison, the madhouse, and poetry readings later recycled; and a touch of the fantastic. Only rare moments between father and daughter supply any quiet and self-sufficient counterpoint to the raucous pitch. The author employs the "I" voice frequently and blends his own name in with the criminal protagonists often enough for an unsettling effect. There is scant distance between the stories of "Charles Bukowski," poet of minor underground repute, and the stories of rapists and madmen and killers.

The fantastic element is used selectively in the stories, but with a growing confidence and effectiveness. Two of the most interesting pieces in the collection are the oddly titled "Animal Crackers in My Soup" and the Kafka fantasy "The Blanket." Both deal with the volume's primary theme: the amorphous definition of a madness that may be necessary for the preservation of the creative individual. "Animal Crackers in My Soup" begins with a typical Bukowski situation that introduces the protagonist's plight: "I had come off a long drinking bout during which time I had lost my petty job, my room, and (perhaps) my mind."[7] The narrator Gordon's possible instability informs the rest of the story. He is taken by Carol into a house where she lives among a menagerie of wild and exotic animals that Gordon discovers are her lovers. Clearly Gordon, too, has been chosen for her zoo, perhaps for a madness that distinguishes him from society. Biblical overtones are obvious, with the sanctuary representing a combination of Edenic passivity and survivalist ark. On successive nights, Gordon watches a snake and a tiger make love to Carol, then he in turn becomes her lover.

> She looked at him and laughed. "Do you think I'm Crazy Carol?"
> "I don't know," I said. "There's no way to tell." (*Tales*, 211)

Even the narrator, himself possibly untrustworthy, can detect that standards of judgment have been inverted.

Although by conventional criteria Carol is insane, the harmony in her zoo is presented as vastly superior to the outside world. To find a paradise, the story suggests, one must construct it interiorly. However, the "mad" individual whose vision threatens society cannot be allowed to continue. "I searched the rooms. Nothing was left alive. All murdered. The black bear. The coyote. The raccoon. All. The whole house was quiet. Nothing moved. There was nothing we could do. I had a large burial project on my hands. The animals had paid for their individuality—and ours" (*Tales*, 214). The narrator concludes that life will all "turn to hate, to dementia, to neurosis, to stupidity, to fear, to murder, to nothing—." These thoughts anticipate the story's expected conclusion, when Carol births a "medically impossible" child: "It was a tiger, a bear, a snake and a human. It was an elk, a coyote, a lynx and a human. It did not cry. Its eyes looked upon me, and I knew it" (*Tales*, 216). The fablelike conclusion of the story, while predictable, is a memorable and eerie consideration of brutality, intolerance, and the consequences of human arrogance. Although on one level the child is suggested as savior, its moment of recognition by one of its fathers coincides with the "first hydrogen bomb" falling on San Francisco. The birth of a new, integrated being is "unbearable" and "impossible" (*Tales*, 216), the narrator's voice is thick with regret, and the story conflates this new beginning with apocalypse.

"The Blanket," which ends *Tales of Ordinary Madness*, also begins simply, although elliptically. "I have not been sleeping well lately but this is not what I'm getting at exactly" (*Tales*, 231). The narrator is apparently Bukowski, adding verisimilitude to the fantastic events. Stranded alone in his room and with his reflections, Hank begins to doubt his sanity. He watches a blanket move. Even tested outside the confines of his room, the madness continues: "Then when I got to the top of the stairway something made me turn and look down the hall. You are right: the blanket was following me, moving in snake-movements, folds and shadows at the front of it making head, mouth, eyes. Let me say that as soon as you begin to believe that a horror is a horror, then it finally becomes LESS horror" (*Tales*, 234). His neighbor Mick verifies the movement of the blanket, although only the men can see it. (Mick's wife attributes their delusions to alcohol.) The story ends with Hank back in his own apartment, burning the blanket and left again with his thoughts.

The mystery lies finally not in the blanket's movement but in its purpose. Is the intent to wrap one in warmth or to strangle? The blanket, cut and then burned, appears to bleed, and the narrator, in a moment of attempted empathy, regrets the destruction of the seemingly benign visitor. "I searched my hands for cuts. The hands of Christ were beautiful hands. I looked at my hands. There was not a scratch. . . . I felt tears coming down my cheeks, crawling like heavy senseless things without legs. I was mad. I must be truly mad" (*Tales*, 238). These last words indicate that the narrator's senseless act against the unknown, his bloody culpability, is more integral to his madness than the ability to recognize a visiting wraith. As is usual in Bukowski's surrealistic stories, the fantastic or sensational element is greeted with acceptance and resignation rather than surprise. This flat reception of the surreal has a startling impact on the reader's perception of the mundane. "Madness? Sure. What isn't madness? Isn't Life madness?" Hank continues: "We walk around and presume things, make plans, elect governors, mow lawns. . . . Madness, surely, what ISN'T madness?" (*Tales*, 238). These lines define the broad thesis of the aptly titled *Tales of Ordinary Madness*. Gareth and Herget explain the effect Bukowski achieves by blending the fantastic with the commonplace: "The unusual and the sensational modulate seamlessly into the familiar and the common thereby producing a banalization of the incredible and at the same time the all too familiar is given a new dimension."[8]

Although "The Blanket" is unusual in that its narrator possibly effects his own spiritual destruction, the point is persistently made throughout *Tales of Ordinary Madness* that the individual is under siege by a frightened status quo, by an armed bureaucracy, by a ravenous and murdering "other." Bukowski's early stories repeatedly focus on the loner fighting a romantic—because it is impossible—war for physical and intellectual independence. Society's brutality is often manifested by the police. "Then they got a white guy, screaming something about

CONSTITUTIONAL RIGHTS . . . and when they brought him back they leaned him against a wall, and he just stood there trembling, these red welts all over his body, he stood there trembling and shivering" (*Tales*, 56). Sometimes the "other" is a more nebulous and unnamed "they": "it's July 1968 and I hit the machine as I wait for the door to break down and see the two green-faced men with eyes the shade of pale jelly, air-cooled hand m.g.'s. I hope they don't show. it's been a lovely evening. and only a few lone partridges will remember the roll of the dice and the way the walls smiled. good night" (*Tales*, 139–40). In "Purple as an Iris," despite the story's humorous tone, even sexual privacy is violated by the Orwellian guards who see all.

> I worked it in. It was great. I just got going good when it seemed as if
> the whole Italian army had burst into the barn—
> "HEY! STOP! STOP! UNHAND THAT WOMAN!"
> "DISMOUNT IMMEDIATELY!"
> "GET YOUR PECKER OUT OF THERE!" (*Tales*, 172–73)

A feeling of justified paranoia pervades the stories; Bukowski illustrates his fears convincingly. Madhouses and prisons constitute the structured, overseen environment where individual liberties are not tolerated. The locations are metaphors for the author's depiction of all society and its often class-based violations.

The poor suffer more frequent and greater humiliations and terrors than the rich, and Bukowski is insistent in his romantic belief that a harder life, lived on the edge of madness, is a purer and truer life. According to Smith, Bukowski posits a comparable belief in the value of marginality when regarding outlaws (who, like the poor, live essentially outside of, and in spite of, the boundaries of law): "Criminals and tyrants supposedly live more authentically (that is, unhampered by moral codes, external authorities) than the solid, law-abiding citizen" (59). In *The Most Beautiful Woman in Town*, an appreciation of renegade behavior is demonstrated in a story such as "A Drinking Partner," in which the narrator only slightly qualifies praise of a violent companion: "I don't suppose Jeff was a very good human being. He made a lot of mistakes, brutal mistakes, but he *had* been interesting. . . . Everybody's asleep and sane and proper. A real son of a bitch like him is needed now and then."[9]

Another story from the second volume, "The Gut-Wringing Machine," considers the mystique of the outlaw and, in a comic treatment, returns to the motif of abolished individuality. A job agency squeezes its victims through a machine until they are banal, obvious, and anxious to enter the workforce. When one of the victims announces a list of heroes that includes Dillinger, Castro, Jersey Joe Walcott, Villon, and Hemingway, he is put back through the wringer until he prefers Bob Hope, Mae West, and Richard Nixon (*Beautiful*, 53). The story is obvious but amusing, with one of the two bosses finally putting the other through the wringer. Ironically, an image of the individual survives, but it is the boss-gangster, the coldhearted hustler who perpetuates bland normality and makes a fortune in the process. The story ends on a satiric yet mercenary note: "he threw out the dollar cigar, lit another, ran the Caddy up to 90, straight at the sun like an arrow, business was good and life, and the tires whirled over the dead and the dying and the dying-to-be" (*Beautiful*, 57).

More than do the stories in *Tales of Ordinary Madness,* the stories in *The Most Beautiful Woman in Town* focus on sexual relationships. Not surprisingly, the message is that healthy and sustainable companionship is practically impossible. The collection begins with the sentimental but poignant title story, in which the narrator falls in love with the darkly mysterious Cass. "She was like a spirit stuck in a form that would not hold her. Her hair was black and long and silken and moved and whirled about as did her body. . . . Some said she was crazy. The dull ones said that" (*Beautiful*, 1). When Cass commits suicide, the narrator considers his own responsibility. "Everything about her had indicated that she had cared. I had simply been too offhand about it, lazy, too unconcerned. I deserved my death and hers" (*Beautiful*, 7). From this point, the stories in the book form a decidedly downward spiral, representing relationships as enervating exercises in power and physical release.

Despite the satiric and light tone of several stories, the overall message in *The Most Beautiful Woman in Town* is downbeat. In the fantasy "Six Inches," a witch-seductress shrinks the protagonist Henry to her desired miniature size, that of a phallus. He dances for her and, as the reader expects, is inserted into her for sexual gratification. The psychological suggestion—that the reduced male suffocates inside the woman—is clear. Sex is torture for him. "Sarah began moving me faster and faster. My skin began to burn, it became harder to breathe; the stench became worse. I could hear her panting" (*Beautiful*, 31). Bukowski's parody of the shrinking man plot, a science fiction staple, makes explicit many suggestions already present in that type of story. The science fiction and folktale element extends even to the tiny man killing the monster, the woman, with a hat pin. "I lifted the pin and plunged it in. Just below the birthmark" (*Beautiful*, 32). Once the beast is eliminated, Henry slowly returns to the size of an adult. This story is followed by Bukowski's infamous "The Fuck Machine," a flawed story that nevertheless makes its point that men prefer a beautiful machine to a real woman. But banalities prevail: the machine cannot be controlled, and the men are susceptible to ruining a good sexual partner with emotional involvement that ends as violence. If she cannot be owned, she will be torn apart.

As the volume progresses, the sexual involvements continue to deteriorate, demonstrating repeatedly the ultimate, inevitable, and unrelenting disappointment of ruined relationships and the perverse effect upon the participants. In "The Copulating Mermaid of Venice, Calif.," two bored and lonely men steal a corpse and discover it to be that of a beautiful woman. Predictably, necrophilia ensues. Tony has never had "such a fuck as this in all his days!" Bill admits it is "the best fuck I *ever* had!" (*Beautiful*, 160). More surprising, however, is the story's sad and touching conclusion. Fearing capture, the men take the corpse to the beach late that night and float it out over the breakers. Tony realizes not the hideousness of their behavior but rather the symbolic potency of the woman as magical "mermaid." She represents an impossible fantasy yet contains the truth of the men's sick emptiness. "They got back to the car. Bill drove. They argued over the final drinks on the way home, then Tony thought about the mermaid. He put his head down and began to cry" (*Beautiful*, 162). This peculiar story hints through its grotesqueness at a sympathy both for the men and for the violated female body. The lives of the forsaken are again contrasted with a stable, churchgoing, middle-class America. "Some were awakening with hangovers. Some were awakening with thoughts of church. Most were still asleep. A Sunday morning. And the mermaid, the mermaid with that dead sweet tail, she was well out to sea. While somewhere a pelican dove, came up with a glittering, guitar-shaped fish" (*Beautiful*, 163). The narrative voice, too, appropriates a sexist tone, and the woman is transformed into an unattainable ideal of fulfillment, unattainable because it is unreal.

The final third of *The Most Beautiful Woman in Town* contains its most violent stories. "The Fiend" is a plausible case study of a child rapist, a man who begins once again in a typical Bukowskian abjection: "Now he was forty-five, lived alone on the fourth floor of an apartment house and had just lost his twenty-seventh job through absenteeism and disinterest" (*Beautiful*, 207). The author is convincing in his portrayal of isolated male characters whose acts, though repugnant, are made understandable. He repeatedly implies that the distance between the rapist and the poet, the killer and the cop or clergyman, is alarmingly small. The difference is a matter of degree and circumstance, of a fortuitously timed moment of kindness or cruelty, and always of luck. "The Murder of Ramon Vasquez" is a graphic recounting of the beating and murder of a male matinee idol past his prime. His only apparent crimes, in the eyes of his torturers, are his homosexuality, his generosity, and his trust. These final stories deal more consistently with male meetings and communities and a growing homosexual theme, as if the woman has been abandoned or excised, or has dismissed herself from the barbaric humiliations ritually imparted between males.

A preoccupation with the male environment is just one area of the early stories that recalls Hemingway. Although Bukowski at times criticizes Hemingway for his lack of humor and the unevenness of his later writing, a debt is nonetheless recognized. Chinaski notes the similarity between Hemingway and a university professor in "Would You Suggest Writing as a Career?": "The professor looked just like Hemingway. Of course, Hemingway was dead. The professor was rather dead too" (*Tales*, 37). The professor's obsession with literary talk seems an oblique criticism of the earlier author, as does Chinaski's kissing of the professor's wife. Nevertheless, Bukowski's continual references to Hemingway keep his begrudgingly recognized mentor in the foreground. In "Night Streets of Madness," Bukowski places himself in the role of sympathetic confidant. When Bukowski asks Hemingway over the telephone why he committed suicide, this exchange follows:

> "when they believed in THE OLD MAN AND THE SEA, I knew that the world was rotten."
> "I know. you went back to your early style, but it wasn't real."
> "I know it wasn't real. and I got the PRIZE. and the tail on me. old age on me. sitting around drinking like an old fuck, telling stale stories to anybody who would listen. I had to blow my brains out."
> "o.k., Ernie, see you later."
> "all right, I know you will, Buk." (*Tales*, 162)

Bukowski's criticism of Hemingway is softened by their shared understanding of life's fickle and destructive demands on the author, and by the ominous, familiar quality of their farewells. In "Notes on the Pest," Bukowski describes the followers of fame who hound him: "these destroyers, although they have no idea of your thought process, they do sense your dislike for them, yet in another way this only encourages them. also they realize that you are a certain type of person—that is, given a choice of hurting or being hurt, you will accept the latter, pests thrive on the best slices of humanity; they know where the good meat is" (*Tales*, 195). The "pest" is reminiscent of the "pilot fish" that Hemingway laments in *A Moveable Feast*, a similarity that highlights a central dilemma for both authors. They desired and cultivated celebrity and yet found it corrupting. "Then you have the rich and nothing is ever as it was again. The pilot fish leaves of course. . . . He is never caught and he is not caught by the rich. Nothing ever catches him and it is only those who trust him who are caught and killed. He has the irreplaceable early training of the bastard."[10]

Although Bukowski's early stories lack the precision and craftsmanship of Hemingway's, they incorporate "a macho role model, an existential material, and an experimental style already pushed in the direction of American 'speech' " (Smith, 57). Smith further contends that Bukowski's rewriting of Hemingway, with humor, qualifies Bukowski as a postmodernist. "We term 'postmodern' those writers who have learned from modernism, and then added extrastylistic components" (56), and Bukowski has "pushed the stripped-down, denotative (classic) style of Hemingway into play, parody, and laughter" (57). A story such as "All the Pussy We Want," with its focus on a male-centered amoralism presented through fragmentary and elliptical conversation, stresses this lineage. Bukowski was from his earliest work a writer of lean and energetic dialogue, a talent that both associates him with and distinguishes him from Hemingway. "What is most striking in Bukowski's use of speech, specifically dialogue, is the dramatic concision it undergoes in what I call 'the routine,' the humorous, formulaic, stereotyped, dialogic interaction derived from some classic American comedians. On more than one occasion, Bukowski has indicated that one of his influences was Jackie Gleason" (Harrison, 243).

The technique of the routine supplies a humorous moment in the story "Goodbye Watson." The narrator suggests that the only lesson he could give a creative-writing class would be to require them to attend the horse races and place win bets. Only experience outside the classroom is significant for the artist. "my students would automatically become better writers, although most of them would begin to dress badly and might have to walk to school" (*Tales*, 73). The 'routine' begins as Bukowski, addressing his imaginary class, criticizes a young woman at length for betting on One-Eyed Jack in the feature race. A lecture ensues on the many technical reasons why this was a "sucker bet" (*Tales*,

73); the punch line is delivered after a student asks which horse, then, the teacher bet:

> "how did you do?"
> "I lost a hundred and forty dollars."
> "who did you bet in the feature race?"
> "One-Eyed Jack. class dismissed." (*Tales*, 74)

His admission of failure collapses the punditry of the preceding lecture. "In the small game, and in the Great Game," David Mamet writes of gambling advice, "the wisdom . . . will, unfortunately, only be appreciated after one has suffered sufficiently to acquire it independently."[11] Bukowski's true lesson is the impossibility of a sure system and the inconsistency of luck. The organization of the comedic routine involves the audience through its superior knowledge, "bonds the speakers" in a community of shared interests, and precludes the possibility of "any kind of serious dialogue" (Harrison, 24). The form, with its implicating constraints, has been used repeatedly by Bukowski for comic and ideological effect.

The racetrack is the most frequent setting in Bukowski's work besides the single room and perhaps the bar. The track location is well represented in the early stories, including a triptych of consecutive treatments in *The Most Beautiful Woman in Town*: "25 Bums in Rags," "Non-Horseshit Horse Advice," and "Another Horse Story." The second is precisely what its title suggests, a short essay of betting advice offered with minimal irony. The author contends that his relationship with the track is analogous to Hemingway's relationship with the bullring: the setting represents a microcosm of human existence beneficial to the writer, a classroom where one learns one's own behavior and how to act with precision and style. "that's what Hem learned at the bullfights and put to work in his work. that's what I learn at the track and put to work in my life" (*Tales*, 161). It is curiously confrontational that Bukowski differentiates the application of principles to Hemingway's "work" from those to his own "life." Bukowski may be in a sense a postmodern Hemingway, his work injected with absurdist laughter, but missing is the earlier writer's eloquently tragic perception. "Bukowski's own writing lacks that sustained fatalism that pervades Hemingway's work, that obsession with our failure to recognize when our luck has run out. In Bukowski's narratives we repeatedly straddle the fine divide between winning and losing, between self-possession and the illusion of control, and it is this that underlies the bitter comedy . . . for in that narrowest of gaps a whole world emerges."[12]

Bukowski refers to luck with conspicuous frequency in his writing. The racetrack crowd, while grotesque and repellent to the author, also amaze him with the persistence of their hope. There is always another day, another racing form, another hopeless dream. One suspects that this human element, as much as the precision and talent involved with the betting act, appealed to Bukowski the writer, the loner, the man of the crowd. The ideal of winning contains a sustaining power, although the rare winner is still a dressed-up clown. "and that Tuesday at Hollywood Park I won $140 at the races and I was once again the quite casual lover, hustler, gambler, reformed pimp and tulip grower" (*Beautiful*, 97). The cycle of fortune dictates that a winning streak is inevitably followed by its opposite. Nevertheless, these moments of respite are crucial in Bukowski's philosophy.

To survive, a man needs sporadic bits of luck, a sense of humor in the face of nothingness, and the ridiculous ability to sustain hope. These are the qualities sought and perpetuated in the author's stories despite their darkness. "He testifies that even under the worst of circumstances people can remain undefeated."[13] Such persistence toward life is perhaps Bukowski's most surprising and salient element. In "Nut Ward Just East of Hollywood," the narrator's laughter is contagious to his community of fellow madmen: "and then they put on some old Laurel and Hardy flicks . . . there was one where the bastards were fighting for covers in the sleeper of a Pullman. I was the only one who laughed. People stared at me. I just cracked peanuts and kept on laughing. Then Izzy began laughing. Then everybody started laughing at them fighting for the covers in the Pullman. . . . Living was easy—all you had to do was let go" (*Tales*, 31).

South of No North

Bukowski's collection *South of No North*, subtitled *Stories of the Buried Life*, was published by Black Sparrow Press in 1973. In the short time that had passed since the City Lights volume, the author's short fiction had tightened and grown more subtle and sophisticated. Harrison identifies "a noticeable change" in *South of No North*, with Bukowski beginning "to achieve a distance from his material, formal evidence of which was his increased use of the third person." Even the first-person accounts begin to be less autobiographical, and *South of No North* forms "a kind of transition" (Harrison, 250) between Bukowski's early stories and his later, strongest two collections. Additionally, the more overtly autobiographical stories begin to mine Bukowski's early years and childhood, material he had previously resisted. The style is increasingly assured, and grammatical and typographical mannerisms have largely disappeared. The greater sharpness of the writing results in stories that are short and succinct.[14]

Several of the stories are also recastings of earlier treatments. In "No Way to Paradise," a woman removes from her purse "a small wire cage and took some little people out and sat them on the bar."[15] The situation is reminiscent of "Six Inches," with the essential difference in the later story being the narrator's distance. The man is not physically reduced himself, but rather enjoys a role of voyeur as the small couples alternately hurt, mistreat, and make love to one another. The later story incriminates male and female alike as it identifies the "small" and abusive rituals of human beings. "I pulled Dawn to me. She was beautiful and young and had insides. I could be in love again. . . . 'I'll kill everybody!' screamed little Anna. She rattled about in her wire cage at 3 a.m. in the morning" (South, 32). In "Love for $17.50," the protagonist Robert initiates a sexual relationship with a store mannequin. This is another of Bukowski's stories, including "Fuck Machine" and "The Copulating Mermaid of Venice, Calif.," in which the male turns to an artificial or inert woman. The irony of such stories is that although the males prefer these inanimate women because they free the men from the baggage of a real relationship—no responsibilities, no emotional burden, no daily trivialities—strong affection, often love, inevitably develops.

Even in perverse circumstances, separating the sex act from personal involvement is difficult. In "Love for $17.50," as in "Fuck Machine," the "perfect" relationship is even more transient than a customary traditional one. Society will not allow such a union. In this case, the human girlfriend, Brenda, explodes against her artificial counterpart, Stella. "Then she leaped at the mannequin and started to claw and beat at it." After Brenda departs, Robert spends a final moment with the decapitated ideal of his dreams. "Robert walked over to Stella. The head had broken off and rolled under a chair. There were spurts of chalky material on the floor. . . . He just stood in the hallway, sobbing and waiting" (South, 42). Robert recalls the death of his parents, but "this was different," and the loneliness, the aloneness of the thawed Bukowski man, is palpable. Companionship with the "other" remains an enigma: "Both of Stella's eyes were open and cool and beautiful. They stared at him"

(*South*, 42). Despite Robert's wishful perceptions, the eyes do not stare in reproach or sadness. They are empty.

Another recurring Bukowski motif, that of women who devour men, is reversed in "Maja Thurup." The story involves an aging socialite who goes into the South American jungle for a "last fling": Hester Adams "entered the jungle with her camera, her portable typewriter, her thickening ankles and her white skin and had gotten herself a cannibal, a black cannibal: Maja Thurup" (*South*, 49). Maja Thurup's great tragedy is that the village has ostracized him for being "vastly overhung" (*South*, 49). After Hester is able to take all of him into her, the two celebrate the "miracle" with a three-day tribal wedding. Her ability to "ingest" his "meat" (*South*, 50) anticipates the story's inverted conclusion. Maja Thurup, displaced in North Hollywood, eats his wife and stores her remains in a refrigerator. The Chinaski persona is distanced, cast as an outsider assigned to cover this great love affair for publication. Despite the goriness of the story's subject matter, it is light and amusing, rendered so primarily by the bland reportage of Chinaski. The female is consumed, and Maja Thurup, a barely modified portrayal of the kept artist, realizes Bukowski's ideals of freedom and leisure: "Maja sat in the middle of the rug with his English grammar books, drinking beer and wine, and singing native chants and playing the bongo" (*South*, 50). "Maja Thurup" is a comic fantasy of the artist as cannibal—indulgent, preoccupied, consuming, and deadly.

The settings in *South of No North* are largely male environments of physicality and labor. Fewer mentions of the racetrack are compensated for by a persistent theme of boxing. These male spheres of action and the stories' clarity and brevity again indicate the Hemingway influence. In his article "*South of No North*: Bukowski in Deadly Earnest," Norman Weinstein warns that such an influence is evident early in the book. "In no other collection of Bukowski's fiction does Ernest Hemingway's ghost play such a major role. Even the book's title, with that flatly articulated oxymoron reminiscent of *Men without Women* and *Winner Take Nothing*, alerts the reader to the Hemingway presence."[16] Hemingway again appears as a character, most fully in the boxing story "Class." Bukowski employs the older writer's own metaphor, estimating prowess in the ring against famous authors, by challenging Papa himself. "Hemingway had just finished a novel, come in from Europe or somewhere, and he was in the ring fighting somebody" (*South*, 65). Bukowski boxes in his own unorthodox manner—no mouthpiece, wearing street shoes, smoking a cigar—and takes punishment in the first round. The second round's outcome, however, is more suggestive. "I had Hemingway up against the ropes. He couldn't fall. Each time he started to fall forward I straightened him with another punch. It was murder. *Death in the Afternoon*" (*South*, 67). Hemingway asks his opponent's name, and, after Hemingway admits that he has never heard of him, Chinaski retorts, "You will" (*South*, 67).

The bravado of the story—its simple title identifies the character of the combatants and the theme of teaching—is clearly parodic. The triumphant Chinaski, with the hindsight of history, shares a sympathetic moment. " 'You're a good man, Papa. Nobody wins them all.' I shook his hand. 'Don't blow your brains out' " (*South*, 68). Weinstein contends that "even the flippancy of the narrator's last line can't erase the sense of tender respect (rare in this book) that Bukowski feels for Papa" (53). Later in the collection, in "No Neck and Bad as Hell," the narrator meets Hemingway in a bar, and the two exchange intellectual barbs, Hemingway scoring with the comment that Chinaski's literary pretensions make him sound "like a character out of early Huxley" (*South*, 138). Despite the ambivalence of the author's feelings and his debt to the earlier writer, the continual mentions and the fact of Bukowski's own rising popularity suggest a position of homage, humility, and recognition of the difficulties of living one's public myth.

Several stories in *South of No North* are specifically reminiscent of particular Hemingway stories. In "Maja Thurup," Hester Adams, whose sexual power and public appeal are fading with age, recalls Margaret Macomber and her comparable predicament. Adams is 35, and "the wrinkles were appearing, the breasts had been sagging for some time, the ankles and calves were thickening, there were signs of a belly" (*South*, 49). The exotic setting also suggests the similarity. In "The Short, Happy Life of Francis Macomber," Margaret "had been a great beauty and she was still a great beauty in Africa, but she was not a great enough beauty any more at home to be able to leave him and better herself and she knew it and he knew it."[17] Such a manipulative, economic equation for relationships is also found in Bukowski's earlier story "The Beginner" following the male's introduction to the racetrack. "As she bent over I looked at her and thought, soon I'll be able to afford something just a little bit better than that. uh huh" (*Beautiful*, 206). The last phrase recognizes the false conceit of the male in the universal transactions of power, money, sex, and love.

Bukowski's western parody, "Stop Staring at My Tits, Mister," concludes with a debased retelling of the famous conclusion of "Short,

Happy Life." Big Bart, the "meanest man in the West" and "well hung" (*South*, 70), represents the cruel natural man, a raw equivalent of the great white hunter. He is caught attempting intercourse with The Kid's wife, Honeydew, and the story ends with a duel. Big Bart is almost certainly about to die. The Kid will be avenged for his wife's humiliation. "Big Bart's hand flicked toward his holster. A shot rang through the twilight. Honeydew lowered her smoking rifle and went back into the covered wagon. The Kid was dead on the ground, a hole in his forehead. Big Bart put his unused gun back in his holster and strode toward the wagon. The moon was up" (*South*, 73). The humor of the scene is the predictable simplicity of the characters' motivations. Honeydew chooses the rough sexuality of Big Bart, a clear choice of physical gratification over ideals, romance, faithfulness, or emotion. Unlike the end of Hemingway's story, no accident is involved, no confused fear by the female regarding the male's bravery. The Kid's idealistic courage marks him as a fool; a real man doesn't waste his "gun" in such a manner.

South of No North continues to explore the author's fascination with criminal outsiders. In "The Killers," the bungling but deadly pair Harry and Bill recall the criminal hopefuls Harry and Duke in the earlier story "All the Pussy We Want." Bukowski's "The Killers" is less oblique and challenging than Hemingway's famous story of the same title, but it and the story "Hit Man," taken together, form a sort of composite of Hemingway's single story and combine its primary element: the introduction of a criminal "evil," banal and presumptuous, into an unwary middle-class setting. In "The Killers," Bukowski demonstrates the fragility of the domestic in horrifying detail, and the reader is incriminated by earlier enjoyment of the outlaws' banter. Humor drains from the story; the clowns have become careless and inhuman killers.

> *"Oh No! Jesus Christ, No! Not my wife, you bastards!"*
> Harry had not heard them enter. The young man let out a scream. Then Harry heard a gurgle. He pulled out and looked around. The young man was on the floor with his throat cut; the blood spurted rhythmically out on the floor. (*South*, 58)

The author's conversations are clipped, tough, sardonic, and often trivial. They reveal the emptiness at the heart of the central characters and show a blasé world of criminal marauders just below the surface of ordinary society.

Bukowski begins the story "Guts" with an explanation of his affinity for the marginalized criminal: "I have always admired the villain, the outlaw, the son of a bitch. . . . I like desperate men, men with broken teeth and broken minds and broken ways. They interest me. They are full of surprises and explosions" (*South*, 119). This sentiment could also be tied to, as in Hemingway, obsession with independence and rebellion against societal restrictions of behavior and belief. "Both authors assert masculine dignity as a necessary rite-of-passage technique in order to survive integrally within an unjust and emasculating socioeconomic system. The ruthless drive to 'act like a man' that all Hemingway and Bukowski characters share leads to a distrust in both authors of any political solutions. . . . Characters in Bukowski and Hemingway are the rugged individualists who defy the utopian schemes of all ideologues. Male character armor held firm by a swaggering boastfulness assures survival" (Weinstein, 53–54). This reading suggests that the most important similarity between the writers may, after all, be ideological rather than stylistic. Weinstein continues that the two authors share "a great deal of eternal youth" (54), which he links to their drifting and the search for singular, unsustainable moments of love. "Is it not precisely this adolescence of vision which makes Hemingway and Bukowski the quintessential American story writers of our age?" (Weinstein, 55).

Bukowski's man alone in a room may finally not be so different from Hemingway's wandering expatriate. The unifying thread, which also explains a preoccupation with criminality, is the preservation of personal freedom. Such an assertion of individuality inevitably involves political choice. Bukowski's aversion to state intervention is summarized in "Remember Pearl Harbor?": "My objection to war was not that I had to kill somebody or be killed senselessly, that hardly mattered. What I objected to was to be denied the right to sit in a small room and starve and drink cheap wine and go crazy in my own way and at my own leisure" (*South*, 85). Hemingway's preoccupation with war signals an important difference between the two authors, yet in this context it is largely irrelevant. Each man owns the right to his own damnation, on his own terms. The two men would certainly agree to such a belief, if not on the type and value of a codified behavior to obtain it.

Hot Water Music

Hot Water Music (1983) is Charles Bukowski's finest collection of short stories and is a seminal volume in his oeuvre. Bukowski recognized the stories as "different than the earlier ones. They're cleaner, closer to the vest. I'm trying for clarity. I think I've really done it here" (quoted in

Cherkovski, *Hank*, 300). More than half of the stories are told in the third person, indicating the author's increased objectivity. Gone is the artificial spontaneity that marred the early short prose. "The stories have been pared down as well. Those in *Hot Water Music* are almost a third shorter than the stories in *Erections*. The titles are shorter and less 'flippant'. . . . Any ideas Bukowski wants to impart are imparted obliquely, through concise description, or short effective dialogue" (Harrison, 259). As the style of the writing changed, so did the focus and tone. The most radical alteration in subject matter is the emphasis on couples and domestic strife. The marginalized individual alone in a room has largely vanished, and when he does appear, the depiction is usually comic, an artist who cannot wrestle privacy from the fans, friends, and lovers who pester him. The last lines of a typical story, "A Working Day," fall incontestably into this ironic mode: "He was Joe Mayer. Freelance writer. He had it made."[18]

In stories where the artist is not hounded by admirers, he is usually presented as grotesque and insensitive to "normal" society. Bukowski's detachment and increased skills allow him to distance these characters, to render them absurd and suspect and yet pitiable in a way seldom achieved earlier. In "Less Delicate than the Locust," the painters Jorg and Serge act reprehensibly, especially in public, and exult in the crass behavior that the mystique of "artist" allows them. "Serge grabbed a half-full bottle of the wine, ripped open the waiter's shirt and poured the wine over his chest. . . . Jorg swung his cane and caught the waiter, hard, just below the left ear" (*Music*, 15). The melodramatic action exploits the story's ribald humor, but subtextually a suggestion remains that minor artistic reputation, once secured, aggrandizes the worst of antisocial behavior. The story ends with a reminder that a less eccentric, middle-class society still exists, and throughout *Hot Water Music* mundane couples are treated much less critically than in Bukowski's earlier work. After Serge and Jorg leave the restaurant without paying, the point of view shifts for the brief conclusion:

> A young couple seated at a table near the door had watched the entire proceedings. The young man looked intelligent, only a rather large mole near the end of his nose marred the effect. His girl was fat but lovable in a dark blue dress. She had once wanted to be a nun.
>
> "Weren't they magnificent?" asked the young man.
>
> "They were assholes," said the girl.
>
> The young man waved for a third bottle of wine. It was going to be another difficult night. (*Music*, 15–16)

The couple's opposed responses summarize the reader's ambivalence toward the artists, and perhaps Bukowski's as well. (The watching male on the sidelines seems at least as representative of the story's author as the painters do.) The artists intrigue as they repulse, and the radicalness of their performance is possibly their most significant art. The author's love for the outlaw is transformed in a satiric critique of personal creative obsession.

In "Head Job," the representation of the poet Marx Renoffski is comparable. Margie is a lonely woman who lives next door. She plays Chopin études, romanticizes the poet's life, and, following one of her neighbors' ferocious arguments, recovers the poet's sculpted bust from their yard. "Head Job" is a cogent example of Bukowski's technical skill and thematic sophistication as a writer. Although the story is written in the third person, the point of view is Margie's, and the author has crafted a rounded and convincing woman. When Renoffski arrives, he is boorish and physically overbearing. He is, in short, the frequent Bukowski persona recast through an outside point of view.

> Marx Renoffski finished his drink and placed it on top of the piano next to the head. He walked over to her and grabbed her. He smelled of vomit, cheap wine and bacon. Needle-like hairs from his beard poked into her face as he kissed her. Then he pulled his face away and looked at her with his tiny eyes. "You don't wanna miss out on life, baby!" She felt his penis rise against her. "I eat pussy too. I never ate pussy until I was 50. Karen taught me. Now I'm the best in the world." (*Music*, 117–18)

The characteristics are classic Chinaski but through a distorted (restored?) lens. Renoffski is mildly comical, yet when violating Margie's apartment, his crassness is neither attractive nor sympathetic.

Another inversion found throughout *Hot Water Music* is the presentation of the male as prostitute, revising Bukowski's depiction of women in the same role. In "A Couple of Gigolos," the narrator introduces himself and his coconspirator. "Comstock wore a beret, a silk scarf, a turquoise necklace, a beard, and he had a silken walk. I was a writer stalled on his second novel" (*Music*, 25). The men discuss "how much longer" they "can go on fooling" (*Music*, 26) the women who support them; the narrator lasts three more months before being forced to leave. Such a dynamic is common in the stories. In "900 Pounds," it is announced that "three-fourths of the writers Eric knew in Los Angeles and Hollywood were supported by women; those writers weren't as talented with the typewriter as they were with their women. They sold themselves to their women spiritually and physically" (*Music*, 51). In the stories, kept men are invariably artists in stages of creative decline.

Although the women can be interpreted as shrews who devour the artistic soul, it is clear that the male's choice is voluntary, and, as in "A Couple of Gigolos," the captives are often grateful and obliging. They are willingly compromised for temporary security and financial peace. The artists portrayed in *Hot Water Music*, although most have achieved a minor fame, still struggle economically. Art doesn't pay, or it doesn't pay well enough. "Have You Read Pirandello?" begins with the writer-narrator's fear of homelessness looming: "My girlfriend had suggested that I move out of her house, a very large house, nice and comfortable, with a backyard a block long, leaking pipes, and frogs and crickets and cats. Anyway, I was out" (*Music*, 63). During the time allotted him, the narrator locates a room in another house with another woman. The spontaneous departure of the male common in earlier stories, usually accompanied by a brief respite in a boarding house, has disappeared.

The middle-aged working artist is a kept man and a whore and does not seem greatly concerned about being so. When the narrator in "Have You Read Pirandello?" meets his new keeper, she informs him twice that "I'm not going to pay you anything" (*Music*, 66). This discussion clearly refers to their earlier phone conversation regarding the sexual gratification of the woman, particularly through cunnilingus. " 'That's all right,' I said. She got her key out of her purse, unlocked the door and I followed her in" (*Music*, 66). The story ends with the woman manipulating the key in the lock, traditional Freudian symbols of penetration. The male is content to hustle his body for room and board. In "Harry Ann Landers," Harry had earlier been kept by a woman for three months and may be the character from "A Couple of Gigolos." When a friend calls to announce his breakup and subsequent suffering, Harry offers ambiguous advice: "Either suck pussy like a man or find a job" (*Music*, 172). In "Scum Grief," the poet Victor Valoff is another writer "supported by his wife" (*Music*, 81). This recurrent theme in the stories offers troubling implications for sincere affection, which has been sacrificed to expedience and economic advantage. "Love is a form of prejudice. You love what you need, you love what makes you feel good, you love what is convenient" (*Music*, 67). Without the security of the woman's protection, the artist's craft is reduced to little more than a vaudeville performance with which to make a buck. After "the writer, Paul" has broken up with

Nancy in "Harry Ann Landers," he introduces his new art: "She started hollering about money. . . . Listen, I been hustling. I got this act. Barney and I, we're both dressed in penguin suits . . . he says one line of a poem, I say the other . . . four microphones . . . we got this jazz group playing in the back of us . . ." (*Music*, 171).

The artist-whore analogy is developed most explicitly in the story "In and Out and Over," which recounts a Chinaski poetry-reading trip. "A few had some of my books and I made drawings in them. It was over. I had hustled my ass" (*Music*, 125). The narrator's feelings toward the event are resigned, defeated, as if the reading were not too far removed from the penguin act in "Harry Ann Landers." The significant difference is that Chinaski has someone to return to, and he is able to endure his "prostitution" because of genuine and dependent affection for a companion. "We floated into L.A. International. Ann, I love you. I hope my car starts. I hope the sink isn't plugged up. I'm glad I didn't fuck a groupie. . . . I'm glad I'm an idiot. I'm glad I don't know anything. I'm glad I haven't been murdered" (*Music*, 129). Bukowski removes the prostitution theme from the context of the relationship and places it squarely on the artist as celebrity-performer. "I'd done my dirty gig. The poetry hustle. I never solicited. They wanted their whore: they had him" (*Music*, 129). The rationalization that he "never solicited" is a wonderful reapplication of the self-preserving cliché of the prostitute.

The shifting in "In and Out and Over" and the representation of the compromised artist-male is not surprising. The stories in *Hot Water Music* present an unstable and problematized world of adult relationships. The persistence of couples in the book is paramount to its approach. Few stories deal with an individual living alone, and even these stories—"The Great Poet," "Not Quite Bernadette"—serve to develop a larger theme of isolation and emphasize the many times couples appear. This focus is a departure from earlier Bukowski short stories. Many of the strongest pieces in *Hot Water Music* do not deal with the artist figure at all but with these male/female couples, often married, and the monotony of their lives. Frequently the introduction of an odd occurrence into the mundane will supply a story's impetus. The ordinary but effective nature of the material indicates "that it was not the ordinariness of the content, per se, that marred a number of the early stories, but, at least in part, Bukowski's defensive stance. One basis for a shift in style, then, was a confidence in the material itself, a confidence that the lack of discipline of the earlier stories undermined, rather than supported" (Harrison, 268).

The flat domestic subjects of *Hot Water Music*, added to the writing's ravaging minimalism, suggest a similarity to the earlier stories of Raymond Carver. Although humor, idiom, and an occasional introduction of the supernatural identify the collection as inimitably by Bukowski, individual stories such as "Some Hangover" and, despite its raunchy title, "Turkeyneck Morning" contain an unmistakably Carver-like flavor. "Turkeyneck Morning" in particular is a powerful study of a deteriorated lower-class relationship, in which the isolation of the woman supplies ironic counterpoint both to the title and to the husband's violating aggression.

> "You like that turkeyneck, kid?"
> The full weight of his heavy body was on her. He was sweating. He offered her no relief.
> "I'm coming, baby, I'm COMING!" (*Music*, 122)

The husband is more horrible than pathetic. The wife Shirley's response is disembodied detachment. "Barney fucked like a machine. She had no feelings for him" (*Music*, 121). Again the female is the central and fuller character. The story is short, three pages, and its understated descriptions of domestic frustration are offered with a stunning sparseness. The story ends after Barney, monstrous and yet strangely ineffective, threatens to kill his wife if another man is responsible for her hesitance in his sexual prerogative. "*Answer me! Got it? Got it? You Got it?*" Her calm and nuanced response, "Yes, I've got it" (*Music*, 123), echoes the futility of the relationship and, perhaps, of her life. Last, her isolation leads to an existential immobility. The unspoken resonance of Bukowski's conclusion is as powerful as Hemingway and Carver at their finest: "He let go of her. He walked out of the bedroom and into the front room. She heard the door close, then heard him walk down the steps. The car was in the driveway, and she listened to it start. Then she heard the sound of it driving away. Then there was silence" (*Music*, 123).

Like several stories in *Hot Water Music*, much of the action in "Turkeyneck Morning" takes place in the kitchen, which replaces the bedroom as the central location where relationships are negotiated. "He hit her then, open-handed, on the side of the face. She dropped the spatula, lost her balance, hit the side of the sink and caught herself. She picked up her spatula, washed it in the sink, came back and turned the eggs over" (*Music*, 123). The combination of discordant events, the nonchalance of the characters' responses, and the story's flat tone again suggest vintage

Carver. The kitchen indicates longer-lasting relationships. Its setting allows Bukowski to reveal both the intimacy characters share and the movement from passion to discourse, with the primary activity a mundane preparation and consumption of food. Boiling coffee signals a relationship's turbulence.

Conversely, daily routines also indicate the comforting, stabilizing effect of long-term involvement. In "Some Hangover," Kevin is accused of sexually molesting two girls at a party the night before. Most of the story takes place in the kitchen the next morning. As his wife, Gwen, authoritatively prepares breakfast, she engineers a method by which to handle the dangerous repercussions of the allegation.

> "Scrambled?"
> "Scrambled."
> "Married ten years and you always say 'scrambled.' "
> "More amazing than that, you always ask." (*Music*, 95)

Such banal conversation contains an ambiguous subtext: the tender reassurance of habits recognized by the other, and yet the necessity to always ask again. Is this man, absolutely, the man I have believed him to be? Gwen is coolheaded and rational, a boon her husband recognizes. "He wasn't sure if he loved Gwen but living with her was comfortable. She took care of all the details and details were what drove a man crazy" (*Music*, 96). Bukowski's earlier equation of love equaling comfort is reiterated, and, in this case, it is a fortuitous equation for the husband.

Similar situations—male dependence centered around the domestic commonplace of meals—are developed in "White Dog Hunch" and "The Man Who Loved Elevators." The latter story, especially, exemplifies the tension in *Hot Water Music* between domestic contentment and the outside encroachments that always threaten. Harry rapes a woman twice in an elevator, then subsequently returns to his wife and apartment. Despite his betrayal and unexplained behavior, he appears to love his wife and enjoy their home life. After the second elevator rape, which is presented as vaguely consensual, Harry returns to his kitchen. "There were steaks and french fries, salad and hot garlic bread. Not bad" (*Music*, 109). His wife, Rochelle, has even remembered to make the coffee. She announces her possible pregnancy, Harry seems genuinely delighted, and the two kiss and celebrate. "It was a good dinner. And a good bottle of wine"(*Music*, 109).

In light of the author's early work, these later stories endorse domesticity at a surprising level, albeit with qualifications. Chinaski ends "In and Out and Over" on a note of homecoming and happy reunion. "The moon stood up, the house smelled of lint and roses, the dog leaped upon me. I pulled his ears, punched him in the belly, his eyes opened wide and he grinned" (*Music*, 130). Mostly gone are the marginalized criminals, killers, and thieves. When a crime is present, as in "Decline and Fall"—in which a couple store a body in their freezer and eat it—the event is typically recalled secondhand, with a mitigating framework that complicates the reader's approach. The world of violence, death, and ordinary madness remains but is rendered only in powerful bits and flashes around the lives of more mundane characters. Instead, domestic life is scrutinized, with its problems and absurd resolutions. "You Kissed Lilly" escalates a tired argument about a husband's affair five years earlier into an unexpected attack of raw domestic violence. The middle-aged couple end up wounding each other with the same gun. The wife shoots the husband in the chest and mouth (with which he had kissed Lilly five years earlier); the husband shoots the wife in both legs. Bukowski achieves a masterful balance between the comic and the horrific and closes the story with the arrival of police:

> Theodore turned his head. His mouth was a blob of red.
> "Skirrr," said Theodore, "skirrr . . ."
> "I hate these domestic quarrels," the other cop said. "Real *messy* . . ."
> "Yeah," said the first cop.
> "I had a fight with my wife just this morning. You can never tell."
> "Skirrr," said Theodore . . . (*Music*, 39–40)

The intrusion of the past is shown to provide a primary danger to current relationships. The world of bars and mad one-night lovers is never fully buried or far from the domestic surface of *Hot Water Music*. This threat forms the catalyst for several stories. Although Bukowski illustrates his distance from his former bar society in "Beer at the Corner Bar," the protagonist Frank in "Broken Merchandise" slips easily back into that street culture. A confluence of work pressure, a fight with youths who chase his car, and a distasteful telephone conversation with his wife is sufficient to transport him to the world of old: "He picked up his bottle of Bud and took a hit. . . . There was somebody sitting next to him. A woman. She was about 38, dirt under her fingernails, her dyed blonde hair piled loosely on top of her head" (*Music*, 203). That a few of Bukowski's aging characters have stepped out of the bar environment certainly does not indicate that it has ceased to exist.

The past is often reintroduced by a ringing telephone, as in "Long Distance Drunk." "The phone rang at 3 a.m. Francine got up and answered it and brought the phone to Tony in bed. It was Francine's phone. Tony answered. It was Joanna long distance from Frisco" (*Music*, 145). Joanna, a lover from the past, begins another secondhand story, as if the telling somehow validates events and speaker. The conversation leaves Tony thoughtful on the difficulty of life, happiness, and enduring relationships, and both nostalgic for and grateful to be out of the stereotypical Bukowski setting. "Some night, some hot summer Thursday night, you became the drunk, you were out there alone in a cheap rented room, and no matter how many times you'd been out there before, it was no help, it was even worse. . . . All you could do was light another cigarette, pour another drink, check the peeling walls for lips and eyes" (*Music*, 147). The second-person pronoun is distanced and yet personal, anticipatory and detached. The man's tone is sympathetic to the situation of loneliness. The impossibility of a lifetime's companionship and of enduring love makes the current shared moment all the more valuable. "Tony drew Francine closer to him, pressed his body quietly against hers and listened to her breathing. It was horrible to have to be serious about shit like this once again" (*Music*, 148). The story implies that Tony's tenderness, understanding, and ability to appreciate his luck have been acquired via the toughness of his earlier life and the dread of returning to that life.

Hot Water Music fluctuates between poles of domestic security and isolated danger. The domestic itself alternates between the comforting and the banal, the nurturing and the enervating. The lure of betrayal is one of danger, of excitement, and of the street. If the past does not cripple the present, then probably the attraction of the other life will. The men routinely go about destroying the very things they crave—home and succoring attention. Bukowski suggests that the swing of desires is unavoidable and is equal parts comic and tragic. A willful self-annihilation by the protagonist adds pathos to many of the stories. "Fooling Marie," which concludes the book, perfectly dramatizes the conflicting impulses of the male. The story is a funny, sad, and finally devastating account of infidelity and lost male potency and one of the author's finest short stories. Three stories earlier, in "Praying Mantis," a woman literally bites off the head of a man's penis during fellatio. This chance liaison occurs while the man waits in a hotel room for his lover to visit him; the attacker returns undisturbed to her own room and to the intellectual speciousness of the Dick Cavett show.

"Fooling Marie" presents a similar plot and theme, but in an understated and far more effective manner. The motif of male victimization begins with its opposite: Ted is having a good night at the track. Luck, so important for survival in Bukowski's work, seems to be with him. Ted's home life is introduced in contrast to his racetrack pastime. "Marie bitched so much about his going to the track that he only went two or three times a week" (*Music*, 215). His winnings attract the attention of the suggestively named Victoria, "a strawberry blonde, about 24, slender hips, surprisingly big breasts; long legs, a cute turned-up nose, flower mouth; dressed in a pale blue dress, wearing white high-heeled shoes" (*Music*, 215). Physically, Victoria epitomizes the magical woman who frequents Bukowski's early stories; her mesmerizing beauty and seeming purity are ordinarily unapproachable. "She was better than some god damned movie starlet, and she didn't look spoiled" (*Music*, 216). Ted's luck empowers him with a boldness susceptible to her flirtations. Because his wife, Marie, has him timed "down to the minute" (*Music*, 217)—Ted is her plodding horse—Ted and Victoria leave the track early for a nearby motel. The unreality of the young woman unnerves the protagonist; she is "a beautiful, maddening dream" (*Music*, 218). Again, the man's good fortune is stressed: he "couldn't believe his luck" and "felt lucky" (*Music*, 218).

Only after Ted begins to undress, to expose his body, age, and hesitation, does his confidence falter and Victoria's harder edge emerge. His justifications for his life and poor condition grow more strained: " 'You know,' he said, 'you're a class act but I'm a class act too. We each have our own way of showing it' " (*Music*, 218). Ted's domination during the subsequent sex act is undercut by his rapid ejaculation. His desire to "rip her" (*Music*, 219) results, as male aggression often does in Bukowski's *Women*, only in displaying his own childish arrogance. She labels him her "big fat Buddha" and compares his sexual performance to the speed of quarter horses. "Victoria came walking out of the bathroom still looking cool, untouched, almost virginal" (*Music*, 220). The dynamic of the relationship, of the luck, has shifted to a degree that even Ted recognizes.

> "Listen, you should have known me when I was young. I was tough, but I was good. I had it. I still have it."
> She smiled at him, "Come on, Buddha, it's not all that bad. You've got a wife, you've got lots of things going for you." (*Music*, 220)

Victoria's solace is shaded with mocking irony. Like her "Praying Mantis" counterpart, she has literally drawn blood during intercourse, and when Ted takes a shower the conclusion is foreshadowed. "He could see the blood in the water running into the drain" (*Music*, 220).

When he returns to the other room, Victoria is gone. Curiously, Ted does not seem overly surprised, intuiting that she has taken "his underwear, his shirt, his pants, his car keys and wallet, his cash, his shoes, his stockings, everything" (*Music*, 221). An odd detachment follows, "a distance between ordinary objects and between events that was remarkable" (*Music*, 221). Common motel objects assume a surreal clarity for him as the distance between the real and ideal, between male dream and male delusion, establishes itself in his consciousness. "Fooling Marie," with its fully ironic title, is a startling revision of the aging Bukowski protagonist. He is weak, foolish, and willing to be defeated. Victoria inconveniences herself to humiliate Ted and ensure his wife's discovery of their fling. There is no logical reason, for the sake of robbery alone, to take more than his money. The young woman has planned this from the beginning to be as personally and domestically damaging to him as possible. Ted is stranded, naked, and as vulnerable as an infant.

Victoria's malice is left as unexplained to him as her dreamlike presence. She leaves a half bottle of Cutty Sark and a lipstick message: "GOODBYE BUDDHA!" (*Music*, 221). She takes his money from him, but, worse, she destroys his conceits of wisdom and experience, of male confidence. "Ted drank the drink, put the glass down and saw himself in the mirror—very fat, very old. He had no idea what to do next. . . . He sat, looking out, not moving, watching the cars passing back and forth" (*Music*, 221). "Fooling Marie" suggests the limits, the physical and thematic exhaustion, of the Bukowskian stereotype of the boozing, aggressive male. Ted's age precludes the possibility of a return to the freedom and independence of street life, yet his proclivity toward past behavior presumably has ruined domestic security. His stoic acceptance indicates his knowledge that a mistake was inevitable. His failure, impotence, isolation, and inability to change complete the story's powerful message. The streets are a young man's game. Luck runs out.

Septuagenarian Stew

Bukowski's unruly, 400-page offering for his 70th birthday was the 1990 volume *Septuagenarian Stew*, a collection of 20 stories interspersed between poems. The author's output of short stories slowed in the mid-1970s and continued to decline during the 1980s. The stories in *Septua-genarian Stew*, therefore, constitute the writer's final testimony in short prose published during his life. The stories are more elaborate than those in *Hot Water Music* and on average lengthier, making several of the stories "longer than anything he had attempted in twenty years" (Harrison, 269). The book was largely applauded by critics. Jack Byrne wrote that, at 70, Bukowski still "knows the elements of our jazzed up society. Knows where the body is buried, he knows where, in town, the games are played, he knows, like a congressional camp follower, 'where it's at.' He's foxy like the old gray fox who won't get his chickens the easy way by working for the farmer."[19] Even a dismissive review in the *New York Times Book Review* notes the "harrowing story 'Son of Satan,' " a bleak childhood reminiscence that begins the collection's prose offerings.[20] Robbins, in an appreciation of Bukowski at 71, contended that the author's central theme had remained the same from the beginning: "passion—and, paradoxically, the butchery done to it, and the butchery endured, by humans" (285). Another reviewer noted in *Septuagenarian Stew* the author's delineation of "the violence at the heart of human relationships."[21]

Passion and violence—both physical and mental—are easily traced in these late stories, and the context, inevitably, is relationships. Sexual tensions are sometimes central, but *Septuagenarian Stew* shifts its primary attention away from the domestic tableaux of *Hot Water Music* to stories centered on the exploitation of workers. In a few stories, such as "A Day," the theme is the traditional Bukowski one of blue-collar labor. "Then, somehow, like awakening from a nightmare, the day was over."[22] However, the protagonist Tom returns not to an empty room but to the older Bukowski's setting of choice: the mortgaged home, the lazing or drunken wife, the hungry and screaming children. After an obligatory argument with his wife, Tom hopes that his offspring have "better luck" in life than he and his wife have had. The barely submerged pathos of their situation emerges in a shared desperation.

> Helena appeared to be crying. "Tom, what are we going to *do?*"
> She turned on the hot water in the pot.
> "Do?" asked Tom. "About what?"
> "About the way we have to *live!*"
> "There's not a hell of a lot we *can* do." (*Stew*, 90)

As is common in such stories, the scene ends with stasis and entropy. They sit immobile in the kitchen while a television laugh track from the adjoining room underscores the situation.

Other stories in the collection, such as "Vengeance of the Damned," focus on lower-class characters. A revolt planned by bums against an expensive department store turns predictably violent, then into an ideologically vapid mob scene. Harrison sees this story as unique in Bukowski in that it "consciously dramatize[s] a political idea" (268); he then develops a lengthy and insightful explication of "The Life of a Bum," which he considers Bukowski's absurd and postmodern masterpiece. The story is stylistically reminiscent of Beckett and Joyce, "the latter in his privileging of ordinary life, and the former in those moments when Beckett uses repetitive and simplified syntactic structures to highlight the banal and the routine" (Harrison, 269). However, stories of the homeless and forgotten are more the exception in *Septuagenarian Stew* than the norm. The pattern of "A Day" is closer to the typical situation: the worlds of work and home exist almost independently, and the domestic life is the waiting reality for the male returning from a humiliating day of work. The implications of this pattern vary according to the depiction of setting—is home a place of sanctuary or a further punishment?

For the most part, the protagonists in *Septuagenarian Stew* are remarkable for their financial success. The author's own rise in celebrity and economic fortune seems paralleled by a comparable shift among his characters. Ironically, the athletes, entertainers, and writers who populate these stories are seldom any more protected from exploitation, failure, and exhaustion than the earlier, threadbare counterparts. The physical presence of the house or home continually looms as a palpable burden in the background of their routines. According to one critic, Bukowski's perpetual losers find "their decaying selves slipping inexorably into oblivion. Life's supposed winners fare no better."[23] The *Septuagenarian Stew* stories frequently expose two sides of each human transaction, often offering little distinction between exploiter and exploited. "Action" focuses on a successful writer whose luck has turned bad. As in many of the author's stories set at the racetrack, the true subject of "Action" is the hopeless hope of the bettor. The crowd's favorite, Red Window, "looked beautiful, so beautiful! The miracle was unfolding. The crowd screamed as one crazy voice. Life was good at last" (*Stew*, 130). As usual, this unified scream of life quickly turns to a "chorus of boos and invectives" and the hopeful crowd to one "insane." "The roar and rattle of agony was everywhere" (*Stew*, 131). The moment's shift from hope to anger is comparable to the mob's recognition and violence in "Vengeance of the Damned." There is no chance against unnamed bureaucracy, and the crowd turns.

In "The Jockey," the story following "Action," the protagonist is thrown from his horse and returns home to a waiting wife. Although Larry is financially above the betting crowd, the track is shown to exploit its employees and visitors in nearly equal measure.

> The right leg had stiffened, and driving in was painful.
> God damn McKelvey, worried about the track take. That track would be there after all of them were gone.
> The house was beautiful. It had cost $300,000 and there was almost no mortgage. (*Stew*, 148)

"The Jockey" is essentially another story of a shrunken man who cannot control his own destiny or the large woman who "owns" him. His wife, Karina, is a "lovely six feet" and remorseful about having married "a miniature man" (*Stew*, 149, 151). A jockey who cannot stay in the saddle is a resourceful variation on Bukowski's theme; the story, unlike "Six Inches," requires no fantasy element. The focus remains on the couple's frustration and the hurtful dynamics of their relationship. After an argument culminates in physical abuse, Larry feels "worse than evil," setting up a conclusion in which he sits unmoving in the bath. "He heard her walking. He heard the water dripping as she walked. He felt her walking up behind him. He waited and looked at the lights of the city" (*Stew*, 151). His detachment recalls the trancelike hyperreality of earlier protagonists, including Ted in "Fooling Marie," left immobile by circumstances. In terms of its sense of impending attack, the ending of "The Jockey" echoes that of "Son of Satan." A boy huddles beneath the bed while the menacing father circles. "I waited, and as I waited all I could hear were strange sounds. . . . I could hear my father breathing, and I moved myself exactly under the center of the bed and waited for the next thing" (*Stew*, 37). The minimalism of such anticipatory and helpless endings is shattering. Neither boy nor man can quite control his actions or the responses these actions initiate.

The steward McKelvey's lack of sympathy for Larry in "The Jockey" exemplifies labor relations throughout *Septuagenarian Stew*. Managers, owners, and trainers show little care for their employees. High-profile employer-employee negotiations may involve celebrity egos and much more money than the blue-collar equivalent, but the brutalizing ethos of work relations does not change. This turbulence is explored in a triad of strong baseball stories. "Strikeout" begins with a pampered batter's irritation at an umpire's marginal call. This routine event escalates to a ludicrous peak of stereotyped comic violence and power maneuvers as players, umpires, and manager crowd the field. The socioeconomic lesson of the story remains clear. Players are the spoiled rich who "invested in commodities and formed corporations," separated from the "poor who came out to watch the millionaires play" and "could have stayed home and gotten drunk and saved some money" (*Stew*, 272). In this instance, the sole middle-class participant in the fray, the umpire Harry who made the original call, is the one who pays the price for doing his job. Players sell tickets and are exempt from punishment. Afterward, Harry returns to a setting that is typical of these stories, "his $65,000 home with its $38,000 mortgage" (*Stew*, 275) and a wife on the couch watching television. Again, the last refuge of the battered male is the womblike bathtub, a numbing submersion after the opposing pulls of work and home.

In ".191," a sophisticated story rendered mostly in dialogue, a player's waning batting skills expose the mercenary subtext of the team "family" (*Stew*, 285). Monty, representing management, brings the negotiation into the player's home. He chews on cigars in Freudian style while denying any racial element of his aggression.

> "Can't we keep racial shit out of this?"
> "It's always been there. Why should it stop now?" (*Stew*, 289)

A man is worth only his current level of consistent performance—that is, his entertainment value for fans. Past performance is irrelevant. Throughout *Septuagenarian Stew*, the individual is sacrificed to the hostile team. "Bukowski redramatizes a view of the solitary nature of existence as well as the individual's inextricable connection to a predatory society" (Harrison, 265). Placing his characters into domestic or labor relationships merely enables Bukowski to heighten, paradoxically, an essential isolation. Monty leaves the black neighborhood grateful that "his car was still in the drive" (*Stew*, 291). The racism, inferred by Harry, manifests itself as self-congratulatory persecution, revealing the management's attitudes and agenda: "That's what you get when you try to go direct to the players. You get a big black dick up your ass" (*Stew*, 291). The story ends from the point of view of the exploiter, champing another cigar and supplying the final irony. "And the worst of all, he hated baseball. What a dog's game, what a celebration for the mindless" (*Stew*, 291). This last comment suggests the crowd from "Strikeout." Bukowski reminds us that exploitation is relative but usually flows from top to bottom economically.

The third baseball story, "Buy Me Some Peanuts and Cracker Jacks," again recalls by its title the working-class fans who finance the indulgences of owners and players. The action concerns an even higher socioeconomic level as it explores the volatile relations between a team owner, Stockmeyer, and his newly rehired manager, Nelson. That the story opens with a press conference announcement introduces its theme of appearances versus submerged reality. "If he was so good, why did you can him twice?" (*Stew*, 321). During subsequent conversations, Stockmeyer stresses to Nelson the importance of his behavior as "a public figure" (*Stew*, 325) and in a fit of rage fires the manager again. The satiric conclusion of the story finds Nelson snorting cocaine—the only ostensibly unpardonable offense for dismissal from the team—as he is hired a fourth time by Stockmeyer. In this story and ".191," only the intricacies of contractual obligation keep human relations functioning. Owners and managers lounge in a fog of indulgence and omnipotence, millionaire players are willingly exploited as commodities until their use and youth run out, and the sucker fans pay for it all.

Only in "The Winner," a boxing story reminiscent of Hemingway's "Fifty Grand," does the reader witness any sympathy between athlete and management. The manager, Harry, seems genuinely concerned for the welfare of his physically overmatched fighter Bobby, who is taking a beating as the story opens. "Next time you go down, *stay* down! The fans don't give a fuck about you. *You've* got to care about yourself!" (*Stew*, 341). Bobby's response to this pragmatic advice is one of criticism: "Jesus, Harry, you're supposed to be my manager" (*Stew*, 341). The story abounds in such ironies. The predatory nature of the event is captured both by the blood lust of the crowd and by the corner man's name, "Buzzard." Harry is incriminated by moving his fighter up too quickly, hopeful for a big payday, and management will be left to pick over the bones of a destroyed career. After reminding Bobby that "this is no 'Rocky' film" (*Stew*, 340), Harry watches Bobby perform a miraculous, Rockylike comeback that ensures another and yet larger payday. They escape the error of overmatching, and, as a result, the boxer can be exploited again for an even bigger profit. After giving the postfight press its required clichés—"Youth and a good fight plan have been served" (*Stew*, 343)—Harry suggests a bout between his fighter and the top-ten opponent Slick Pettis. If any lesson is learned, or affirmed, it is that "America is a great place to be when you were winning" (*Stew*, 343). Buzzard opens the door for the victorious entourage. As in Hemingway's story, where the stoic fighter Jack has to think quickly to preserve his loss and keep from being swindled in a double cross, the characters in "The Winner" maneuver through their society and capitalize on its corruption. As Jack notes with understatement in "Fifty Grand," "It's funny how fast you can think when it means that much money."[24] Whether the fight is actually rigged seems negligible in the larger scramble for dominance and survival.

Bukowski once commented on his ambivalence for human beings, "I have compassion for almost all the individuals in the world; at the same time, they repulse me" (*NYQ*, 320). The stories in *Septuagenarian Stew* avoid simplistic alliances and easy sympathy. In "Lonely at the Top," a killer is killed by the killer who employs him until "he knows too much" (*Stew*, 304). The gullible fans who waste their cash for the luxury of the rich are also the menacing fanatics in "Fame." Audiences proliferate in these stories, from the crowds in the stands to the heckling nightclub customers in "There's No Business." The washed-up comedian Manny Hyman just isn't drawing them in anymore, and his "stuff seems real bitter" (*Stew*, 350). He is laughed at, but not with, and both the hotel management booker and the audience supply fresher punch lines. The final story in the book, "Mad Enough," is a fictionalized account of the making and release of *Tales of Ordinary Madness*, a film based on Bukowski's short fiction. The story, a precursor of *Hollywood*, further concerns the theme of performance. "But he wasn't the right guy to play Chinaski. He was dozing inside" (*Stew*, 364). An actor portrays Chinaski, while Chinaski, always cultivating his own crazy myth, portrays himself. He is up on the screen and in the audience, heckling his butchered representation.

The layers of artifice and reality that cover these stories are intricately wrought. Bukowski suggests that our daily lives are illusion, façade, and dissembling. "Bring Me Your Love" begins with yet another Harry (a name indicative of "hairy," primitive men?), this one visiting his wife in the sanatorium. Her greeting is peculiar: "Are you the conductor? . . . The conductor of verisimilitude?" (*Stew*, 222). Behind this seeming obscurity is the wisdom of the insane. It is appropriate that the author places the words that define his theme into the mouth of madness. Whether inside or outside the walls, at the job or returned to the mortgaged home, one finds only a fabrication of reality. This shared illusion maintains the appearance of a stable world. Regarding the "truth" of race and class and empowerment, Bukowski appears dedicated to the old dictum of mystery solving: Follow the money.

Chapter Four
Early Poems

Burning in Water, Drowning in Flame

By his own account, Charles Bukowski quit writing in his mid-twenties and spent 10 years drinking and alternating unemployment with short stints of unskilled labor. When he returned to writing at the age of 35, he wrote poetry rather than fiction. In retrospect, the author explained that "poetry is the shortest, sweetest, bangingest way. Why write a novel when you can say it in ten lines?"[1] Len Fulton recalls that Bukowski's "first poems were published in 1957, but it was not until the early Sixties that you began to run up against him everywhere in the small magazines. His rise correlates strikingly with the proliferation of the small presses of the decade" (Fulton, 27). Bukowski's return to the written word was also historically fortuitous for other reasons. His early success spans two conflicting decades, "the blackness and despair of the 1950s with the rebellious cry of the 1960s for freedom."[2] The technological printing advances that allowed the burgeoning of America's small presses coalesced with a dissatisfied underground ready for Bukowski's brand of tough, direct poems. His long-desired appreciation was beginning in earnest. In 1963, Jon and Louise Webb selected Bukowski as "Outsider of the Year," with an accompanying special issue of their *Outsider* magazine.

The Webbs were to become even greater benefactors of the "new" poet. The same year, under the imprint of the Loujon Press, they published Bukowski's first full collection of poetry, *It Catches My Heart in Its Hands*. The production of the book, elaborately hand printed by the Webbs in their New Orleans apartment, was an act of love (of poetry and of bookmaking) that the writer never forgot. A companion volume, *Crucifix in a Deathhand*, followed from Loujon Press in 1965. Bukowski described the second book as "a groaning monster, $7.50, drawings and cover by Noel Rockmore, paper you can eat and all that. I don't know about the poems."[3] The volume's substantial print run of 3,100 solidified and extended the attention accrued by the earlier Loujon projects.

Undertaking a critical consideration of Charles Bukowski's poetry is a daunting task. His mammoth poetic output is nearly impossible to catalog either stylistically or bibliographically. Of the thousands of poems by Bukowski that appeared in predominately small-press and underground publications over five decades, only approximately 50% are collected in the standard editions published by Black Sparrow Press. As integral as Bukowski was in the proliferation of the American small presses from the mid-1960s onward, his primary and most important literary relationship was with John Martin, editor and founder of Black Sparrow Press. The artistic and financial benefits of the relationship were reciprocal. Black Sparrow began book publication with Bukowski's third collection, *At Terror Street and Agony Way* (1968), and, with Bukowski as its primary talent, subsequently grew into arguably the most successful independent publisher of alternative poetry in America. The advantage of a reliable publisher and discriminating editor was, in turn, liberating for Bukowski and of inestimable value to his work and reputation. At the time of the author's death, the Black Sparrow relationship had been an equitable and lucky marriage for 30 years. John Martin's sure handling of the poet's posthumous work is currently under way.

In 1974, Black Sparrow released *Burning in Water, Drowning in Flame: Selected Poems 1955–1973*, an invaluable volume collecting many poems from Bukowski's two Loujon Press books, his first with Black Sparrow, and the book's title poems from 1972 to 1973. Readers familiar primarily with the short-lined, lengthy narrative poems of the 1980s, which frequently and often matter-of-factly concern the author's growing fame and movement into old age, will be jolted by the intense, surrealistic poems of the early books. The debate over what constitutes "vintage" Bukowski continues to rage, and the radical differences in style and subject are indisputable. Even within the confines of *Burning in Water, Drowning in Flame,* changes are occurring, although these seem minimal compared to poems of subsequent decades.[4] The poet's early influences may also surprise the later reader, but they are inevitable: Walt Whitman and Pablo Neruda primarily, William Carlos Williams and e. e. cummings to a lesser degree, and, in sensibility more than style, Bukowski's poetic god Robinson Jeffers.

Although Bukowski's tone varies significantly from Whitman's, the debt to the earlier poet is clear. From Whitman, Bukowski inherited an openness of line, an embrace of direct experience, and the central incorporation of the "I." The father of American poetry writes: "One's-Self I sing, a simple separate person, / Yet utter the word Democratic, the word En-Mass. / Of physiology from top to bottom I sing."[5] Bukowski must have been attracted to the older poet's intimately personal yet paradoxically comprehensive voice, to his emphasis on the physical and the immediate, and to his loose, free-ranging and breathing verse. In *Whitman's Wild Children*, Cherkovski confirms the connection between Whitman and Bukowski: "From the earlier poems, Bukowski has affirmed the call Walt Whitman made for a clear, articulate voice wholly indigenous to the American earth. Beyond that, Bukowski's own insistence that a poem be devoid of tricks, that it not be in line with a standardized literary tradition, is precisely the same note that Whitman struck in the preface to *Leaves of Grass*. . . . He often spoke of Whitman as the one who opened the door to a freer style and to an unabashed sense of selfness in the poem."[6]

The explosive Bukowski "I" is prominent even in the earliest poems: "then, I'll rise with a roar, / rant, rage— / curse them and the universe / as I send them scattering over the / lawn."[7] Although Whitman is a huge influence stylistically, the earlier writer's "good fellowship of the road" (*Purdy*, 13), to quote poet Al Purdy, is foreign and often anathema to the battered Bukowski "I." At times, however, Bukowski, like the Whitman in "Song of Myself," opts for expansiveness and acceptance over judgment: "it is justified / all dying is justified / all killing all death all / passing, / nothing is in vain" (*Burning*, 152). In the labor poem "the workers," the detached "they" is introduced to the narrator's "I"—"but now I see / it all has meaning" (*Burning*, 60)—merging finally into a democratic "we" to end the poem: "we laughed / all 4000 of us" (*Burning*, 61). The pieces often contain Whitman-like catalogs, such as in the apocalyptic "something for the touts, the nuns, the grocery clerks and you . . .":

> and nothing, and nothing. the days of
> the bosses, yellow men
> with bad breath and big feet, men
> who look like frogs, hyenas, men who walk
> as if melody had never been invented, men
> who think it is intelligent to hire and fire and
> profit, men with expensive wives they possess (*Burning*, 68)

A distancing skepticism almost always remains. Rarely present are Whitman's spirituality and optimism.

Bukowski's relationship with William Carlos Williams is related to their mutual debt to Whitman. The poetic line "beginning with Whitman and extending through Williams, had broad sympathies and generous ideas as to what constituted proper content and did not fetishize its mode of production" (Harrison, 32). Harrison compares such an openness with, for example, the fastidious aesthetic of Flaubert and concludes that Bukowski's "almost industrial" (32) production of poems not only stylistically but ideologically links him with a notion that poetry be unrestricted in its subject matter. The primary lesson Bukowski learned from Whitman, Bukowski himself takes credit for bringing to contemporary verse: "My contribution was to loosen and simplify poetry, to make it more humane. I made it easy for them to follow."[8] In particular, the emphasis on simplicity indicates an influence besides Whitman. When Bukowski describes his cat as "alive and / plush and / final as a plum tree" (*Burning*, 76), the homage to Williams is explicit. Bukowski rejects the "emphasis on irony and the impersonal stance" (Harrison, 33) emphasized by the high modernists and, likewise, disdains the New Critics' calls for detachment of feeling and objective reading. His impulse was essentially the opposite: a subjective, emotional rendering of experience with a minimum of linguistic self-consciousness. Although Williams at first glance seems a gentler, more genteel poet, more insistent upon craft than is the profane and seemingly spontaneous Bukowski, their similarity is rooted in directness of language. Bukowski updates "his predecessor's demands with an infusion of contemporary speech."[9]

Bukowski consciously eschews psychological explanations and relies on clear observation and precise images to convey his concerns. He, like Williams, "never tires of looking at himself" (Fulton, 28) as crucible for contemporary experience, and this self-referential filtering suggests a shared theme of the two poets: voyeurism. One paradox of the central "I" is its persistent emphasis on its own subjective outwardness. From the vantage point of his languor, Bukowski continually "eyes" the world: "I am watching a girl dressed in a / light green sweater, blue shorts, long black stockings" (*Burning*, 17). Often the narrator is engaged at the beginning of a poem, only to retreat by the end to the sanctity of his isolation. "then I took a bath and went back to / bed" (*Burning*, 120). Both sleeping and bathing are common as suspension of involvement, of the I/eye retreat into self. During the interim, the narrator walks "in the sun and streets / of this city: seeing nothing, learning nothing, being / nothing, and coming back to my room" (*Burning*, 133).

The land itself is cut off, curtailed, "divided, / held like a crucifix in a deathhand" (*Burning*, 52). Only back in the tub or the bed, bottle nearby, is there any cessation of an assaulting exteriority that is inextricable from hyper-self-consciousness. For Bukowski, the "I" represents both a miracle and a curse. A will for isolation, with its misanthropy and its tired disappointment, is, as in Henry David Thoreau, the shadow side of the personality's need for involvement and study:

> go away, it is not the day
> the night, the hour;
> it is not the ignorance of impoliteness,
> I wish to hurt nothing, not even a bug
> but sometimes I gather evidence of a kind
> that takes some sorting . . . (*Burning*, 75)

Whereas Bukowski was influenced by the open form of Whitman and the imagist precision of Williams, and the voyeurism of both, his primary predecessor in temperament remains Robinson Jeffers. Only Hemingway and perhaps Céline are mentioned as frequently by Bukowski, and no other poet comes close in references. After laboring over a title for his first full-length book, Bukowski returned to Jeffers's "Hellenistics": "Whatever it is catches my heart in its hands, whatever it is makes / me shudder with love / And painful joy and the tears prickle."[10] He refers to Jeffers deferentially throughout his letters and at least once in print labels Jeffers his "god."[11] "Jeffers is stronger, darker, more exploratatively modern and mad" (*Screams*, 13) than the best of the other twentieth-century poets. Bukowski particularly admired the longer narrative poems, "where everything is up against the knife and very real" (*Screams*, 57). He frequently indicates the other's ideological attractiveness to him: "I go with Jeffers—the best friend is a rock wall" (*Screams*, 245). Pages of Jeffers's are "like warm things" (*Screams*, 57) in your hands, suggesting Bukowski's desire for a poetry of comparable heat and passion. In similar language, Jeffers described his elemental theory that poetry "should be a blending of fire and earth—should be made of solid and immediate things . . . set on fire by human passion."[12] Moreover, it was not until his late thirties, with *Tamar*, that Jeffers's full talent began to emerge. He acknowledged, "Great men have done their work before they were thirty, but I wasn't born yet" (Jeffers, *Selected Letters,* 108). This relatively late blooming as a poet undoubtedly solaced Bukowski, a "new" poet approaching middle age.

Although Bukowski drunkenly wandering the Los Angeles streets may seem far removed from Jeffers contemplating the hawks and sea from Tor House, much of the attraction is apparent. In "Hellenistics," Jeffers charts "the new barbarism, the night of time" (Jeffers, *Collected Poems,* 528), the passing of a romanticized golden age in exchange for a present in which "freedom has died, slowly the machines break / down, slowly the wilderness returns" (Jeffers, *Collected Poems,* 527). Such entropy corresponds to Bukowski's often bleak depiction of contemporary society. Both poets, pushed to the edge of the country, speculate on dead myths of expansion and frontier and contemplate a disappointment with modern man. Both demand isolation, lament the deleterious encroachment of the city (although Bukowski is inextricable from its environs), and finally hold a romantic view of the necessity of spiritual strength. Jeffers envisions an idealized future in which his distant children are "not to be fractional supported people but complete men" (Jeffers, *Collected Poems,* 528). In *"poverty,"* Bukowski attempts and fails to locate Jeffers's "complete" man in the present.

> I have looked almost half a century
> and he has not been seen.
>
> a living man, truly alive,
> say when he brings his hands down
> from lighting a cigarette
> you see his eyes
> like the eyes of a tiger staring past
> into the wind. (*Burning*, 128)

The truly living man, Bukowski tells us, could be recognized by his wildness. The complete man not found in this world is ruled by the primitive, by the purely instinctive and visceral rather than the intellectual. He stares past the world of men into the natural wind.

However, unlike Jeffers, Bukowski often armors himself with self-effacing humility. Although he occasionally suggests himself as the complete man, he is more often the anticipatory, searching prophet, himself defeated by the minutiae of the society in which he participates. "poverty" ends with the narrator's recognition of his failure:

> and soon it will be too late for me
> and I will have lived a life
> with drugstores, cats, sheets, saliva,
> newspapers, women, doors and other assortments,
> but nowhere
> a living man. (*Burning*, 129)

Hugh Fox notes that the Bukowski persona has, ironically, "survived the essential Terror only to be destroyed by trivia."[13] However, such a daily confrontation in itself may constitute "the greatest moments of heroism" (Fox, 35). Bukowski admires endurance, which complements, rather than contradicts, an admiration for surrender. "I don't know why people think effort and energy / have anything to do with / creation" (*Burning*, 214). He respected Jeffers's physical escape from the intrusions of man, intrusions that Bukowski resented. His "living" man, in fact, seems close to an evocation of the myth of Jeffers himself—wild, isolated, iconoclastic, creative, and superhuman.

Each prophetic call of extinction by the earlier poet finds its continuation in Bukowski. In "The Purse Seine," Jeffers explains that there is no escape now that "we have built the great cities" where "insulated / From the strong earth, each person in himself helpless." The poem's famous closing lines criticize both the fraudulent reasoning and the hysteria of contemporary verse and then conclude: "There is no reason for amazement: surely one always / knew that cultures decay, and life's end is death" (Jeffers, *Collected Poems,* 518). Bukowski answers Jeffers in a personalized context that reveals leisure as an ideal:

> well, I suppose the days were made
> to be wasted
> the years and the loves were made
> to be wasted. (*Burning*, 165)

He encourages the reader to laugh at the "terrible joke" while also incriminating his audience by naming them: "now there are more killers than ever / and I write poems for them" (*Burning*, 165).

A final similarity between the two poets is the preoccupation with and anticipation of death. Jeffers's "Original Sin" ends with this advice: "And not fear death; it is the only way to be cleansed."[14] One recalls

Bukowski's predilection for suicide and his notion of life as preparation for the end. He equates his own death with peaceful release:

> when my heart stops
> the whole world will get quicker
> better
> warmer
> summer will follow summer
> the air will be lake clear
> and the meaning
> too (*Burning*, 131)

The world will be improved by his passing, and the poem deftly includes the ambiguity of who the receiver of the "quicker / better / warmer" world will be; who except the poet in his imaginative forecast? For both Jeffers and Bukowski, the idea of a future without human beings, of a savage and regenerative world, is solacing.

Bukowski's debt to Pablo Neruda is not surprising when one considers the diverse circle of poets influenced by Whitman, a circle that includes the surrealists. Neruda explains that Whitman "had eyes open to the world and he taught us about poetry and many other things. We have loved him very much. Eliot never had much influence on us. He's too intellectual perhaps, we are too primitive."[15] Bukowski in turn complimented Neruda: "Outside of myself, I don't know anyone with such a clean line. When he says 'blue' he means blue" (Cherkovski, *Whitman's Wild Children,* 13). Robert Bly, however, articulates a fundamental difference between Neruda and Whitman, a difference that accounts for the surrealists' appeal to Bukowski. "The *Residencia* poems are weighed down by harshness, despair, loneliness, death, constant anxiety, loss. Whitman also wrote magnificently of the black emotions, but when Neruda in *Residencia* looks at the suicides, the drowning seamen, the blood-stained hair of the murdered girl, the scenes are not lightened by any sense of brotherhood."[16]

Neruda's masterpiece *Residencia en la Tierra* and Bukowski's early poems share a dark tone, preoccupations with death, women, and sexuality, and a powerful juxtaposition of discordant images. In "Walking Around," Neruda's narrator begins, "It so happens I am sick of being a man. / And it happens that I walk into tailorshops and movie houses / dried up, waterproof, like a swan made of felt / steering my way in a

water of wombs and ashes" (Neruda, 29). In "machineguns towers &
timeclocks," Bukowski's speaker experiences a comparable lassitude and
disenchantment and is likewise ravaged by trivialities.

> to be a lizard would be
> bad enough
> to be scalding in the sun
> would be bad enough
> but not so bad
> as being built up to
> Man-size and Man-life
> . . . .
> not wanting a carwash
> a toothpull
> a wristwatch, cufflinks
> a pocket radio
> tweezers and cotton
> a cabinet full of iodine (*Burning*, 64)

Neruda's "Sexual Water" is convincing evidence of the Chilean poet's
great impact on Bukowski's early poems. "I look at blood, daggers and
women's stockings, / and men's hair, / I look at beds, I look at corridors
where a virgin is sobbing, / I look at blankets and organs and hotels"
(Neruda, 55). Neruda's "red noise of bones" (55) parallels Bukowski's
nights of contemplation. The poets share "a sense of reportorialism
struggling for the present tense, and in both cases also a Romantic jun-
ket into the possible avenues of the mind" (Fulton, 28).

The shocking, subconscious surrealism of several poems in *Burning in
Water, Drowning in Flame* shows an artist struggling for an anti-rational
language to truthfully represent his existence. "a nice day" and "the
rent's high too," with their ironically mundane titles, are among the
most effective examples of such poems. In Bukowski's "i am dead but i
know the dead are not like this," the title anticipates the poem's elliptical approach:

> the curtain smokes a cigarette
> and a moth dies in a
> freeway crash

as I examine the shadows of my
hands. (*Burning*, 82)

Finally, the narrator approaches the bed and the waiting woman, who "mumbles a rosy gratitude / as I stretch my legs / to coffin length / get in and swim away / from frogs and fortunes" (*Burning*, 82). The poet demonstrates his skill with fragmentation and the intuitive sense necessary for effective surrealistic comparisons.

Surrealism is risky in that at its most powerful and evocative, it most defies explication. More often than not in these poems, Bukowski succeeds impressively. The personification and burning of the revealing curtain, the discordance of a moth's involvement with an auto crash, the menacing unknown of the speaker's own dark hands, all are bound by a theme of the death and surrender, in sleep, of consciousness. Fox likens such techniques in Bukowski to a sort of literary cubism, where "the obvious things disappear, the image is fractured" (47) and the individual speaker dissolves to allow "the prototypical voices of primal emotions and primordial things to flow through him" (51). Far-reaching connections are suggested by "i am dead but i know the dead are not like this" between moth and madman, between coffin and woman. Bly compares conjuring a convincing surrealism to living "briefly in what we might call the unconscious present" and "like a deep-sea crab" being able to "breathe in the heavy substances that lie beneath the daylight consciousness." Neruda, he adds, is one of the few poets who has the ability to stay "on the bottom for hours . . . calmly and without hysteria" (Bly, *Neruda and Vallejo,* 3). Bukowski, perhaps as much as any English-speaking poet, could also linger effectively in the dark bottom waters. "I hear the death-whisper of the heron / the bone-thoughts of sea-things / that are almost rock" (*Burning*, 51).

Influences notwithstanding, the finest of Bukowski's early poems are shocking, fresh, and inimitable. His rapid reputation among the small presses is no surprise. The best poems contain an insuppressible wildness and energy, are nonacademic and non-intellectual in the best sense, and roar with the emotional necessity of their own existence. In John William Corrington's original foreword to *It Catches My Heart in Its Hands*, he wrote that "without theorizing, without plans or schools or manifestos, Bukowski has begun the long awaited return to a poetic language free of literary pretense and supple enough to adapt itself to whatever matter he chooses to handle."[17] Bukowski arrived sui generis and a bit older than the pack, an artist of enormous energy and diverse influences. "There's a time-bomb inside his chest," contended Robert Peters, "and if it doesn't go off as a poem it will explode in drunkenness, despair, vomiting, or rage. As long as he writes he leashes terror."[18] Even in the earliest poems, many Bukowskian trademarks are in place: suicide, music, Los Angeles, cars, cats, boxing, flowers, Christ, horses, baths, women, booze, muddy oceans, sympathy for outlaws and the self-mutilated, madness, labor, and a longing for grace, luck, courage, creation, and laughter.

The last section of poems in *Burning in Water, Drowning in Flame* (from 1972 and 1973, a five-year leap from the poems that precede this section in the volume), already contains traces of the changes in style and perception that will generally mark the later poems from the earlier. They move away from surrealism and metaphor toward a concentration on narrative, dialogue, and intentional mundanity. More references are made to the author's own writing and to the burden of his growing celebrity. This latter concern is handled humorously in the poem "deathbed blues," in which the writer's editor threatens him over the phone: "you're not hitting the ball anymore. you *are* hitting the / bottle and fighting with all these / women. you know we got a good kid on the bench, / he's aching to get in there" (*Burning*, 196). Already the poet is struggling with his myth. In the introduction to the collection, Bukowski writes that he likes "the last poems best" (10) and, in a sentiment reminiscent of Hemingway, hopes for a few more years to write.

Bukowski's optimism toward his later work was not unwarranted. The unsparing directness of the last poems is at times powerful. Two of the book's most forceful pieces, in fact, appear in its final pages: "pull a string, a puppet moves . . ." contains the sobering reminder "that it can all disappear very / quickly" and that everything, "all our necessities / including love, / rest on foundations of sand—" (*Burning*, 221). Bukowski's vision remains wide and intact, as does his ability to see the relations of the "unrelated: / the death of a boy in Hong Kong / or a blizzard in Omaha." Any randomness can serve as a man's undoing, and the cause, unknown and unknowable, is answered only with "I don't know, / I don't know . . ." (*Burning*, 221). This short, stark lyric is among the strongest in the collection. "dreamlessly," the book's penultimate poem, evokes the walking dead and the society that created them. The ending sounds a note of tenderness and sympathy even as it again reminds of its bestial connotations:

they feel no terror
at not loving
or at not
being loved

so many many many
of my fellow
creatures. (*Burning*, 230–31)

The Roominghouse Madrigals

In 1988 Black Sparrow released Bukowski's *The Roominghouse Madrigals: Early Selected Poems 1946–1966*. Although the majority of these poems likely come from the second of the two decades (the earlier constituting Bukowski's documented hiatus from serious writing), any historical or scholarly interest in the book seems intentionally stymied. The collection presumably contains the best of the early poems that do not appear in other Black Sparrow editions and is lengthier than any single early volume of the author's poetry. However, no specific citations to earlier books or magazine publications are given. Additionally, no composition dates are offered. The effect is that of a single, disjointed volume written over 20 years. Many individual poems in the collection, however, are remarkable. One reviewer added: "The poems included here are pure, raw Bukowski from a time when fame, even solvency, seemed remote if not unattainable possibilities."[19]

Although a few pieces address the author's own notoriety and disruptive visits by fans, such intrusions are minimal. *The Roominghouse Madrigals* assembles, instead, a fascinating collection of studies on death, apocalypse, the poet's disappointment with mankind, and a persistent ambivalence toward art that nevertheless finally endorses the creation act as a noble enterprise. Considering the generally somber tone of the pieces and the many years involved in their composition, the ragged edges of the book are perhaps unavoidable. As Bukowski wrote concerning *Crucifix in a Deathhand*, "It is hard to scream or bayonet and still retain the vindictive and cool Art-form" (*Screams*, 231). In the brief foreword to *The Roominghouse Madrigals*, the poet simply states that "the early poems are more lyrical than where I am at now."[20] Although these poems contain less surrealism than some others, their density, tendency toward stream of consciousness, darkness of tone, and reliance on surprising metaphor rather than narrative all mark them as early Bukowski.

Many poems in *The Roominghouse Madrigals* blend the author's primary concerns of death, art, and the necessity of hard living into a troubling amalgam of willful destruction of both self and other. "Old Man, Dead in a Room" is one of the book's better-known and most brilliant poems.[21]

> it's not death
> but dying will solve its power
> and as my grey hands
> drop a last desperate pen
> in some cheap room
> they will find me there
> and never know
> my name
> my meaning
> nor the treasure
> of my escape. (*Madrigals*, 54)

The lines are romantic, indeed lyrical, and isolate the prototypical Bukowski image of a man writing alone in a small room. Written by an obscure, middle-aged poet, the poem is presumptuous, yet excruciatingly poignant. It attempts to answer an implied riddle: "this thing upon me is not death / but it's as real." The enigmatic "thing" is what "some call Art / some call Poetry" and "crawls like a snake" of temptation to terrify the speaker's "love of commonness" (*Madrigals*, 53–54).

Bukowski is fascinated with death and its corollary peace, a fascination that also accounts for his preoccupation with suicide. Not until the later poems is suicide consistently treated with humor. Death, while perhaps not a friend, nevertheless brings a gift of annihilation to the individual: "as the wind breaks in from the sea / and time goes on / flushing your bones with soft peace" (*Madrigals*, 64). The poem "The Gift" ends with the narrator's pronouncement that "certainly the charm of dying / lies in the fact / that very little / is lost" (*Madrigals*, 81). In the occasionally stunning poem "Practice," Bukowski presents his preparation for death as integral to life. "I practice for you, death: / your wig / that dress

/ your eyes / these teeth" (*Madrigals*, 151). As in "Old Man, Dead in a Room," anticipation of death is nearly inseparable from the artist's craft of performance and representation, and the speaker practices "for everybody, / but for myself mostly" (*Madrigals*, 152). In "Everything," the poet's incarnation of the dead renders them as as needful and vibrant as the living: "but the dead might need / each / other. // in fact, the dead might need / everything we / need // and / we need so much" (*Madrigals*, 185–86). Again echoing Jeffers, Bukowski suggests the falsity of the egotism that drives him. True peace, as explained in "Regard Me," may be possible only through surrender and passage:

> regard me, even as dead, more alive than
> many of the living, •
> and regard me, as I fumble with flat breasts,
> regard me as nothing
> so we may have peace
> and forget. (*Madrigals*, 176)

The poet's interest in an imagined rest beyond this life is related to a theme of ennui. The narrator in the room sits alone, watches, and withdraws again from the world of labor and knowledge. This point of view is nicely modulated in "Hangover and Sick Leave," in which the speaker, aware that "there are universities and / books full of men and / places like / Rome and Madrid—" chooses instead to "stay in bed / and watch the light rise in the curtains / and listen to the sounds / that I dislike" (*Madrigals*, 169). "Books full of men" is doubly suggestive, indicating both a fuller life within literature and a literature that consumes. The narrator's "beautiful cardboard day of / the mole" (*Madrigals*, 169) evokes an attitude of withdrawal more than a bit reminiscent of Emily Dickinson. In fact, the dark tone of *The Roominghouse Madrigals*, its fascination with death, its isolated speakers, and its tendency to focus on a microcosm through the window to represent a macrocosm of experience all indicate a perhaps unlikely similarity between the central personae of Dickinson and Bukowski. Curiously, such an influence aligns Bukowski with both traditions of American poetry, traditions generally considered quite opposite: the expansiveness of Whitman is wedded to the exquisite isolation of Dickinson.

The world that the speaker watches is often one apparently approaching its end, and the voice is in turn apocalyptic. The collection opens with the intriguing poem "22,000 Dollars in 3 Months," a first-person account of third-world exploitation that ends in flames and death. The cost of ravaging the earth and its cultures is annihilation. The narrator captures and kisses a small snake, symbolically embracing his temptation, and in the final moments recalls "dead communists, dead fascists, dead democrats, dead gods" (*Madrigals*, 14). It is an unusual and effective poem for Bukowski and establishes the tone of what follows. Throughout *The Roominghouse Madrigals,* the seeming randomness in a suffering world is portentous, interdependent, and inescapable. "I hear a voice singing. / I open a window. / a dog barks. / in Amsterdam a holy man trembles" (*Madrigals*, 165). In the chilling "Saying Goodbye to Love," the contemporary man leaving for work is indistinguishable from the ancient warrior departing for a final brutal crusade. "no more stalling, / the war torch is lit / and all over the neighborhood / men rattle in their irons"; the speaker says farewell to "wife and hound," both of them "like two jellychildren / lost in smoke" (*Madrigals*, 182). The destruction of man seems imminent, his goals dubious and unnamed. It is a willed demise, the coveted death-peace.

When effective, Bukowski's masculine posing is undercut by his skepticism of such behavior, of the very assertions of male ego that constitute a personal mythos:

> one-third of the world starving while
> I am indecent enough to worry about my own death
> like some monkey engrossed with his flea,
> I am sad because my manliness chokes me down
> to the nakedness of revulsion (*Madrigals*, 192)

In a lighter mode, "Winter Comes to a Lot of Places in August" satirically represents the blue-collar warrior. Hundreds of workers march "like cattle, / like Hannibal victorious" with lunch pails of wives' bologna sandwiches "to warm our gross man-bones / and prove to us that love / is not clipped out like a coupon" (*Madrigals*, 228). The routine of labor that deadens also measures and determines machismo. In "One Hundred and Ninety-Nine Pounds of Clay Leaning Forward," the speaker succinctly offers that "our dirty time is just about / served and done" (*Madrigals*, 190). In poem after poem, nature lurks just out of the frame of human idiocy. The hungry sharks, notable for their cold nonhumanness, wait "beyond the rocks / thrashing for our silly blood" (*Madri-*

gals, 239). The earth itself possesses a patient sentience: "and the sea waits / as the land waits, / amused and perfect" (*Madrigals*, 199). Although some of Jeffers persists, the landscape of the coming oblivion is Bukowski's own. In "It's Not Who Lived Here," the death of man initiates a time when "the insect / and the fire and / the flood / will become / truth" (*Madrigals*, 21).

In addition to violence, fire, and dark predictions, two other notable preoccupations persist in *The Roominghouse Madrigals*. One is the intrusion of art and artistic process into the banalities of quotidian society. A classical composer, a modernist author, Bukowski's own poetic composition and the outsider status he relishes, these continually offer counterpoint to the madness both seen outside the window and battled within. Despite the author's disappointment with the artistic output of the centuries, the attempt itself of creation in the face of circumstances is one he idealizes and admires. Artists have produced despite the "nature of their / brothers" and "it's more than good / that some of them, / (closer really to field-mouse than / falcon) / have been bold enough to try" (*Madrigals*, 49). Bukowski tends to romanticize and identify with the artist of the ages, at the same time lamenting again the absence of the whole man he seeks. It is not a privileging of experience that distinguishes an artistic viewpoint, but a privileging of discipline, vision, endurance, and finally excellence. The ideology of the Chinaski persona is latent in such a philosophy. The poet, too, wants the whole world or nothing. "I know / that there is nothing more incomplete than a / half-talent; / a man should either be a genius / or nothing at all" (*Madrigals*, 229).

Bukowski's obsession with the power of art to salvage an otherwise unredeemed life is frustrating to reconcile with his suspicion of charlatans, his demand for excellence, and his disgust with the approved literary canon. He writes that "people who dabble in the Arts / are misfits in a misshapen society" (*Madrigals*, 229) and "practically speaking / the great words of great men / are not so great" (*Madrigals*, 245). In the next moment, the speaker may recall with admiration "Segovia / who practices 5 hours a day" (*Madrigals*, 198) as an antidote to a burdensome and unimaginative society. The seemingly contradictory sensibilities reveal, most significantly, the centrality of art and creative process to Bukowski's vision. Writing is tonic to his demons. The wistful poem "Seahorse" relates the author's transportation to a better world through art. He will ride his horse "up the mountain / down the valley" to an imagined land:

> we will go to where kings eat
> dandelions
> in the giant sea
> where thinking is not terror
> where eyes do not go out
> like Saturday night children (*Madrigals*, 100)

The poet effects a utopian return: "the horse I own and the myself I own / will become blue and nice and clean / again" (*Madrigals*, 100).

Men march to work with dull faces and lunch pails, and Bukowski, despite his artistic concerns, often places himself among them. Such an inclusion both palliates and legitimizes what is often perceived as a misanthropic vein in the poet's work. The artist is voyeur, but also weary and disenfranchised laborer. The attractive destruction of self to achieve peace is also the chronicling of the violent and absurd extinction of the race. Within this paradox, Bukowski clings to a notion that he also ridicules: a life of physical labor, which destroys, is also a life that can purify and demand artistic honesty. In "A Word on the Quick and Modern Poem-Makers," the speaker defines himself: "I have an honesty self-born of whores and hospitals / that will not allow me to pretend to be / something which I am not—" (*Madrigals*, 99). This "double failure," he continues, is "the failure of people / in poetry / and the failure of people / in life" (*Madrigals*, 99). The slightly garbled syntax is intentional. Life and labor, art and artisan, are not easily separated. Bukowski recognizes the complexity of this interrelatedness and also the impossible distinction between choice and fate, will and determinism. The essay "He Beats His Women" addresses these contradictions:

> That most men don't gamble with their lives or their creativity is not my fault. And it makes for dull writing and duller writers.
>   The factories, the slaughterhouses, the warehouses were not exactly a choice and then they were a choice. . . . The gods were good to me. They kept me under. They made me live the life. It was very difficult for me to walk out of a slaughterhouse or a factory and come home and write a poem I didn't quite mean. And many people write poems they don't quite mean. I do too, sometimes. ("His Women," 67–68)

The Days Run Away like Wild Horses over the Hills

The Days Run Away like Wild Horses over the Hills contains, according to the author, "poems from late 1968 and most of 1969, plus selections from five early chapbooks" (*Burning*, 5). The collection is a strong one, dealing extensively with Bukowski's themes of ironized machismo, the transportative power of artistic imagination, a surprised response to fatherhood and, extensively, the pain and limitation of male-female relationships. This last subject is heartbreakingly rendered in several poems lamenting the death of his lover Jane. The publication of the collection in 1969 also roughly coincided with the author's attempt to write full-time and professionally. In January 1970 he shared his apprehensions in a letter: "I am a member of the unemployed now with nothing but a typer and a couple of paint brushes to hold off the world. So keep your fingers crossed for me and hope the gods are on my side. There's my 5 year old daughter involved and if I lost her, that would do me in. But things have a way of working. There's no need to lay it down yet. There's a novel in mind and *The Days Run Away* . . . moving along nicely" (*Screams*, 354). The book makes increasing use of narration and dialogue, and some of these longer narrative poems represent the weakest sections in the volume. Two poems in particular fall into this category: "Did I Ever Tell You" is an eight-page poem in the voice of a lover who cannot help recounting her former men at length. The technique of the poem, that the woman's voice drowns out Bukowski's own, is also its greatest handicap, resulting in monotonous repetition. "The Seminar" is a six-page satire of writers' conferences, again told exclusively in a voice other than the poet's usual persona, this time a conference participant observing the "great American poets"; the irony intended in the depiction of the self-important proceedings is clear, but, in the end, the poem seems obvious and overwrought.

These glitches aside, *The Days Run Away like Wild Horses over the Hills* contains memorable work. The book opens with a complementary triptych of poems worth scrutiny. "What a Man I Was" is another of Bukowski's parodic westerns, this time rendered from the point of view of a blasé outlaw. The tone is burlesque. "I shot off his left ear / then his right, / and then tore off this belt buckle / with hot lead, / and then / I shot off everything that counts."[22] The poem's amoralism is tongue-in-cheek, the killing more a result of boredom than any meaningful cause: "Didn't seem to be no one around / so I shot my horse / (poor critter)" (*Days*, 13). The killer's disingenuous compassion is underscored by his lack of concern for consequences, even concerning his own self-preservation and escape (his horse). When every animate thing around him has been killed, the narrator's impulse for destruction enlarges with a self-deifying zest that includes the universe: "and I shot out the stars one

by one / and then / I shot out the moon" (*Days*, 14). The will and power
to destroy are here aligned with the creative urge, the indivisible sides of
a coin that partly explains Bukowski's continual fascination with the
criminal and killer. Even at the speaker's hanging, all reality is filtered
through ego: "and though they was moanin' / other men's names / I just
know they was cryin' / for me (poor critters)" (*Days*, 15). To the killer,
victims are confused with self, and his last earthly act is to stare "down /
into Nellie Adam's breasts." Unrepentant, his actions unexamined, the
speaker and his watering mouth close the poem, suggesting a victory of
instinct and animality over intellect, morality, and human sociality.

Although a silly poem, and one of the few light moments in an otherwise grim collection, "What a Man I Was" sets the tone for its author's
examination of masculine myths, their absurdity and their danger. In
"Down thru the Marching," the speaker is a sniper firing into a military
parade in the American South, with the innovation that he fires not
from rooftop but from cellar: "and when the legs / came walking by on
top of my head, / I got a colonel, a major and 3 lts. / before the band
stopped playing" (*Days*, 21). The tone here is more intentional and
pointed than in the gunslinger poem, yet the situation is comparable.
Bukowski neither condones nor condemns the sniper and eschews psychological examination in favor of reportage. The primary difference
between the lone madman and the war hero, the author suggests
throughout his work, is the endorsement of government and the public's gullibility.

The book's second poem, "Mine," is disguised as a short, lyric love
poem, but beginning even with the piece's possessive title (coming
directly after the godlike egotism of the outlaw), troubling subtextual
rumblings are heard. The unnamed woman "lays like a lump" and has a
"great empty mountain" for a head, yet the speaker recognizes her as a
living being, implies the value of this, and indicates the primacy of her
presence: "She yawns and / scratches her nose and / pulls up the cover"
(*Days*, 16). Before kissing her good night, he thinks of "Scotland / and
under the ground the / gophers run." All is not well or as it appears. The
foreign, "other" place beckons as the animals of memory and longing
dig below a surface of contented appearance. The man hears "engines in
the night" and sees an ambiguous white hand in the night sky. The
poem's last line, "good night, dear, goodnight" (*Days*, 16) is unclear: Is
the white hand that of a lost lover waving farewell forever? Is the
speaker addressing his ghosts or merely kissing his current partner as
closure to the evening? "Mine" concisely but effectively articulates the

troubling difficulty of relationships apparent in much of *The Days Run Away*. The speaker is torn between disappointment and appreciation, between the living and the dead, between sexist ownership and an acute awareness of his sexism. The carefully modulated tone of "Mine" renders it powerful both as embrace and as denial of the man's relationship with the woman beside him.

The following poem, "freedom," is the narrative of a man who emasculates himself with a butcher knife while forcing his lover to watch as payment for her nightly indiscretions. The self-inflicted disfiguration accomplishes its perverse purpose; when the poem ends, the woman is screaming, on the verge of incoherence, and the man assumes a new composure as "one hand holding and one hand / lifting he poured / another wine" (*Days*, 18). "freedom" is disturbing, with hateful and melodramatic action overwhelming the sketchy characters, but completes a circle begun by the two preceding poems. Male dominance is reasserted only, and ironically, through an extreme, perverse act of violence that damages the other through masculine self-destruction. The woman's yellow dress, his favorite, is rendered meaningless as sex is made impossible. Even survival is uncertain, and the male's absurd "victory" is most costly to himself.

> and he sat there holding 3 towels
> between his legs
> not caring now whether she left or
> stayed
> wore yellow or green or
> anything at all. (*Days*, 18)

Each life-embracing poem in the collection is subtly undercut by the poems surrounding it. The color yellow is again prominent later, in the love poem "All-Yellow Flowers":

> she went on singing but I wanted to die
> I wanted yellow flowers like her golden hair
> I wanted yellow-singing and the sun.
> this is true, and that is what makes it so strange:
> I wanted to be opened and untangled, and
> tossed away. (*Days*, 49)

Even without the echoes the yellow dress brings, the ending of the poem is typically ambiguous. In one sense a lyrical embrace of lover, warmth, and surrender, still the poem associates the speaker's happiness with death, penetration, and a discarding of self that seems far removed from a reciprocally nurturing and sustainable relationship. Another poem, "Yellow," associates that color with pusillanimous male behavior. Told from the harsh point of view of the assistant coach of a professional football team, this poem chronicles the running back Seivers's injury and subsequent loss of nerve. The coach's disgust takes the form of ritual humiliation. "I got him in the locker room the other day when the whole / squad was in there. I told him, 'Seivers, you used to be a player / but now you're chickenshit' " (*Days*, 114). This is followed by a physical assault and finally abandonment by the team. "guys like Seivers end up washing dishes for a buck an hour / and that's just what they deserve" (*Days*, 114). The poem's sneering cruelty never relents. Although the poem "Yellow" has no explicit connection to "All-Yellow Flowers," the repetition of the color in radically different contexts is indicative of *The Days Run Away*'s circularity. Sexual love is inevitably superseded by distance (often spiritual, as in the superb poem "The Screw-Game," but physical in the Jane elegies). This distance, several poems suggest, is either created or at least increased by the barbaric myopia of the male.

At times, the coupling of male assertion and female stereotype results in sexist language on Bukowski's part. In the best such poems, however, these sentiments are countered by recognition. In "sleeping woman," for example, the troubling midpoem proclamation "yet you cannot help being a / woman" is modified by the speaker's final focus on the woman's fragmented but individual reality, on the value of companionship, and on an acceptance of imperfection.

> I can see $\frac{1}{2}$ a mouth, one eye and
> almost a nose.
> the rest of you hidden
> out of sight
> but I know that you are a
> contemporary, a modern living
> work
> perhaps not immortal
> but we have
> loved.

> please continue to
> snore. (*Days*, 72)

In his calmer and fairer moments, the speaker recognizes his own defi-
ciency in perception and the likely possibility of his own anachronistic
approach. The poems of requiem to Jane, moreover, are among
Bukowski's most tender, revealing, and painful.

Five poems of memory and loss are collected together early in the
volume, and their melancholy pervades much of what follows. In the
brief apostrophe "I Taste the Ashes of Your Death," the narrator suffers
the bittersweet addiction of a loss he will not let go. "the blossoms shake
/ sudden water / down my sleeve, / sudden water / cool and clean / as
snow—"; he is emptied, and to that extent cleansed, of the trivialities of
ordinary life. The severity of the emotions is purifying. "and the sweet
wild / rocks / leap over / and / lock us in" (*Days*, 31), the poem concludes, indicating burial and finality, yet at the same time life, fluidity,
and a primitive energy that signifies the animating power of love and
loss. "For Jane: With all the Love I had, which was Not Enough:—"
finds the speaker among the physical reminders of the dead woman:

> I pick up the skirt,
> I pick up the sparkling beads
> in black,
> this thing that moved once
> around flesh,
> and I call God a liar (*Days*, 32)

The narrator suffers and indulges the limitations of his own understanding, culminating in the shocking directness of the poem's conclusion.

> I lean upon all of this
> and I know:
> her dress upon my arm:
> but
> they will not
> give her back to me. (*Days*, 32)

Each colon represents a chasm, but only the man remains to supply the next word, the next gesture. One accepts what must be accepted.

The Days Run Away counterbalances the weight of loss with the appearance of Bukowski's daughter. The arrival of the infant frequently confuses and delights the new father, forcing him to reexamine his bleakness and to continue to live and hope. "birth" is a determinedly unsentimental poem, yet in the poet's first sight of his daughter—tellingly, without the mother—a sure knowledge of the world's cruelty is mediated by hopefulness and affection: "I am called upstairs. they show me the thing through glass. / it's red as a boiled crab and tough. it will make / it. it will see it through" (*Days*, 109). The speaker's limited perceptions of women are recast as a humorous extrapolation of his daughter's future. "I can see her now on some Sunday afternoon / shaking it in a tight skirt / making Boulevards of young men warble in their / guts" (*Days*, 109–10). When Bukowski speaks of his daughter, his tone lightens. He is clearly aware that his customary severity diminishes, and he welcomes the change.

In "kaakaa & other immolations," told from the voice of father to daughter against the backdrop of the parents' failed relationship, paternal advice devolves into silliness and enjoyment of a simple moment of togetherness. "you say *I'm* kaakaa! / hey that's / good! I like that! / very funny. // now let's go get some more beer and / applejuice" (*Days*, 149). The father's vulgarity becomes childlike in the daughter's presence. A previous acceptance of destruction is now a feared annihilation of his child's future: "I tickle again, say / crazy / words, and and and and / hope / all the while / that this / very unappetizing / world / does not blow up / in all our / laughing / faces" (*Days*, 132). The death of Jane and the birth of the daughter are the two poles between which *The Days Run Away* fluctuates. Both extremes cause Bukowski to question his beliefs, and both, it seems, cause him to value life as a fragile and transitory gift. In this context, the collection's other concerns—"learning" death, the police at the door, the indulgent madness of artists and the suffering of the laborer—carry altered implications. The presence of the daughter may instill enough responsibility and wishfulness in the father to ensure his continued struggle, but otherwise much remains the same.

The collection's last lengthy poem, "Even the Sun was Afraid," finds the speaker back in a world of violence and male domination. A stark, colloquial voice effectively deconstructs the myth of the bullfight, its rituals and supposed dignity.

we had another
drink. we knew the plot, the hero, the whole
fucking thing. the sword went
in. (*Days*, 137–38)

Exhausted by the banality of the situation and disgusted even by his own
clichéd sympathy for the bull, the narrator aligns himself with the American crowd. He is, after all, willing audience to the spectacle. "kaakaa &
other immolations" shortly follows, and the juxtaposition of the opposed
settings is clear. In Bukowski's work, the bull is often admired for its
ferocity, directness, and primitive honesty and is often associated with
light and the sun. The paradox is that the bull is the artist, wild and necessary to itself, yet it is also a stupid, brutal beast representative of man.
The father recognizes himself as participant in a world of inflicted pain, a
world he must bequeath to the daughter. "you could SEE the bull / die.
the bull gave it / up. the crowd / cheered" (*Days*, 139).

Mockingbird Wish Me Luck

Mockingbird Wish Me Luck collects Bukowski's poems "from late 1969 to
early 1972" (*Burning*, 5). Taken with *The Days Run Away,* the poems
complete the four-year gap between *At Terror Street and Agony Way* and
the poems concluding *Burning in Water, Drowning in Flame*. Like the
pieces contained in the latter selection, those constituting *Mockingbird
Wish Me Luck* move closer to Bukowski's persona and style from the late
1970s onward. There is a tendency toward shorter lines, less lyrical and
more narrative content than before, and, in spots, a troubling verbosity.
The 10-page "ww2," while an interesting blurring of verse and short
story, seems nevertheless bloated, its parenthetical asides more typical of
the author's journalistic prose. Section 3 collects the bulk of the book's
volatile love poems to Linda King—a woman fictionalized in *Women* and
to whom *Mockingbird Wish Me Luck* is dedicated—and odes and reflections to the author's daughter, Marina.

Throughout the volume, and concentrated especially in the earlier
sections, Bukowski again associates himself with the mad, the tor-
mented, and the powerless. He associates, in short, with the poor, and
they populate this collection. The poet diligently and convincingly pursues his long-held belief that poverty and labor are closer to the reality

that identifies the truly living, and he inevitably portrays the rich as callous and deadened. Sometimes Bukowski's use of personal pronouns reveals his sympathies. In the racetrack poem "the world's greatest loser," he writes: "I guess nothing ever works for us. we're fools, of course—."[23] The author cherishes the idea of luck, which often seems nearly synonymous with grace and seldom comes to the poor. The poem continues:

> bucking the inside plus a 15 percent take,
> but how are you going to tell a dreamer
> there's a 15 percent take on the
> dream? he'll just laugh and say,
> is that all? (*Mockingbird*, 15)

Losers, laborers, and dreamers are each the same, a group that often to Bukowski contains a kind of bruised beauty, a tough survivalism that the poet recognizes and sometimes includes himself in. Although many poems concern the violation of the poet's private space and thoughts, one notices in the racetrack poems that Bukowski continues to throw himself into the crowd, revealing his own incriminating participation in an impossible gamble of long odds.

"a day at the oak tree meet" chronicles a series of unwise bets and common susceptibilities. The narrator recovers from his losses in the ninth race. The sudden shift in tone, from loser to winner, argues for skill and persistence, while the possibility remains that the speaker's turn of fortune is random and arbitrary (that is, lucky). "There are thorough— / bred horses and thoroughbred bettors. What you do is / stay with your plays and let them come to you. Loving / a woman is the same way, or loving life" (*Mockingbird*, 24). Bukowski, by the chance of a late winner, assumes the world-weary swagger of the survivor imparting wisdom. The distance that separates victors, a distance of money, is reestablished. "You'll see me that night having a / quiet drink at the track bar as the losers run for the / parking lot. Don't talk to me or bother me and I won't / bother you. All right?" (*Mockingbird*, 24). This arrogance is miles from the author's portrayal of himself as social barfly, and the separation between the two roles is primarily financial.

Although a reliance on luck, style, and persistence pervades Bukowski's work, the arrogant class distinction that ends "a day at the oak tree meet" is undercut by the population of losers present throughout the collection. Similarly, in "moyamensing prison:", the speaker separates himself from other inmates by his luck with dice.

> "Mr. Bukowski," ace-crapshooter,
> money-man in a world of almost no
> money.
> immortality. (*Mockingbird*, 18)

After Bukowski is thrown back "on the streets," normal social stratifications resume, and he is "innocent, lazy, frightened and mortal / again" (*Mockingbird*, 18). This event is significant enough to its author that it is related twice in the book, appearing later as one of several ironic class incidents in "ww2." Even among losers, the criminals and convicts of society, a hierarchy is present, and the poet's enjoyment of his temporary elevated status is tinged with a large degree of ironic self-awareness.

Mockingbird Wish Me Luck's numerous references to the poor are gradually revealed as the book's central concern. "funhouse" and "another academy" are adjacent poems that document, through the example of homelessness, the dismal failure of the American dream of richness, growth, and physical prowess. "another academy" begins with vagrants waiting to enter a mission shelter for the night, "700 of them / quiet as oxen." It ends with a refutation of the Hollywood frontier hero:

> out in front of the Mission I heard one guy say to
> another:
> "John Wayne won it."
> "Won what?" said the other guy
> tossing the last of his rolled cigarette into the
> street.
>
> I thought that was
> rather good. (*Mockingbird*, 21–22)

The narrator stands with and among the others, sharing in the joke of a decimated dream in which they constitute the punch line.

Even those lucky enough to hold a job typically suffer under the same burden of distorted achievement, with the added travail of soul-shredding menial labor: "or making it / as a waitress at Norm's on the split shift, /

or as an emptier of / bedpans, / or as a carwash or a busboy" (*Mocking-bird*, 115). The ironic emphasis on "making it," with its echo of commercial jargon, is reminiscent of the fraudulent assertion that John Wayne has "won it." Won what? Bukowski asks. Made what? The short, brutal poem "making it," which co-opts this phrase as its title, directly addresses this rhetoric of a self-deluded success fueled by propaganda, consumption, and a national idea of "action":

> ignore all possible concepts and possibilities—
> ignore Beethoven, the spider, the damnation of Faust—
> just *make* it, babe, make it:
> a house   a car   a belly full of beans (*Mockingbird*, 29)

As Bukowski explicates the tenets of capitalistic "success," he manifests disgust for such pursuit. Contemplation, art, recognition of death and loss, all are curtailed by the achievement of a fake utopia. Despite this harsh recognition, perhaps informed by it, *Mockingbird Wish Me Luck* revolves around a simple equation of suppression and suffering: "he was rich and I was poor / and the sea rolled in / and I turned the / white / pages" (*Mockingbird*, 60).

The critical depiction of the rich in the book is a case study of waste and excess, frequently at the expense of the poor. In "the hunt," sandwiched between a "long day" at the track and a final image of "unemployed drunks / with flopping canvas hats," is a sighting of the blasé upper class: "offshore you could see the lights of a / passing yacht / with a party on board, / lots of girls and jokes and the / rest" (*Mockingbird*, 87). In "the golfers," the narrator again identifies at a distance the rich in their insulated lives: "driving through the park / I notice men and women playing golf / driving in their powered carts / over billiard table lawns" (*Mockingbird*, 67). A class-conscious mentality increasingly informs Bukowski's poetry throughout his career, and Harrison argues that this emphasis is one of two reasons that the author has received little serious critical attention from academics: "The first is the sheer volume of his poetry and the attitude such a production bespeaks . . . the second, subtler and more important reason arises out of a failure to appreciate the significance of, or to react against, the class content of Bukowski's poetry. . . . More than anything else, he is a proletarian poet, but a proletarian poet of a special sensibility" (29). Concerning the author's prodigious output, Harrison continues that "the amount of poetry Bukowski has published and the apparent ease with which he has produced it offend against certain tenets of modernism and his work provides a sharp contrast to the production of many 20th-century poets" (30). Moreover, contemporary poets for the most part conspicuously lack a legitimate, convincing working-class component in their work.

Critics' dismissal of Bukowski's emphasis on the everyday and the mundane as the paranoia of a single eccentric artist overlooks the frequent empathy between the poet and his characteristic setting. "The attempt to marginalize the experience that is at the core of Bukowski's poetry, to rob it of its significance, is an attempt to deny the validity of that experience which is, in the main, not marginal but that of the American working-class" (Harrison, 40). Especially in poems that recall his years as a young man, such as "hot," Bukowski categorizes himself as a vagrant. In "the rat" he recalls that "we slept in rented rooms that weren't rented" while "the rich pawed away at their many / choices" (*Mockingbird*, 78). Young men may choose patriotism and war as an alternative to poverty, but the poet's sharp juxtapositions expose the fraudulence of that method of escape: "3 of us . . . were killed in World War II. / another one is now manager of a mattress / company" (*Mockingbird*, 79). Only Bukowski, the member of the "we" who rejects participation, survives recognizably whole. The poems further indicate a connection between the artist's lifestyle and that of the jobless. The voice in "vacancy" proclaims that "the good days are / over. / you can't tell an unemployed man / from an artist anymore, / they all look alike" (*Mockingbird*, 76). Such a comparison allows Bukowski, even as a modestly famous poet, to retain and cultivate a pertinent connection with the unemployed. In "happy new year" the speaker contrasts his lifestyle with that of his silently antagonistic neighbor: "We test each other, / never speak—I live without working, / he works without / living" (*Mockingbird*, 113).

The sentiment of "happy new year" is typical of *Mockingbird Wish Me Luck* and is its most cogent argument. Despite the hard dues of membership in the lower class, that group shares with the artist the boon of leisure, a freedom Bukowski feels is inestimable. In "the millionaires," the poet addresses an audience with "no faces / at all / laughing at nothing" and remembers

> imbecile winos
> whose cause was better

whose eyes still held some light
whose voices retained some sensibility,
and when the morning came
we were sick but not ill,
poor but not deluded,
and we stretched in our beds and rose
in the late afternoons
like millionaires. (*Mockingbird*, 54)

This brief, direct poem could serve as a thesis for the best work in the collection. The repetition of the title word in the last line nicely refocuses the poem from its presumed subject to, instead, the speaker and his fellow poor. Bukowski embraces personal leisure. In "the golfers," the narrator is relieved not to be among the elite who, in his estimation, isolate themselves from a direct and honest involvement with life. "I drive on and start singing / making up the sound / a war chant / and there is the sun / and the sun says, good, I know you" (*Mockingbird*, 67). The calibrated aggression of the war chant and the heat of the sun (both warming and searing) link the narrator's animosity with his celebration of self-liberty.

The poems in *Mockingbird Wish Me Luck* include several instances of cleansing or apocalyptic fire. In "the golfers," the speaker notes that the fire of the sun "burns the trees and the people and the city" (*Mockingbird*, 67). A blaze of retribution and devastation frequently consumes the last people sitting in the last rooms. "burning," "carnival," and "climax" deal extensively with variations on this theme. In "the big fire," Bukowski writes

I'm on fire like a beggar in India
a beggar in New York
a beggar in Los Angeles . . .
the smoke and burning rises
and the ash is crushed under . . . (*Mockingbird*, 89)

The fire is in and of the individual, endemic to a culture burning from within and from without. To the poet, the fire both cleanses and annihilates and is integral to his themes of class, justice, relief, and regret. It is the great equalizing fire of nature that warms and burns, and it is, as the title of another poem indicates, a "consummation of grief." Bukowski admits with a combination of disgust, disappointment, and pride that he "was born to hustle roses down the avenues of the dead" (*Mockingbird*, 85). The dead are the dead, and, he paradoxically argues, the dead are the living—corrupted by wealth or twisted by its absence.

Play the Piano Drunk like a Percussion Instrument Until the Fingers Begin to Bleed a Bit

Play the Piano Drunk like a Percussion Instrument Until the Fingers Begin to Bleed a Bit—a perorational title even by Bukowski's standards—was not released until 1979 but was assembled "from Bukowski's earlier work that had not yet been collected. A reader familiar with the poet's output will encounter poems that are typical of his earlier poems" (Cherkovski, *Hank*, 265). Even a cursory glance at the book reveals it to be a peculiar follow-up to *Love Is a Dog from Hell* (1977); *Play the Piano Drunk* is slim, its 125 pages of verse the fewest of any Bukowski volume available from Black Sparrow. Its poems, moreover, seem an odd mixture of work culled from many years. "12-24-78" indicates by its title a poem contemporaneous with the book's publication, while "a little atomic bomb" is cited by Cherkovski as a popular poem from the 1960s. As a result, the collection is an uneven mix of work containing numerous strong poems but sitting uncomfortably on the border of the "new" Bukowski territory. Many of the pieces seem uncharacteristically sparse, like the volume itself, and this too complicates a unified impression.

The poems contain several recurrent themes. Ironic portraits of tough guys are offered: "a killer gets ready" and "the loner" are typical. "the apple" returns to a treatment of voyeurism reminiscent of William Carlos Williams's work. The poem considers temptation and imperfectibility as the poet's eye moves from "a girl in a white dress" passing by his window to "a dirty / ashtray."[24] The apple's savoriness ends as a belch. The following poem, "the violin player," coalesces Bukowski's concerns with luck and style as a day at the racetrack is transformed by a pauper musician beautiful to the author:

> after Dumpty's Goddess took the last
> and they began their long slow walk to their cars
> beaten and broken again
> the violin player continued

sending his music after them
and I sat there listening (*Piano*, 62)

The poet's deference is displayed in allowing the other man "a few minutes" before he follows (*Piano*, 62). "the red porsche" reconsiders
Bukowski's class theme as a recognition of the poet's peculiar fortune:
"it's better to be driven around in a / red porsche / than to own / one. the
luck of the fool is / inviolate" (*Piano*, 23). The poem idealizes an escape
from the yoke of ownership, modernizing a Thoreau-like sensibility. The
fool—that is, the artist—owns all he surveys.

Other poems explicitly reject the mendacity of ordinary social values,
either by the author's alternative example ("the sandwich") or by the
failures demonstrated in others' cyclical patterns ("the proud thin
dying"). "the drill" and "dow average down" are convincing variations
on the difficulty of sexual relationships, while the ironically titled "I love
you" and "I'm in love" both reveal romantic betrayal by the speaker.
"I'm in love" is particularly self-incriminating:

> her arms were thin, very thin and when
> she screamed and started beating me I held her
> wrists and then I got it through the eyes: hatred,
> centuries deep and true. I was wrong and graceless and
> sick. all the things I had learned had been wasted.
> there was no living creature as foul as I
> and all my poems were
> false. (*Piano*, 58)

Although the narrator undoubtedly recognizes his hyperbole, the con-
demning sentiment convinces: the severity of blame itself cannot be
escaped aesthetically or intellectually, and escape is not desired. Pain,
throughout these poems, signifies being alive: "agony can kill / or /
agony can sustain life / but peace is always horrifying" (*Piano*, 113).
Especially in his earlier poems, peace is a façade that Bukowski is wary
of and denies.

The abrupt mention of the writer's poems into the penultimate line
of "I'm in love" indicates the nearest idea to a unifying theme in *Play the
Piano Drunk*: the continual encroachment of art into life, and vice versa.
Although Bukowski customarily aligns himself staunchly with art (as an

escape from the banal and as a pursuable perfectibility), many of the poems in this volume betray an opposite loyalty. The tedium of life seems a necessity that must be confronted. The toughness of artistic creation may represent a pose. "40,000 flies" ends with a distillation of this idea: "it's so easy to be a poet / and so hard to be / a man" (*Piano*, 27). The conclusion is reached after the poetic conceits in the middle of the poem are interrupted by the writer's own (and seemingly sudden) recognition of his failure to simply and directly capture life. "arms of my soul? / flies? / singing? / what kind of shit is / this?" (*Piano*, 27). A similar event occurs in "through the streets of anywhere":

> *I say that*
> *the backalleys will arrive upon*
> *the bloodyapes*
> *as noon arrives upon the Salinas*
> *fieldhands. . . .*

> bullshit. I rip the page once, twice,
> three times, then check for matches and
> icecubes, hot and cold (*Piano,* 37)

Such conflicting voices may be Bukowski's recognition of his own evolving style, a conscious movement from the more lyrical, surrealistic, and "poetic" techniques of earlier books to a simpler narrative approach. In *Play the Piano Drunk,* the poet struggles between artistic coyness and direct apprehension of life.

"interviews" apparently finds the "new" Bukowski close to fully formed, rejecting literary pretense even as he asserts his own literary authority:

> forget that shit I told you about
> Dos Passos. or was it
> Mailer? it's hot tonight
> and half the neighborhood is
> drunk. the other half is
> dead.
> if I have any advice about writing

poetry, it's—

don't. (*Piano*, 76)

Tellingly, this "note" to an admirer is signed "buk," the signature appellation of Bukowski's self-perpetuated persona. Even an appreciation, that of D. H. Lawrence in "I liked him," is qualified by the poet's suspicion that the man is inferior to his writing. "I liked D. H. Lawrence / but I'm glad I never met him / in some bistro / him lifting his tiny hot cup of / tea / and looking at me / with his worm-hole eyes" (*Piano*, 106). The idea of flawed artists as inferior to their work is commonplace, but one that Bukowski doggedly pursues in these poems. He is troubled that even the few men he admires—inevitably authors, painters, and musicians of the past—are failed men as men, and this failure isolates rather than endears them to him.

they pulled Ezra through the streets

in a wooden cage.

Blake was sure of God.

Villon was a mugger.

Lorca sucked cock.

T.S. Eliot worked a teller's cage.

most poets are swans,

egrets. (*Piano*, 102)

This harsh, belittling criticism found in "junk," finally irrelevant to artistic product, should not be taken entirely as bravado on Bukowski's part. One senses in such indictments the struggle of the poet in his own life, the attendant difficulties and disappointments of attempting to live worthily of his talent. "junk" concludes, "I believe in a simple violence. // this is / some of it" (*Piano*, 103). Bukowski's narrator, the "poetry junkie" of that poem, does not allow us to separate the poem from its disturbing setting. Following shortly after his dismissive list of artists' faults and foibles, the conclusion of "junk" should be read as partly self-indicting.

Faced with the dilemma of being alive, Bukowski struggles with his fallibility as a man. It is a romantic struggle and at its core concerns how these flaws will damage his art. One of the *Play the Piano Drunk*'s last and most moving poems is "to weep," in which the speaker laments the deterioration of the "great soprano" and sees in her his own humbling humanness. "sweating in the kitchen / I don't want to murder art." Lorca is offered a more heroic fate, "down in the road / eating Spanish bullets in the dust" (*Piano*, 122). The "best poet" the author ever knew is dead, and the living write "useless things / dull things / vain things," and "the great soprano has never read my poems / but we both know how to murder art / drink and mourn" (*Piano*, 123). To Bukowski, wasted talent is infuriating and sublimely tragic. Death ends, but life destroys, and only in the amber of history is the artistic moment preserved. He fears the deceptions of intellect far more than those of emotion. The development of a simpler, more direct style was the poet's attempt to find an approach true to his art and to his life.

Chapter Five

Later Poems

Love Is a Dog from Hell

Love Is a Dog from Hell marks, by its physical appearance, a divisive point in Charles Bukowski's poetic career. This thick collection of work from 1974 to 1977 brings together 160 poems in over 300 pages of text and sets the standard for all subsequent Black Sparrow volumes of the author's poems. "Early" and "late" Bukowski are distinguishable in part by the sheer size of the later collections.[1] Their effect is novelistic; we follow the picaresque development of the Bukowski persona within each book and from one book to the next. "Poetic" material is neither privileged nor distinguished from a "novelistic" attention to the most minute aspects of the speaker's life.

Love Is a Dog from Hell as a collection is unusually consistent in its subject, which is, as the title suggests, the poet's numerous relationships during the years of these poems, his struggles understanding love and sex, and the impact of such turmoil on the work of an aging writer just coming to national prominence. The book's ironic title recalls *The Love Tale of the Hyena*, the working title of the novel *Women*, and the volume generally serves as a companion piece to that novel. In a letter in 1977, at the close of the years that the two books chronicle, Bukowski wrote that "I realize I must have been crazy from 1970–1977."[2] Many of the poems composed during that period overlapped with the writing of the novel. "Got first copy of *Love Is a Dog from Hell* in mail yesterday. Finished the novel *Women* last night" (*Luck*, 232). And unlike the author's finest work, his most nuanced and controlled, both books share a problem of distance.

Bukowski thought highly of *Women*—his letters of the time call the book his best work. That novel alone of his first four was written during the time it was also being lived, albeit near the end of Bukowski's fabled period of promiscuity, and this closeness mars the novel. The writer himself, in 1976, feared that his "nose was too close to the mirror at the moment" (*Luck*, 221) to treat such complex and emotionally charged material with an effective artistic objectivity. This same dilemma

116

informs and flaws many of the poems in *Love Is a Dog from Hell*. The collection contains some fine poems, but the author seems unusually exposed, at times confused by and victim to the volatile shifts of response and emotion that the relationships bring. He rages with wounded male bravado one moment, romantic sentimentality the next. He seems, in short, uncomfortable in the philandering role in which he casts himself. In a later interview, Bukowski admitted, "I'm soft man! I can't be a lady's man. You've got to be a hard number to do that deal. . . . Fuck this, fuck that. If you get emotionally involved, you can't do that" (Andrews, 174). While this hints at the exaggerations of persona found even in the most seemingly autobiographical work, still the reader cannot get over the feeling that in *Love Is a Dog from Hell* the author is not entirely in control of his material, as during that period he was perhaps not entirely in control of his life. The result is a sympathy—perhaps partly unintended by the poet—for the wounded, befuddled, and aging narrator. He is not always sympathetic in his attitude toward women but seems at least open and sincere. Curiously, one reviewer of the collection contended that "Bukowski has committed himself to living and writing without illusions."[3] Even the narrator of *Women* arrives at a self-understanding that may initiate change. The speaker in *Love Is a Dog from Hell*, however, is not shown to transcend his Dantean circles of mating, deterioration, and self-recrimination.

The collection finds the Bukowski persona at his most emotional, with reason, intellect, and self-restraint infrequent. Although this stance serves the speaker well in calmer instances, during a whirlwind of love and sex—the book's primary question is how these may be separated—the confused male flounders. Despite the curtailed perspective in many of the poems, the organization of the book is clearly intentional: an ironic title followed by four loosely thematic sections. Section 1 contains almost exclusively poems of love's magic and subsequent hurt, with the burden of blame falling primarily on the woman's shoulders. Section 2 mixes more love poems with a selection of poems concerning lonely men. These consider both sides of the isolation equation—the self-willed and necessary isolation of the artist and the desperate, helpless isolation of the forsaken male.

Section 3 begins with the epigraph and title "Scarlet," suggesting the proper emotional color of love and its relationship with blood (both as liquid of life and symbol of violence). The poems in this short section deal exclusively with the author's turbulent relationship with the young woman of the title.[4] Section 4 concludes the book with a focus on the marginalized, including the speaker, and develops a motif of voyeurism that signals the author's failure and a retreat from the book's love battle zone. In 1970, already anticipating a tumultuous period beginning, Bukowski wrote: "The most beautiful woman is the one who walks past your window and then she is gone" (*Luck*, 102). Such a recognition encapsulates both chivalric romanticism and the artist's predisposition for watching—Raymond Chandler crossed with William Carlos Williams—but also contains the latent paranoia, stung apprehension, and wariness of commitment that pervades much of the poet's work during this time. Reluctance toward intimacy is integral to Bukowski's theme, which is the refusal of exploitation. "Relationships are treacherous because, owing to the power struggle on which they are based, they inevitably end up in one person exploiting and/or dominating the other; mutuality, rather than dominance, is rare" (Harrison, 63–64).

The epigraph that begins section 1 identifies the book's tone and subject: "one more creature / dizzy with love."[5] Vertigo—sickness caused by an overload of emotion—and animality recur in the collection. Bukowski is clear that love is a disease unavoidable to those who remain engaged in the social world. When the narrator of "sexpot" informs us that he is "feeling much better / now" (*Love*, 22), the sentiment is ironic. There is no true cure; even self-imposed isolation is temporary and unsatisfying. *Love Is a Dog from Hell* is as preoccupied with sexual intercourse as it is with love, and the narrator, confused by every woman, is alternately the innocent, the wronged, the perpetrator, and the redresser.

> when I got back there was a letter from a
> lady in Eureka. she said she wanted me
> to fuck her until she couldn't
> walk anymore.
>
> I stretched out and whacked-off
> thinking about a little girl I had seen
> on a red bicycle about a week ago. (*Love*, 185)

These lines from "waving and waving goodbye" exemplify the narrator throughout the collection—dizzy with the idea of women and sexuality, confused, indulgent, immediate, physical, and lacking psychological scrutiny. Alternately, there are romantic moments of bonding, as in "like a flower in the rain": "I mounted / my face falling into the mass / of red hair that overflowed / from her head / and my fattened cock entered / into the miracle" (*Love*, 173). The poem ends in domestic tranquillity and sensual satiation:

> she told me
> how good she felt and I told her
> how good I felt and we ate
> the chicken and the shrimp and the
> french fries and the buns and the
> mashed potatoes and the gravy and
> the cole slaw too. (*Love*, 174)

The repetitive and childlike syntax dramatizes, without explanation, the natural, easy sharing of the couple's postcoital warmth.

However, the collected "Scarlet" poems demonstrate from the beginning the control of the young female. Section 3's final poem, "I made a mistake," ends with inevitable separation:

> I drive around the streets
> an inch away from weeping,
> ashamed of my sentimentality and
> possible love.
>
> a confused old man driving in the rain
> wondering where the good luck
> went. (*Luck*, 200)

These lines are touching, sincere, and guilty of the very sentimentality of which the speaker accuses himself. In a sense, Bukowski's scrupulous dedication to his shaky emotional states disarms criticism, yet often his confusion and pain seem no more fated and natural than his domestic longings and his postures of male dominance. One supersedes another in a repetitive, tiring, and dubious ritual. This circularity is the collection's primary point, one it drives home relentlessly. "you were once strong enough to live alone. / for a man nearing sixty you should be more / sensible" (*Love*, 34). Age brings little wisdom, and the narrator, rebounding from a lifetime of poverty, obscurity, and loneliness, cannot say no to the ringing telephone or to the knock on the door. Dizzy with the sex game, he dismisses serious introspection: "it's probably some deeply-rooted childhood fuckup / that makes me vulnerable, I thought" (*Love*, 60). To feel is enough, to compensate for lost time an adequate justification.

> for a man of 55 who didn't get laid
> until he was 23
> and not very often until he was 50
> I think that I should stay listed
> via Pacific Telephone
> until I get as much as
> the average man has had.
>
> of course, I'll have to keep
> writing immortal poems
> but the inspiration is there. (*Love*, 153)

The narrator's sexual gamesmanship and the objectification of the female are unattractive and only partially redeemed by the implication of a reciprocal objectification—the women come to glow in the poet's fame. Even this justification is unsatisfying, as it causes Bukowski to trivialize the importance of creation and writing in his own life. In poems such as "a good one" and "artist," the value exchange of art for sex is explicit; that this is what artistic creation is "good for" is the troubling subtext. The narrator proceeds through the majority of the poems in an emotional fog, unable for long to escape a context of sexuality that colors even topics ordinarily inviolate. "drunk and writing poems / at 3 a.m. // what counts now / is one more / tight / pussy // before the light / tilts out" (*Love*, 252). The narrator's priority here is less than compelling. At best he seems pitiably confused, at worst willfully coarse. Only rarely does the creative act rise to redemptive prominence, and then exclusively in terms of emotional recovery, as in the poem "me":

> I'm still alive
> and have the ability to expel
> wastes from my body.
> and poems.

and as long as that's happening
I have the ability to handle
betrayal (*Love*, 31)

Vital signs are present, and a recognition that the creative act is as natural to Bukowski as breathing or bodily functions. The necessity of writing, usually predominant, is among the poet's most attractive qualities.
Peters argues that the scatological analogy is a meaningful one, that
"Bukowski's urge to write, prompted by a mix of sardonicism and angst,
is as natural as defecation. An image allows him to translate pain into a
testimony of his spirit, one fought with 'madness and terror' along
'agony way' " (60–61).

Women in *Love Is a Dog from Hell*, when not compliant with the
male's emotional and sexual needs, are portrayed as predatory, cold, cal-
culating, and bestial. They are witches and spiders and, importantly in
Bukowski's vocabulary, beings that drain luck from the victim. In two
particularly effective poems, "longshot" and "Hawley's leaving town,"
the setting is again the racetrack, depicted now as a male sanctuary. The
luck, however, seems to have gone elsewhere. Advice is useless, the track
ritual vacuous.

he got up and bet the 6
and I got up and bet the 4.
the 5 horse won
by 3 lengths
at 15 to one.

she's got red hair
like lightning from heaven,
I said. (*Love*, 181)

Without control and knowledge, the men wonder at their vanished fortune. The witch from heaven, a paradox, strikes like lightning. She is
unpredictable, arbitrary, and possibly deadly.

Occasionally the poems in *Love Is a Dog from Hell* do achieve an
effective authorial distance, a fuller articulation of both sides of the relationship struggle, and these moments represent the highlights of the
collection. "turnabout" charts the process that its title describes. The

narrator's glib dismissal of a former lover—"it's all quite dramatic and I
enjoy it" (*Love*, 63)—is followed by a flash forward in time and the same
careless behavior perpetrated against the male.

> it's very quiet and I feel like I have a spear
> rammed into the center of my gut.
> . . . .
> mercy, I think, doesn't the human race know anything
> about mercy? (*Love*, 64)

In "one for old snaggle-tooth," Bukowski sifts the wreckage of another
relationship, finally applauding the woman for creating "a better world"
and hurting "fewer people than / anybody I have ever known" (*Love*, 66).
Even the deceptively titled "fuck" reveals beneath its toughness pity for
both sexes, trapped in a ritual of flesh in the push not to be alone.

> it's only human.
> now we've got to do it.
> I've got to do it
> after all that bluff.
> it's like a party—
> two trapped
> idiots. (*Love*, 29)

The narrator performs desultorily, caught in the sad consequence of his
own mating dance, and recognizes that he and the woman share the
same plight: "I can't blame her," he acknowledges, then identifies her as
"someone the / others have abandoned" (*Love*, 29). The title of the
poem, more than an explanation of the physical event, is a statement of
resignation.

The theme of voyeurism developed in the collection's final section is
tied closely to the narrator's increasing hesitation, doubt, and withdrawal. In almost all cases, these issues are dealt with somberly, without
Bukowski's typical humor. This seriousness is typical of *Love Is a Dog
from Hell* and is attributable, again, to a lack of distance apparent
between author and material. One of the more effective pieces in this
section, "the beautiful young girl walking past the graveyard—", com-
bines the poet's watching with concerns of aging and death.

as she walks past the iron fence
I can see through the iron fence
and I see the headstones
and the green lawn.

her body moves in front of the iron fence
the headstones do not move.

I think,
doesn't anybody else see this?

I think,
does she see those headstones? (*Love*, 286)

This sequence is nicely accomplished. The moment of youth contrasts with the stasis of death; the repetition of "the iron fence" creates a mantric effect indicative of the speaker's reverie. Further, the syntactic redundancy of the two couplets beginning with "I think" suggests intellectual isolation against a background of death. A psychological corollary to the poem's voyeurism is found in "an almost made up poem," concerning an epistolary relationship. The safe distance of letter writing, coupled with the narrator's confidence with the written word, empowers him as advisor and mentor. "kid, I wrote back, all / lovers betray. it didn't help" (*Love*, 47). The poem ends with the woman's suicide, discovered by the narrator in a third party's letter months afterward, and the recognition that "if I had met you / I would probably have been unfair to you or you / to me" (*Love*, 48).[6]

In *Love Is a Dog from Hell*, Bukowski tackles a turbulent period of his life with a directness typical of his work and with as much honesty as he can muster under unnerving circumstances. Several poems indicate the poet's awareness of his fevered limitations. "I can't imagine the people. / it's hard for me to imagine the people" (*Love*, 154). For a writer, lack of empathy is deleterious. Much of the collection is unpleasant, with both its immediacy and its lack of humor signaling a damaging lack of aesthetic distance. What emerges, however, is Bukowski's awareness of the necessity of risk, of a mysterious and incredible drive within the living despite evidence of certain failure. In "the crunch," the author recognizes that "people are not so good to each other. / perhaps if they were /

our deaths would not be so sad." Yet the young girls continue to be "flowers of chance" in his search for "a way we have not yet / thought of" (*Love*, 164). The reasonable and sensible are submerged beneath the rush of the instinctive.

> who put this brain inside of me?
>
> it cries
> it demands
> it says there is a chance.
>
> it will not say
> "no." (*Love*, 164)

Even the brain serves an idea of redemptive union, unattainable except in fleeting moments or in dreams. This idea seems comparable to the creative impulse ordinarily so primary in Bukowski's writing. "When you're with a woman and the sex is good, there's something that takes place beyond the act itself, some sort of exchange of soul that makes all the trouble worthwhile—at least for the rest of the night."[7]

Dangling in the Tournefortia

Bukowski, as if exemplifying his best late-round boxing analogy, rebounded from the overwrought *Love Is a Dog from Hell* and the erratic *Play the Piano Drunk* with the strong 1981 collection *Dangling in the Tournefortia*.[8] Shaking off the last tremors of the 1970s—when Bukowski had at last become a professional writer and had subsequently indulged in his late-blossoming celebrity—the poet entered the next decade with new aplomb. Distance and control return to the poems. Bukowski considers himself and the accoutrements of his late financial security with humor. He develops tax shelters with his accountants, lounges in his new home in San Pedro, and drives laughing into the sunlight in a BMW. In 1979, the poet wrote to John Martin, "We'll just have to forget about 'the image.' I never hide anything. The car is a 1979 black BMW, sun roof and all. 320I. (52% tax write-off)" (*Screams*, 267). Bukowski traveled to Germany and Paris, in the latter location was the featured guest on a national television talk show, and began to mingle with personalities from the film and entertainment industries. Aware of both the irony and the great luck of recognition, and tempering this awareness with a healthy skepticism as to both the worth and the endurance of acclaim, Bukowski not only survived success but continued to evolve and grow. *Dangling in the Tournefortia* begins, in earnest, the author's later period, years of relative peace and of domestic and financial stability.

As *Love Is a Dog from Hell* is the poetic counterpart of *Women, Dangling in the Tournefortia* shares thematic considerations fully realized in Bukowski's best novel, *Ham on Rye*, published in 1982. In short, the relative quiet of his life during these years gave the author time to reflect on the past and to approach his experiences, both past and present, with a high degree of thought and artfulness. The first five poems in *Dangling in the Tournefortia* all deal with Bukowski's adolescence, a subject approached infrequently in earlier work. The tone is nostalgic, even elegiac, recalling a 1930s America remembered as tougher and more independent than the present, a leaner, more honest, and more efficient time. The opening poem, "the lady in red," creates its sprawling, dreamlike effect through long unpunctuated lines and a montage of memories. "The '30s were a time when people had very little and there was / nothing to hide behind" (*Dangling*, 13). The romance of the outlaw is present, as is regret over the betrayal of such fierce lawlessness. Bukowski depicts the time as one of anticipation, a "glorious / non-bullshit time" (*Dangling*, 13). Another poem, "silk," laments the passing of stocking and garters, "silken legs for / Cagney and Gable and / all the boys in the neighborhood" (17).

The meditative tone of such pieces, however, almost always resonates with the social and financial hardship of that period. Beneath the idealization of gangsters and movie stars and stockings lurk barely submerged desperation, impending war, and, most important, class distinctions. "You" and "we" are prominent pronouns in Bukowski poems depicting the past, and such treatments are easily related to his most effective poems concerning labor. Tracing his life from childhood to adolescence to adulthood, Bukowski, in his best work, transcends self to create a startling national history of hardship, depression, and labor delineated by a remarkable understanding of class tensions. In "the weather's been fair" an oblique reference to material in "the lady in red" reveals the speaker's allegiance to values rare in the 1980s. "I can roll a smoke with 2 fingers of my left hand / that's good enough for me" (*Dangling*, 162).

In general, *Dangling in the Tournefortia* tends toward the longer narrative poems that are the hallmark of the author's later work. Such poems are often difficult to quote meaningfully, as they contain a gradual building of tone or action crucial to their effect. Locklin equates quoting a single line of Bukowski to telling "a punch line without the build-up."[9] Bukowski is a fine storyteller, and both Jackie Gleason and W. C. Fields have been suggested as influences on his comedy. The longer poems also partially create the nearly novelistic effect of the later books of poems. Although occasionally other characters are substituted, the voice is mostly the consistent Bukowski persona, alternately celebratory and skeptical, lonely yet antisocial. Overall, the poems in the collection are leaner in their syntax, less discursive than much of his earlier work despite their humor, and sometimes contain a gentleness not typical earlier. "two drunks" is a touching recollection of a painter acquaintance and the poet's own inadequate gestures of friendship. "laugh" is a mature, nuanced, and balanced look at a lost relationship. "meeting is more exciting than parting but parting is / important if you want to stay human in a certain way" (*Dangling*, 105). This Bukowski is aging, reflective, and more open to reciprocal companionship. "there is much good in being alone / but there is a strange warmth in not being alone" (*Dangling*, 139). In "guava tree" the poet marvels at his own leisure and his escape from labor.

> now under the pineapple guava tree I am still sucking at
> the free hours
> I can never suck enough free hours, blinking at the
> sun, scratching my nose, nowhere to go and nothing to do
> glorious (*Dangling*, 232)

Dangling in the Tournefortia is marked by the narrator's awe and wonder. He is alive, mostly complete, and relishing a languorous mix of contemplation of the past and enjoyment of the present. "for the little one" is a lovely poem to Linda Lee Beighle, Bukowski's subsequent wife and the woman responsible for the author's domestic stability. He overhears her singing and is clearly amazed by the ebullience of life, the woman's voice, the lights of the city, their home, and finally his own room "calm / so strange / as if magic had / become normal" (*Dangling*, 276). The tone is slightly sentimental, but only slightly, and few admirers of Bukowski's work would resent him a moment of peace. The ironically titled "my big fling" conveys the extent of the poet's changed life. Following an argument, the speaker leaves his house, checks into a hotel, and considers the women he might still know in the city. The situation seems at first typical, even classic, Bukowski. However, he decides that any new involvement would only mean more of "what I had gotten away / from." He instead chooses isolation: "it felt good / in that dark room, / it was quiet, far away / from war / of any sort" (*Dangling*, 259). Although the situation and setting are recognizable from countless earlier treatments, the particulars are importantly altered. Drinking is mentioned only peripherally. Second, rather than write or pursue a rowdy night of sex, the narrator selects the mundane alternative of watching television. Neither party makes good on the threat of unfaithfulness, and finally, happy to be reunited, the couple debate the relative merits of the same television programs they had separately watched. This is a quieter, domesticated Bukowski persona, one willing to receive good luck and companionship. Leisure, freedom from work, and domestic stability are the foundations on which the author, like a true descendent of Thoreau, will mine his last and most deeply buried gems.

Still, it is a mistake to equate Bukowski's more placid life with a taming of his artistic ambitions. One persistent idea in all of the author's writings, that of retreat from society and its values, is again evoked in *Dangling in the Tournefortia*. The need of a balancing "other" is undercut by the artist's requirement to remain distant and complete. Locklin observes that Bukowski "is simply an abhorrer of orthodoxies" and "seldom initiates a relationship" (Locklin, *Tournefortia*, 6). The poet casts himself in contradictory roles—romantic innocent and weary traveler of life, passive yet aggressively watchful. Such personal aloofness is inseparable from the central theme in Bukowski's poetry, the fear of "involvement in a system of domination. The stoic, unflinching attitude of his protagonist . . . is cognate to this refusal. . . . The fear of intimacy is the same as the fear of speech. It is a fear of vulnerability" (Harrison, 66–67).

Some poems in *Dangling in the Tournefortia* reflect a fuller openness toward romantic relationships, but others are still marked by a conspicuous regularity of, perhaps reliance on, retreat. "I didn't want to" is a searing and systematic catalog of the author's life of refusal, from adolescence to self-incriminating failure with the woman Jane. "I should have loved her more than I did but I didn't want / to" (*Dangling*, 38). These lines conclude and complete the poem, resonating with their connotative meaning: "Because I couldn't," the author seems to say, equating denial with, finally, impossibility. Refusal in the poem frequently links the poet with that which is denied. "I disdained money and my first wife was a millionairess," he writes, and "I hated poets and I hated poetry and I began to write / poetry" (*Dangling*, 35). For the "frozen" man, each denial cloaks a desire, each attempt at freedom from exploitation supplies its entrapment. Poems are routinely concerned with withdrawal or leaving. "the new woman," "we both knew him," and "culture" are examples of this movement, of a consciousness locked into embattled repetition. "discard or be discarded. / it was endless" (*Dangling*, 122), the poet laments in "we both knew him," and there is no joy in the recognition.

Poetry readings continue in the book to supply a setting representative of Bukowski's ambivalence toward fame and the siphoning relationship between poet and audience. Always, escape is cherished. "read to them and drink your wine, get paid in cash, / leave and let somebody else drive the car" (*Dangling*, 166). Although these concerns are not new in his work, in *Dangling in the Tournefortia* the author seems rejuvenated, lucid, and calm, a writer pursuing his craft with skill and clarity. For example, a technique with which Bukowski had had uneven results in the past, allowing the male persona to be overwhelmed by a female voice, is adeptly handled in "we've got to communicate." The poet, withdrawn from language and involvement, exists only as refracted through the voice of the berating woman. The three pages of dense text are both funny and troubling, ending with a last reflected image of the author and the woman's unintentionally ironic summary of her interrogations:

> but look at you *now!* all you want is one more drink and then
> one *more* drink and you won't talk to me, you just keep
> lighting cigarettes and looking around the room . . .
> don't you *want* to work at making our relationship better?
> tell me, why are you afraid of a woman's pussy? (*Dangling*, 94)

That the woman's questions are answered, although the man never speaks, testifies to the poem's craft.

Bukowski's continual withdrawal is related to a lifelong feeling of marginalization, beautifully rendered in a poem such as "out of the mainstream." However, a semblance of normality must be preserved, as the author reminds himself in "let nothing ever happen," if one expects to remain on the streets. And Bukowski always, despite his disappointment with fellow humans, requires society, if only to pull away from it. "Bukowski's poetry of the 1980s showed an increasing awareness of the dialectical nature of the relationship between the self and the other, the individual and the social," writes Harrison. In the poet's work, the "social world and the narrator are often mutually defined through their interaction. Moreover, there is no attempt to transcend the social world" (Harrison, 47–48). Any reader familiar with Bukowski's oeuvre will readily recognize such a dependence. There can be no "outsider" without an "inside" to depart from, and this impulse distinguishes Bukowski's work from, for example, the isolationism in much of Jeffers's poetry. The persona is predicated on society, and the poet continues to look for the full, complete human being. "Sometimes there's a small chance, you can see it for a moment in the face of a waitress in a cheap cafe, an old waitress, nowhere to go, there is some truth in that face. . . . Of course, she can't speak to you and you can't speak to her. Words would mutilate, words have too long been used the wrong way. You put in your order and wait" (*Screams*, 272).

At several points in *Dangling in the Tournefortia,* the poet is struck with a feeling of oddness, of dislocation, as he proceeds dangerously through the mangled daily events of his society. "another day" is a fine example of this new, more subtle surrealism in which the otherness becomes the real. "the waitress comes with the sandwich and she asks you / if there will be anything else? and you tell her, / no no, this will be fine" (*Dangling*, 149). The flatness of tone and the struggle of the poet to remain calm and normal while eating a sandwich—"a minor, frustrating, and sensible act" of self-consciousness—reveal the unacknowledged madness of "ordinary" life. The environment is a freak show in which all participate. One man has "hands . . . down almost to / his ankles and he's whistling," (*Dangling*, 149). Outside, three others have "heads like ostriches" and "drive away first. they're the best. / it's a first stage smog alert. all the birds are dead. / you start the engine" (*Dangling*, 150). The poet follows the pattern of exit initiated by the ostrichmen. The world is sick, dying, or dead. He adds his share to the smog. Hyperawareness is stultifying yet fills one with wonder.

Dangling in the Tournefortia is weighted with the mutilated and the mad, the freakish and misbegotten. The racetrack poem "pick six" is a horror show rendered in verse. The speaker is approached by a "headless" man. "somebody / has sliced his head / entirely off and / I look down / into dark bubbles of / blood. / 'hey, buddy,' / he asks, 'where's / the nearest crapper?' " (*Dangling*, 179–80). The decapitated are "everywhere," the narrator notes, and he is among them, probably of them. In "table for two," the mundane incident of waiting for a dinner table will not maintain its seeming stability. In the men's room, the narrator witnesses "a midget" with an orange tennis ball. "he cocked his arm and threw a / line drive at the mirror. / the mirror didn't break" (*Dangling*, 243). In the context of the collection, this Fellini-like encounter is hardly surprising. Bukowski has raised the level of his eccentric perceptions into a commentary on the grotesqueness of contemporary urban life in America. He passes the freaks of society nonchalantly. Before he can leave the restaurant, a door is thrown open against him by a man who has a "a head like a pumpkin" and accompanies "a woman whose face looked like a seal's." Further description is worthy of a Dali painting: the woman "had on a little hat / only the little hat looked like a large / wristwatch had been fastened to the top of it" (*Dangling*, 244). The peculiar couple continue to stare at the narrator, indicating a mutual surprise.

These are haunting portrayals of the mundane. If the poet is to speak clearly and simply of what he sees, suggests Bukowski, then his own marginalization must be reflected through the mutilated and absurd everywhere, those elements usually not spoken of in our decayed contemporary life. "Sometimes," the author explained, "I feel like I'm not really part of this world. . . . I say I don't like people, but really I get kinda charged up when I'm around 'em" (Esterly, 34). These poems are filled with terror and humor, but with noticeably less animosity. Something like affection, and at least amazement, lurks behind the poet's continued involvement with society, a circus of recognition and need.

War All the Time

Bukowski's next collection, *War All the Time: Poems 1981–1984*, continued to fulfill the unlikely expectation that the 1980s would be the most productive and impressive decade of the author's career. The collection is one of his most powerful, although its 280 pages may represent, shockingly, only "a sixth of his poems composed during this time period."[10] This suggests the considerable credit due to John Martin in selecting and arranging the poems. Locklin applauds Bukowski for "leading us in a new direction in American poetry with his direct, spontaneous, conversational free-form style. Many poets have been talking for a long time about getting more of a narrative quality into their work," but it was finally Bukowski, naturally and with seeming ease, who "really succeeded" (Esterly, 30).

In particular, the lengthy poem "Horsemeat" is exemplary for Bukowski's assimilation of narrative techniques—storytelling and dialogue—and his blending of genres. The 28-page poem is divided into 30 brief sections set in or near the racetrack and its society. The title of the poem is a double entendre indicating both the racing animals and the shuffling, hopeful losers who finance the racing industry. Each of the 30 poems could stand alone, but, by combining them, the author has woven a fascinating tapestry of images and people, of contrasts and concerns. Prose and poetry blend easily, sometimes almost imperceptibly shifting within the same short section. However, such shifting reflects not a stance of artistic carelessness but rather a conscious, effective melding of approaches. Bukowski contended that his fiction and poems came from basically the same source. "Yes, they do, there's not much difference—line and line length" (*NYQ,* 321). Likewise both genres are pointed toward the same goal, to illustrate "how many different things could happen to the same man on the way to suicide, madness, old age, natural and unnatural death" (*NYQ,* 322).

An apparent theme throughout "Horsemeat" is the subject's qualified attitude toward the crowd. Section 2 begins, "Being alone has always been very necessary to me."[11] Nevertheless, the entire dramatic impetus of "Horsemeat" is its narrator's daily merging into a group that he criticizes. Locklin suggests that the racetrack is a microcosm where "stories offer themselves—it is a world of inherent narrative tensions" (Locklin, *War All the Time,* 34), and, indeed, Bukowski desires the "common" crowd even as his income and celebrity might naturally turn him away. "I would like to be human / if they would only let me" (*War,* 45) is an assertion rendered perverse by the author's willful participation in the track ritual. Part of what the narrator craves is clearly anonymity, to be literally "lost forever in the crowd" (*War,* 51) of unskilled wagerers and gamblers and to put aside self-conscious perceptions of himself as an author. In "a valentine gift" he relates this attraction: "I think the idea of the track . . . / . . . is / so that we don't have to sit around all day / thinking, I am a writer" (*War,* 189). This explains why being recognized at the track by a fan, and labeled by his profession, is always the worst violation for Bukowski, whereas recognition by someone who knows him from a different context—for example, an old labor acquaintance—is generally accepted more generously. At the same time, the writer watches the people and accumulates poetic "moments," an inescapable double bind of "passive" voyeurism that frequently erupts into aggressive involvement. "I dug my elbow into his gut. / I felt it sink in like it was / entering a sack of dirty / laundry"; this violence is followed by disingenuous concern: " 'you all right, buddy?' I / asked" (*War*, 54).

Bukowski is alternately one of the mass of inevitable losers and the detached observer and social critic. The impossible obstacle of the track "take" does not matter because "the people continue to play. Check the faces at any track going into the last race. You will see the story" (*War*, 39). In section 18, the narrator objectively watches two old men delude themselves with consecutive bad bets. They lose their money then rise again on a crest of foolish optimism. In the subsequent section, the narrator explains he has "evolved an astonishing / new theory on / how to beat the races" (*War*, 61). The juxtaposition makes its point. The narrator's actions, his participation in an unbeatable system, identify him as one of the masses. Only a slightly heightened level of self-awareness, an ironic level, separates him. "You can have isolation, or you can have the crowd. I tend to mix the two, with a preference for isolation" (Wennersten, 38), Bukowski explained. Harrison has written extensively on this dialectical relationship between self and other in Bukowski's work, particularly how such a tension grows stronger in the later writings. During the 1980s, the author's poetry increasingly lacked "what we so closely associate with poetry, metaphor and the kind of transcendence it implies" (Harrison, 52). Instead, the presence of the Bukowski "I" increasingly presents a concern for the individual and society, a reciprocity of seeing and being seen, of signifier and object: "This further refraction of the narrator constitutes a mutuality of characterization where neither subject nor object can be examined independently of one another. Such a characterization is integral to Bukowski's poetry and lends it greater objectivity than would any (specious) impersonality" (Harrison, 53).

Bukowski's observations on the racetrack inhabitants are often linked to social commentary, an element Harrison feels has often been overlooked by readers distracted by the poet's ostensible "emphasis on the individual." In actuality, the "self in Bukowski's poetry is inevitably defined through the other" (Harrison, 47). Such a relationship goes a long way to explain the poet's daily interaction with a crowd that largely repulses him. His observation of a track workman leads the narrator to note that "I'm one of those who doesn't think there is much difference / between an atomic scientist and a man who cleans the crappers"; one keen difference, of course, is "the luck of the draw" (*War*, 41).

The racetrack gives Bukowski an opportunity to test continuously two elements he finds crucial to a full life or art—luck and gamble. The stretch run of a race is described in section 17 as "rapidly closing the space," language identical to that which the author often employs to describe death. The rush of the finish is followed by another 30 minutes of waiting.

> such is the life of a gambler: to go away then and wait
> to return.
>
> not all of us are gamblers; those who aren't don't
> matter. (*War*, 58)

"Waiting" he adds, "is the greater portion of being around" (*War*, 58), delineating an analogy between the horse race and the creative surge of writing, both of which are delayed and fleeting.

Despite Bukowski's desire to escape professional identification, the time at the track, mostly spent wandering or waiting, is aptly comparable to the writer's life. "Time is made to be wasted" (*War*, 40), he informs us, and, moreover, the interim allows him to think "of all the rotten jobs and how glad I had been to have them" (*War*, 42). Waiting is life, and waiting, for the writer, is when crucial prework rumination occurs. "I took a sip off the top and waited for the action, thinking of many things, too many things" (*War*, 43). Such reflection could as easily describe the action of writing as of racing, and as the mind wanders into reverie, so too the poet's vision shifts from the immediate setting, and the writing subtly changes from prose to verse. His thoughts move out "into the grass and / trees and dirt out there, one mile, the dirty shades in / dirty rooming houses flapping back and forth in a light wind" (*War*, 43). This masterful section, with its tour de force writing, demonstrates both Bukowski's sure handling of his stylistic blending and the close linking of the track time between races to the writer's mental preparation.

The racetrack offers enough dislocation and randomness that Bukowski can be constantly working as he surrenders to external and internal stimuli. The author's predilection for writing in front of windows or in busy environments reveals a similar process. "I like interruptions, as long as they're natural and aren't total and continuous" (Wennersten, 51). As "Horsemeat" powerfully demonstrates, the track is a location that simultaneously allows Bukowski to escape and to practice his craft, to gather material, to comment implicitly as social critic, to define and refine his relationship with society, and, nine times each day, to test his aesthetic of luck, gamble, grace, and style against long odds. Winning is most worthwhile when you beat the favorite.

> and when your figures
> select only *one* horse,
> it is a very curious and
> magic feeling, of course,
> and you learn to apply
> the same simplicity to
> other areas of existence (*War*, 62)

In the poem "an old buddy," he posits a nearly Aristotelian notion of action to indicate character and, properly enacted, to manifest luck in all areas of life. "class under duress / often creates a / strange and lucky kind / of nobility" (*War*, 140).

With the arrival of Bukowski's affluence, the poet alone in a room is increasingly replaced with the poet driving a car, a more aggressive, involved act of involvement cum retreat. "Horsemeat" begins with the narrator arriving and locking his automobile and closes with his return to the vehicle. Another driver has blocked the poet's exit, a situation that allows a gleeful release of aggression. "I started my engine / put it in reverse and / jammed my bumper against him" (*War*, 62). The narrator pushes the car in front of another, not only perpetuating the cycle of conflict but worsening it by letting the air out of two tires. This is equivalent to his ambiguous relationship to the track crowd—hostile, involved, and finally dependent on entrapment for escape to be fully enjoyed. "it felt good to / drive out of that racetrack" (*War*, 63). The poem "jack-knife" amplifies Bukowski's association of driving with danger and a sense of manipulating destiny: "then you feel shame for / such conservatism / hit the throttle and / begin weaving through and / past the others" (*War*, 67). Such action is representative of social relationships. He moves in and among the group, consistently jockeying for position and power in a race that cannot be won. The poem concludes "as the signal changes / and we move onto / the boulevard" (*War*, 68), wary, aggressive, each driver part of the flow of movement yet separated by glass and steel. Only luck, chance, and a bit of skill protect the individual from collision.

War All the Time's final poem, the magnificent "eating my senior citizen's dinner at the Sizzler," concludes with a similar rejection by the narrator, in this instance of the aged and dying:

> I rise
> make it to the door
> into stunning sunlight
> make it to the car
> get in
> roar the engine into
> life
> rip it into reverse
> with a quick back turn of squealing
> tires (*War*, 279)

The accumulating pace and speed of the passage accomplishes its refutation of the previous sedentary scene. That the narrator is conscious of "making" it to the exit door and "making" it to his car indicates both his creation of the act and his gratitude for a small accomplishment. "I am up to / 50 mph in a flash / moving through / them. / who can turn the stream / of destiny?" (*War*, 279). The answer to this rhetorical question is, of course, no one can.

The volume contains many poems concerned with the maintenance and violation of social normality. The narrator in "frozen food section" acts on a long and inexplicable desire when he molests a woman shopper: "and he saw his hand / go out— / there it goes, he / thought— / and the hand / grabbed / one of the buttocks / and squeezed" (*War*, 177–78). The act is impulsive, with little sexual motivation, and finally seems almost innocent. Yet the social response is severe: "he was dragged through the / supermarket / and then outside. / it was early evening going into / night / and he was shoved into / the back seat of / the police car" (*War*, 179). Like several of Bukowski's earlier characters, the man acts unconsciously, without understanding and without malice. However, unlike those earlier characters, he is neither rapist nor killer, sociopath nor severely marginalized outsider. His last thought, of his wife Meg's warning not to forget paprika, locates him in a bland domestic sphere. One intuits the author's sympathy for the man and for an act that embraces life in an immediate way of the flesh. The scene

constitutes the sort of moment the author has warned of, when momentary evidence that one is outside the norm may sacrifice an entire life.

True normality remains enigmatic and troubling for Bukowski, as he
relates in the humorous poem "the puzzle." He expects a revealing
break in the surface of his neighbors' routine, "lights at 3 a.m." or "flying bottles," but this anticipation is frustrated: "for 5 years now / his
routine has remained the / same" (*War*, 251). For the author, the normal
equals the banal. He loathes routine and obviousness and aligns these
with stillness, acceptance, and death.

> I'd like to call the
> cops on them
> but I don't think the cops
> would understand my
> complaint
>
> their red lights flashing,
> white-faced in
> dark blue:
>
> "Sir, there's no
> *law*
> against what they
> are
> doing . . ." (*War*, 252)

Bukowski's success, domestic stability, and age softened his physical life
and in turn allowed distance, objectivity, and balance in his creative life.
The wild nights continue in the mind, where for the artist they are most
useful.

Despite its nostalgia for dead authors and a lost country, despite its
pain, its cynicism toward society, and its occasionally apocalyptic tone,
War All the Time achieves a kind of optimism. If the poet is not exceed-
ingly grateful to be still alive, working, and walking in the smog-choked
sunlight, the older author at least appreciates the luck and humor of
his situation. His recollections of visiting John Fante in the hospital
when his idol was "blind, and cut away, again and again" (*War*, 156)

distill a complicated acceptance. Fante continued to work from his bed by dictation, and his energy and Miltonic compulsion for creation, for life, are analogous to Bukowski's passions. Like the racetrack, human life remains a valuable race for the fully alive individual. The honest toughness of the Bukowski gaze affirms a free, spontaneous, and creative existence. In "suggestion for an arrangement," the poet imagines Fante returning to him, and imagination makes it so:

> at his funeral
> I expected him to rise from his
> coffin and say, "Chinaski,
> it was a good run, well
> worth it." (*War*, 158)

You Get So Alone at Times That It Just Makes Sense

The 1989 volume *You Get So Alone at Times That It Just Makes Sense* shows its author entrenched in the comparatively simple domestic lifestyle of his later years. In 1978, Paul Ciotti wrote in the *Los Angeles Times Magazine* that Bukowski "at his wife's urging . . . has given up hard liquor and red meat. Now he takes 40 vitamin pills a day, eats lots of fish and drinks red wine" (13). As early as 1973, Bukowski had acknowledged that his style was evolving as his life changed: "But I am still the best Charles Bukowski around and my style keeps adjusting and changing as my life does, so they just aren't going to catch me. Only Papa Death will catch me" ("His Women," 69). The poet was apprehensive that his sedate later years might damage his myth; he encouraged a journalist not to make him "a congenial soul. Insult me a little bit. Put some salt on me. Make me dangerous. Help sell my books" (Ciotti, 14).

As the peculiar title of Bukowski's 1989 collection suggests, although the physical abuse of earlier years may have mellowed into quiet comfort for the older man, the interior life remained turbulent. "In contrast to the airy spaciousness" of the Bukowskis' home in San Pedro, the poet's workroom was "a dingy cell, not unlike the rooms in which he had spent most of his life" (Ciotti, 13). This observation is congruent with one of *You Get So Alone*'s predominant concerns, the nagging incompleteness that mars even the richest, most comfortable moments of life. Bukowski's new stature was the proper place from which to address this. In the sparse and powerful lyric "no help for that," he writes that

there is a space in the heart that
will never be filled

a space

and even during the
best moments
and
the greatest
times

we will know it (*Alone*, 26)

The lines dissolve, seemingly overcome by the white space that
encroaches upon the thought, the physical poem itself representing the
difficulty of filling a smothering area. "we will wait / and / wait // in that
/ space" (*Alone*, 26).

The experience of incompleteness in *You Get So Alone* frequently takes
the form of an address to readers wary of the mellowing Bukowski:

for those readers now
sick at heart
believing that I'm a contented
man—
please have some
cheer: agony sometimes changes
form
but
it never ceases for
anybody. (*Alone*, 123)

Again, the skeletal lines suggest the difficulty of speech against an
oppressive otherness. In "relentless as the tarantula," emptiness is manifested as the aggressive "it," allowing one perhaps "ten lucky minutes /
here / or maybe an hour / there" but always "working toward you."
Bukowski's insistence on the second-person pronoun in this poem

reminds that the awareness of the approaching "it" is not merely the artist's indulgence, but a dilemma of each thoughtful human being: "I mean you / and nobody but / you" (*Alone,* 196).

The space that is the unfilled subtext of each moment is inextricable from the approach of death. Throughout his work, Bukowski is waiting, and this habit grows more pronounced in later work. In "a magician, gone . . ." death is irrevocable and democratic, taking "one by one / presidents / garbage men / killers / actors" (*Alone,* 63) without discrimination. "the gods play no / favorites" (*Alone,* 149), he writes in reference to Fante's slow, horrific death. The touching and ironic poem "helping the old" finds the narrator picking up glasses and cane for "an old fellow" in line at the bank and standing "behind him waiting / my turn" (*Alone,* 91). Death skirts the edge of the poem and is rarely absent in the book. However, the pendulum sometimes swings back to poems that recollect a virile young man. "garbage" ends with the unknown narrator on his bed: with "the ceiling up there above me, / I waited" (*Alone,* 98). The poem conflates the anticipation of the fully lived life with the anticipation of its conclusion. There is no winning, he asserts, only passing of one's allotted time with style and the burden of monotonous waiting. What happened to the confident Bukowski is "what / has happened to / all of / us" (*Alone,* 136).

> I remember your
> saying: "make it or
> break it."
>
> neither happened and
> it
> won't. (*Alone,* 136)

The poem "January" is another example of the excruciatingly short lines that are a trademark of Bukowski's late style. Fragmented images barely hold their position as the reader's eye tumbles down the page. The inevitability of unchanged human behavior crashes into an incontrovertible nonhuman level of consciousness so frequently unacknowledged by society.

> as
> the junkies junk

as the alkies drink
as the whores whore
as the killers kill

the albatross blinks its
eyes (*Alone*, 56)

Redundant behavior is met by the ambiguous gaze of nature. Does the blinking eye suggest boredom, disbelief, or even an eradication of the human? The following poem, "sunny side down," weighs the limits of history and supposed human achievement against the ennui of a constant "now." The poem's opening lines immediately establish this contrast:

NOTHING. sitting in a cafe having breakfast. NOTHING. the
        waitress,
and the people eating. the traffic runs by. doesn't matter what
Napoleon did, what Plato said. Turgenev could have been a fly.
        we are worn-
down, hope stamped out. we reach for coffee cups like the
        robots about
to replace us. (*Alone*, 57)

The attitude is consonant with the apocalyptic tone of many of the poems. Human life is, for practical purposes, a dubious and completed story. Entropy is so pronounced in American society that it is difficult to distinguish from personal disharmony. Harrison argues that "one of Bukowski's strengths" is "acceptance and an absence of moralizing" (56). The poet's obviousness is problematic: "Apparently simple, even transparent, Bukowski's poems often have an 'undecidable' quality when it comes to interpreting them: subjective expression or objective comment? In the best there is a mutuality which precludes easy dichotomizing" (Harrison, 57).

Although Bukowski agrees with Sartre's determination that hell is other people, he also concludes a seeming opposite: "each man's hell is in a different / place: mine is just up and / behind / my ruined / face" (*Alone*, 102). The muddle of consciousness is a tiring and inescapable burden. By contrast, the knowledge of death can serve as an antidote.

"my vanishing act" recalls the young barfly's need to rest and take nourishment away from human company, in the "tall field of grass" of "an abandoned graveyard." This setting seemed "the best / place to be" and "offered a generous cure to / the vicious hangover" (*Alone*, 99) that drinking, in this context a social activity, caused. Death is more often a soothing tonic than a source of existential disquietude. Resignation, rather than despair, prevails, and occasionally even resignation blooms into a quiet, determined hope. The poem "it's ours" closes *You Get So Alone*. It is a paean, after all, to continuance, struggle, and the victory gained by a life undertaken with courage. The approach of death is transformed into "that / gentle pure / space" of an easy, accepting peace. Paradoxically, the space of death also enables an inviolate personal space:

> that space
>
> there
>
> before they get to us
>
> ensures
>
> that
>
> when they do
>
> they won't
>
> get it all
>
>
> ever. (*Alone*, 313)

As the lines succumb to whiteness, to nothingness, the poet's voice offers a last assertion. The space that renders us incomplete also ensures a minor spiritual victory.

"it's ours" presents another seeming contradiction in Bukowski's philosophy—the dichotomy between self-definitive struggle and liberating surrender. "it's worth // centuries of / existence // say // just to scratch your neck / while looking out the window at / a bare branch" (*Alone*, 312). In a manner still skeptical of human history, the poet asserts the worthwhile primacy of the immediate in a way that modifies the wearisome toil of "sunny side down." Bukowski's father appears in several poems in the collection, partly for the purpose of delineating the poet's choice of a different kind of life, one eschewing traditional American values of participation, productivity, and material consumption. "retired," where a grotesque intake of food ends with sudden death, articulates a rejection of the father's values. The poem's last lines, "never missing a day / of work" (*Alone*, 18) are pointedly critical of a restricted, cruel, and wasted life. In "my non-ambitious ambition" the writer describes his early choice:

> and I thought, if being a bum is to be the
> opposite of what this son-of-a-bitch
> is, then that's what I'm going to
> be. (*Alone*, 28)

Similarly, the poem "education" is a powerful polemic against the educational system and the values that it supports, these again represented by the brutalizing father. "father, my mind said, / father and father and / father. // words like that. // I decided not to learn anything / in that / school" (*Alone*, 31). It is a compelling narrative of a boy's struggle with words, with signs, and with the distance between these indicators and the hard reality of his perceptions. "my mother walked along / beside me. / she wasn't anything at / all" (*Alone*, 31). The supposed real world, with its standards of dutiful study and family values, is hardly perceptible to the dislocated youth. Moreover, the mother is nonexistent in the father's universe of arbitrary judgment and harsh physical punishment.

Bukowski indicates his conscious choice, made as a young man, for poverty and disenfranchisement. This anticipates a withdrawal from potentially exploitative relationships that is central in his work.

> I was young but always alone—I felt that I needed the
> time to get something done and the only way I could buy time
> was with
> poverty. (*Alone*, 208)

The paradisiacal late nights of Bukowski's later years, those hours of peace and thoughtful creativity containing the "power of sanity" (*Alone*, 20), are the descendants of early nights of poverty and haunting isolation. From a young age, the author's impulse was to withdraw from commitments that handicapped individual leisure. Thorstein Veblen's classic study *The Theory of the Leisure Class* offers insight to Bukowski's proclivity for withdrawal, aligning the poet with the barbarian state rather than the predatory, although the latter is more typical of competitive industrial society.

The most imperative of these secondary demands of emulation, as well as the one of widest scope, is the requirement of abstention from productive work. This is true in an especial degree for the barbarian stage of culture. During the predatory culture labour comes to be associated in men's habits of thought with weakness and subjection to a master. . . . It . . . becomes impracticable to accumulate wealth by simple seizure, and, in logical consistency, acquisition by industry is equally impossible for high-minded and impecunious men. The alternative open to them is beggary or privation.[12]

Bukowski's treatment of work in many of his poems makes apparent its deleterious effect. Absence from blue-collar manual employment is of conspicuous value. Absence equals leisure, defined by Veblen as the "non-productive consumption of time" (43).

Bukowski's work places a high premium on free/freed time. Although mandatory for the writer's craft, leisure constitutes a crucial ideological component in his chosen lifestyle, a passive aggression toward a society it implicitly rejects. In "the finest of the breed" the poet summarizes that "the / most sensible / thing / a person can / do / is / sit / with drink in / hand / as the walls / wave / their goodbye / smiles" (*Alone*, 131). Bukowski suggests a surrogate father, one whose values of withdrawal are amenable to his own, in the recollection "my buddy":

> I liked him: he never questioned me about
> what I was or wasn't
> doing.
>
> he should have been my father, and I liked
> best what he said over and
> over: "Nothing is worth
> it." (*Alone*, 226)

The word "nothing" is employed throughout *You Get So Alone*, and its meaning is twofold. Human endeavors are illusions, not worth the life and time they demand. On the other hand, the word approaches optimism. Nothingness, which is all that exists including tedious human life, "is worth it."

"my buddy" recalls the poetry of Raymond Carver, particularly his later poems. Carver's narrator also craves found moments of quiet and introspection. He too lives his best time in an isolation that implicitly criticizes involvement. Such withdrawal permeates a collection such as *Ultramarine*. Carver's poem "Shiftless" embraces the ethic of leisure over an idea of self-definitive labor.

> I never liked work. My goal was always
> to be shiftless. I saw the merit in that.
> I liked the idea of sitting in a chair
> in front of your house for hours, doing nothing
> but wearing a hat and drinking cola.
> . . . .
> Once in a while hailing a fat, blond kid like me
> and saying, "Don't I know you?"
> Not, "What are you going to be when you grow up?"[13]

The philosophy and reminiscent tone of "Shiftless" are remarkably close to those of "my buddy," suggesting a comparable point in the poets' philosophies and, perhaps, Carver's debt to the older poet.

For Bukowski, the income that ensures his writing nights and his leisure is a "cockeyed miracle": "the gods have been kind to me through this / life-style that would have killed / an ox of a man" (*Alone*, 107). As much as persistence and talent may have influenced his success, he equates the "miracle" with "luck / this absolute shot of / grace" (*Alone*, 108). According to Veblen, an allegiance to gambling and its notion of luck is a form of withdrawal from predatory society. "The gambling propensity is another subsidiary trait of the barbarian temperament. . . . It is recognised to be a hindrance to the highest industrial efficiency of the aggregate in any community where it prevails in an appreciable degree," and "the belief in luck is in substance a habit of more ancient date than the predatory culture" (Veblen, 276). Appropriately, this links the gambler with "an incipient animistic belief, or an animistic sense of relations and things, that imputes a quasi-personal character to all facts" (Veblen, 279). Such an argument seems readily applicable to Bukowski, the consciously "archaic man": "all the obtrusive and obviously conse-quential objects and facts in his environment . . . are conceived to be possessed of volition, or rather of propensities, which enter into the com-plex of causes and affect events in an inscrutable manner. The sporting man's sense of luck and chance, or of fortuitous necessity, is an inarticu-late or inchoate animism" (Veblen, 279).

Bukowski argues continually that only the gambling life is worth living and that he wants all or nothing, an impossible assertion that is simultaneously aggressive and regressive. Behind the façade of accepted sociability is an unnamed otherness, the poet tells us, an essence that is and is not nothingness, that contains but is not wholly death. In this space, impossible to fill, is the means to a private liberation. Struggle and risk are necessary for the subversive leisure that is a reclamation of one's life.

Septuagenarian Stew

Poems constitute half of *Septuagenarian Stew* and deal primarily with Bukowski's contemplation of his advancing age. He seems surprised and delighted to enter his fifth decade as a poet, and these poems consider that durability in the context of childhood reminiscences, literary nostalgia, hospitals, and failing health. One critic noted Bukowski's "marvelous way with narrative" in the collection, how the poet can sustain "a poem of several pages through short lines and dialogue, sometimes exuberant and sometimes hard-bitten."[14] The theme of the poems, congruous with this tendency throughout the 1980s, is acceptance of oneself and of others. "this old man" has "finally found out / how to be / kind to / himself" (*Stew*, 78), the poet writes, and this generosity extends to others, as in a tender and hopeless recollection of his mother's death, "cancer." Finding a locked hospital door that he knows signifies the passing of a woman he hardly knows, the son disperses a wreath to girls "6 or 7 years old / walking home from school. // 'pardon me, ladies, but would you / like some flowers?' " (*Stew*, 51). The poem is not ironic or angry, simply sad and tired by death.

The hospital setting of "cancer" anticipates the discussion of Bukowski's own failing health. Humor is still present in the poems, as are disgust and disappointment for the state of society and the average man, but also included are acceptance and an appreciation of being alive. In "a friend," the domesticated narrator greets his neighbor and double, the 93-year-old "Charles," and then notes "sometimes it takes more courage / to live / than to die" (*Stew*, 296). His detached apprehension that he is alive in that moment contains amazement. "I walk back into the / house. / the wife is / there." As she prepares breakfast, he walks "upstairs gladly to / shave and / primp / up" (*Stew*, 296–97). In "a bit of gardening" the poet finds himself in a previously unlikely setting.

> I kick the weed to one
> side, lean on the
> pitchfork: all the waiting's
> not
> much: just part of the
> space between
> agonies. (*Stew*, 333)

The "closing space" so common in Bukowski's later writing necessitates acceptance, a weary peace, and a time for recollection and preparation. "we must bring / our own light / to the / darkness" (*Stew*, 100), he advises, and "as the final season / leaps into / focus" (*Stew*, 101), the private and the public are united.

The poem "the summing up" is another meditation on leisure, the generosity of the poor, and freedom from labor restraints. The title also suggests the writer's activity in poems beginning to form the closing bookend of his career. *Septuagenarian Stew* has a strong sense of taking stock, of viewing one's writing life in a larger context. Through looking back, Bukowski considers his place. In the momentary peace of "the space between spaces" (372), he anticipates his passage into history:

> resting quietly here in the
> afterdusk as the sound of the centuries run
> through my body . . .
> this
> old dog
> resting in the shade
> peaceful
> but ready. (*Stew*, 372)

A conspicuous number of pieces reveal the author's preoccupation with his final literary worth. A full and final catalog of influences is offered in the collection, including homages to Hemingway, Jeffers, Céline, Li Po, Fante, and Tolstoy. More than ever, Bukowski identifies himself as a writer, without distancing effects or ironic undercutting. "well, Li Po, the wine is still / good, and in spite of it all, there is / still some / time / to / sit alone / and / think" (*Stew*, 337). Simplicity, solitude, silence, reflection, the relaxed and altered consciousness of drink, these are the values that the older poet embraces.

Although a suspicion of fame and an ironic perception of artistic immortality still pervade the poems, the overriding feeling is of acceptance of a modest place in literature. When Bukowski laments, "I look around and / I look / and / I say: where are the / writers?" (*Stew*, 161), a congregation of former creators stand behind him. He stresses again his suspicion of a prevailing academic poetry that is "secretive / soft and / nearly indecipherable" (*Stew*, 230). The decay of society is saliently reflected in the absence of direct and genuine artists, and vice-versa. This sentiment is movingly reflected in "the burning of the dream," an evocative and nostalgic recreation of the Los Angeles Public Library. The seven-page poem alternately catalogs names and titles in recollecting an imaginative world that transported the young man from his immediate life. "my greatest problem was / stamps, envelopes, paper / and / wine, / with the world on the edge / of World War II" (*Stew*, 44). Before a final list of titles, the narrator returns to the present with an understated explanation to his wife: "I used to spend my / time / there . . ." (*Stew*, 48). The past persists, of course, in the memories of the living. Reciprocally, the persistence of the past problematizes the present. The question "where have / my people / gone?" (*Stew*, 310) is echoed by the self-accusing "where / did I / go?" The poet stares at a face he hardly recognizes, an old face seemingly unrelated to a man "20 years old / drunk at / 10 a.m. / staring into / a cracked / New Orleans / mirror" (*Stew*, 204).

The motif of disfigurement common in Bukowski is persistent in *Septuagenarian Stew* and is linked to concerns of aging, deterioration, and entropy. "an angel and an asshole" and "not from the same mould" are typical of poems that depict the mutilated. In "postcard," time is condensed, causing a friend's unfortunate life to be reenacted as a swift, horrible transfiguration:

> he looked stranger and stranger, finally no longer spoke,
> simply sat there, very upright, not moving his eyes
> seemed to be losing color, then
> I never saw him again. (*Stew*, 199)

Always, another apparition appears. One is reminded of Sherwood Anderson, a writer Bukowski admired and thought underacknowledged. Ghosts parade across the mind of the old writer in *Winesburg,*

Ohio. "Some were amusing, some almost beautiful, and one, a woman all drawn out of shape, hurt the old man by her grotesqueness."[15] For the aging poet it is the same:

> yes, I almost visualized them, one at a time: an old woman with a
> grey shawl about her neck, a middle-aged drunk, a repressed child-
> rapist with a long yellow nose, a man with one eye, a young girl
>   who
> sometimes imagined she was a swan . . . (*Stew,* 94)

These characters, like Anderson's, are rendered grotesque by the truths they take as their own. Bukowski, however, wary of answers, avoids the trap of bitterness. He raises a late, last pagan drink to luck and, in *Septuagenarian Stew*'s terse final lines, offers an act of creation that

> makes each word
> drill
> into the
> paper
>
> clear
>
> fast
>
> hard
>
> feeding a
> closing
> space. (*Stew,* 374–75)

The Last Night of the Earth Poems

The 1992 collection *The Last Night of the Earth Poems* continues the elegiac nature so evident in *Septuagenarian Stew*. One critic locates this shift in voice even earlier, arguing that these poems "enlarge the meditative tone begun in *You Get So Alone at Times That It Just Makes Sense*."[16] *The Last Night of the Earth Poems* is the last collection published during Bukowski's life, and it is a massive volume of over 400 pages, "the size of a more cautious author's *Collected Poems*."[17] The poems are marked by the aging poet's preoccupations with hell, death, illness, and the spiritual poverty of contemporary artists and society. The stance is one of preparation and closure, one, in short, of good-bye.

> now, all there is to do is
> reset
> broken moments.
>
> when even to exist seems a
> victory
> then surely our luck has
> run thin.[18]

The book is full of summaries, summings-up, and parting invective against mediocrity and the offense of wasted life. In "be kind," Bukowski concludes "age is no crime // but the shame / of a deliberately / wasted / life // among so many / deliberately / wasted / lives // is" (*Night*, 43). The truncated lines tumble down the page, ending, like many of the poems, with a sense of language as depleted, ended, and surrendered to whiteness. "Bukowski's septuagenarian existence has mellowed down to typing and drinking wine while listening to classical music, the company of his wife and cats, and going to the racetrack, aware that he is running out of days" (Smith, "Bad Times Again, 19). The author of these poems seems tired, angry at ruined potential, a bit sad, and acutely aware of the increasing value of time as it passes. "each person is only given so many / evenings / and each wasted evening is / a gross violation against the / natural course of / your only / life" (*Night*, 25). Bukowski guards his moments and has learned how to say no to the ring of the telephone, to the door buzzer, and to the intrusive approach of a stranger at the racetrack. The hours of labor are vividly recalled, "every minute as it was / mutilated" (*Night*, 158); the philosophy of conspicuous leisure, ensured by a commitment to poverty, is recalled and reaffirmed. In the bar, "time came under your / control, time to wade / in, time to do nothing / in" (*Night*, 328). Being poor and crazy was, he

suggests, partly an ideological choice, "a / celebration / of something not
to / do / but only / know" (*Night*, 355).

The theme of illness is prominent in *The Last Night of the Earth Poems*.
In "upon this time," the narrator, propped in bed as he writes in a notebook, compares himself with the older, disoriented Hemingway. Despite
his impulse to write, the poet apologizes: "I have TB and the / antibi-
otics dull the / brain" (*Night*, 185). In the poem's understated and ravaging conclusion, Bukowski notes his impossible predicament:

> I've got to do a
> Lazarus
> and I can't even
> shine
> my shoes. (*Night*, 186)

Although humor is present, such as in the rude conclusion of "8 count"
and the baseball analogy developed in "finished"—"my batting average
has dropped to / .231" (*Night*, 177)—the poems concerning illness are
predominantly grim. They present a Bukowski who, after so many
decades of remarkable endurance, is at last physically weakened, his
weight dropping, his mind sometimes unclear, and his expectations
minimal. Even the racetrack "seems meaningless" as he is distracted by
a pattern of illness. "washed-up, on shore, the old yellow notebook / out
again / I write from the bed / as I did last / year" (*Night*, 196). As always
he writes of his life, and through a consideration of aging, illness, dying,
and death attempts to craft experience into art.

> this year
> 1988
> all these months
> have had
> a terribleness to them
> that I have never felt
> before.
>
> I light a cigarette and
> wait. (*Night*, 242)

He is "weary with the continuation" (*Night*, 242) and, considering the collection's consistent tone, this weariness seems to reflect a sincere physical tiredness.

Although Bukowski did not die until 1994, and then of leukemia rather than tuberculosis, *The Last Night of the Earth Poems* has the unshakable feeling of a last testimony. Following the poet's "ungodly durability" and "almost heroic perseverance and strength of purpose," it was "perhaps inevitable that a life-centred author ends up being fixated on death" (Smith, "Bad Times Again," 19). Death is a palpable, often personified presence in the book. The author is "waiting for extinction" (Smith, "Bad Times Again," 19) and sometimes, as in the poem "Dinosauria, we," makes little separation between the world's demise and his own. The opening poem, "jam," contains one of Bukowski's favorite later images, the crowd of automobiles, here described with a self-inclusive pronoun:

> we were like some last, vast
> final dinosaur
> crawling feebly home somewhere,
> somehow, maybe
> to
> die. (*Night*, 17)

The enjambed "maybe" refers as much to the uncertainty of returning home as to the inevitability of death, but death is never far from these poems.

The personification "Mrs. Death," appears both in "Dinosauria, we" and in "the creative act." The figure of Mrs. Death seems an homage to e. e. cummings, who himself is mentioned with admiration more than once in the volume. In particular, the last lines of "the creative act" echo cummings's "Buffalo Bill's defunct":

> this life dancing in front of
> Mrs. Death. (*Night*, 204)

> how do you like your blueeyed boy
> Mister Death[19]

In the surreal poem "freaky time," death again appears as a woman, in this instance as an attractive "lady down at the end of the bar" (*Night*, 229) who finds the narrator appealing. The man is angered, although not especially surprised, to discover that the departed woman is death. He adds the punch line: "knew it all along: she was a / whore" (*Night*, 230).

Although *The Last Night of the Earth Poems* shows Bukowski writing almost obsessively about death and dying, the writing itself is a creative act that gradually reveals itself as death's antithesis. The name "Mrs. Death" suggests the existence of a husband, and frequently this other is represented by art, which generates life and meaning. Even ill, as he proclaims his inability to write, the author stills compulsively writes of these frustrations. "As it did for Hemingway, writing has become Bukowski's greatest vice and greatest pleasure, and only death can stop it" (Smith, "Bad Times Again," 19). Bukowski concurred with each poem he completed. Ritualized creation, reenacted during countless nights in small rooms of smoke and music, has a transforming, redemptive effect for the creator:

> it has saved my ass from the worst of women and the
> worst of men and the
> worst of jobs, it has mellowed my nightmares into a gentle
> sanity, it has loved me at my lowest and it has made me
> seem to be a greater soul than I ever
> was. (*Night*, 311)

Bukowski asserts that his creative nights have in turn assaulted the assailant: "death, I have chopped off your arms and your legs and your / head" (*Night*, 311).

The notion of cheating death is associated with the preservation of privacy and with submission to the process of a creative unconscious. In the lyric "victory," the poet notes that "the dogs of the hours / close in," but for those who have properly and fully lived, "nothing / can be taken / from us / but / our lives" (*Night*, 163). In "death is smoking my cigars," the narrator's visitor is sardonic, garrulous, and ominous, the possessor of secret knowledge but also jovial antagonist:

> no matter what you've been:
> writer, cab-driver, pimp, butcher

sky-diver, I'm going to get

you . . .

o.k. baby, I tell him. (*Night*, 73)

Of crucial importance to Bukowski's response is his argument for preserved isolation, creativity, diligence, and personal integrity: "I got my /
5 god-damned minutes / and much / more" (*Night*, 73). The epithet in
this instance is tellingly placed. Except during the author's famed 10-
year hiatus, writing was the obsession that unified his life, and this last
volume continually takes stock of writing's redemptive power. As a
young man, sick and starving in rooming houses across the country, the
poet would "get out of bed / find a piece of / paper / and start / writing /
again" (*Night*, 145). Clearly the act itself, that process of engagement
and exploration, is of greater value to the artist than any resulting arti-
facts. In "only one Cervantes," the poet is respectful, full of gratitude
and memories: "writing has been my fountain / of youth, / my whore, /
my love, / my gamble," and even with writer's block and failing health,
he is "still / lucky" (*Night*, 194).

The power of the creative act for the individual is distinguished
from the limited results of language. "yet / none of us come / near /
none of us even / close" (*Night*, 205), Bukowski writes, during his last
days more than ever aware of art's final, frustrating failure at transcendence: "and the worst thing / of course / is that the words will never /
truly break through for any of / us" (*Night*, 224). Such incomplete discourse is linked with the ineffectiveness of human life, as in "cut while
shaving": "It's never quite right, he said, the way the people look, /
the way the music sounds, the way the words are / written." This
tedious cycle of lives can end only in the grave. The narrator simplifies
the riddle of the sphinx: "it was morning, it was afternoon, it was /
night." Lack of imagination and courage is waste. Yet as the poem
concludes, the speaker continues, descending into renewed engagement: "I walked down the stairway and / into it" (*Night*, 322). For
individuals truly alive, continuation's meaning is within its struggle
toward unachievable goals.

While waiting "for the whole thing to go / one way or the / other"
(*Night*, 191), Bukowski, as his health allows, continues the evenings of
creative solitude that sustained him for decades.

another still, hot summer night,
the small insects circle my wineglass, my
winebottle.

I once again consider my death
as a Brahms symphony ends upon the
radio. (*Night*, 223)

The repetition of the solitary event is indisputably worthwhile.[20] Integral
to the scene, as always, is the author's boon companion, classical music.
Robert Sandarg wrote in 1991 that Bukowski's "oeuvre contains nearly
300 references to no less than 50 composers. Their works have buoyed
Bukowski during good times, drowned the dissonance of bad times, and
inspired his literary creation."[21] The poet corroborates this early influence:
"I sucked mostly at the classical music boys. It was good to come home
from the factories at night, take off my clothes, climb on the bed in the
dark, get drunk on beer and listen to them" (*NYQ*, 319–20). The tinny
radio rattling with symphonic energy represents for Bukowski an immediate link with centuries of composition and creation.[22]

   Classical music is also a conspicuously non-American tradition and
one commonly associated with aristocracy, allowing Bukowski historical,
geographic, and social transcendence. "the soldier, the wife and the
bum," set during World War II, highlights the music's solace and its
greater implications. Disappointed with the artificiality of the crowd at
a live performance, the narrator returns to his room and his radio; he listens as if in prayer. Music permeates the tableau—next door, a young
soldier who will soon depart for war embraces his girlfriend—with
meaning, sadness, and history:

and as I listened to the classical music I
heard them making love, desperately and
mournfully, through Shostakovich, Brahms,
Mozart, through crescendo and climax,
and through the shared
wall of our darkness. (*Night*, 293–94)

Magically, the European composers play music for the present, their
war-torn continent persisting through dark walls.

"classical music and me" is a touching account of Bukowski's history with the poem's subject, from a first accidental encounter to decades of nightly listening that "gave heart" (*Night*, 374) to his life. Music also contributes the planned interruption that Bukowski likes when writing. Rhythms seep into the poems. "Instead of a hindrance, it's an aid. . . . It doesn't engulf the work, but it's there" (Wennersten, 51). The immediacy of sound, the courage of composers as they struggle with notes as comparably restrictive as words, remained crucial to the author's method, tying him as well to an older, different world. "my German buddy," an homage to Wagner, recalls Bukowski's own heritage as it pays tribute to artistic grace, power, and immediacy:

> I can't believe that
> he is not in
> the other
> room
> or around the
> corner
> or alive
> someplace
> tonight (*Night*, 22)

The poet concludes that "he is / of course / as I am taken / by the sound of / him" and "he's here // now" (*Night*, 22).

To the extent that music speaks through the poems, Bukowski serves as mediator for artistic spirits. In the poet's mind, each note (or poem) is a further strike against the disappointments of common human behavior, against flawed art, against butchered lives, against unavoidable loss, and against his nemesis, death. "the open canvas" is ostensibly the narrative of a musician at a keyboard, fully alive only when "the music seeps through his / bones" and "centuries bend" (*Night*, 403). The organist, however, is actually the writer at his machine, and the poem represents the process and transportation of the artist who surrenders to the music of his work as he "touches the keys and / is taken / again" (*Night*, 404). The word "taken" supplies an effective double meaning: a notion of being "taken," or exploited, by art is swept away in the flight and primacy of process. Bukowski sits, listens, questions, and waits. Writing for him was as necessary as breathing or eating, as ethereal as

music. "His best poems discharge energy. We are touched by a vital creative mind prizing the creative act. Nothing . . . can diminish it" (Peters,
61). Only that old whore Mrs. Death could stop him from composing,
and her victory would not be a proud one.

> now
> I drink cabernet sauvignon while
> listening to
> Bach: it's
> most curious: this
> continuing death
>   this
> continuing life
>
> as
> I look at this hand
> holding a cigarette
> I feel as if
> I have been here
> forever. (*Night*, 59)

Chapter Six

Barfly, Fame, and Concluding Novels

Shakespeare Never Did This

Throughout his life, Bukowski remained suspicious of literary fame. As early as 1962, with his underground reputation beginning to consolidate, he wrote in a letter of his uneasiness over the growing attention. "They are putting a lot of light on me right now, and it is the test. There is little doubt that obscurity and aloneness are the agents and angels of the good Art, and I am being tested here" (*Luck*, 30–31). However, Bukowski also sought recognition and in large part enjoyed it. He later defined being a professional: "You send it out and get it paid for. Professional is one who gets paid for doing his work" (Andrews, 166). Such a definition was still a distant goal for the underground poet of 1962, and he could hardly have anticipated the success that would accrue by the late 1970s. The Bukowski phenomenon outside of America, especially in his native country of Germany, is well documented. In 1987, *Interview* suggested that the author was "the most widely read living American writer in translation in the world today. More than 2.2 million copies of his works have been sold in Germany alone" (Penn, 94). Other unlikely reports filter in: "In 1983–84, three Bukowski titles appeared on the best-seller list in Brazil, two of them simultaneously" (Dougherty, 69). Carl Weissner, Bukowski's translator and foreign agent, credits the writer with "triggering a poetry renaissance" in Germany. "All of a sudden there were lots of very personal, narrative poems, loose, colloquial, even tough."[1] To Bukowski, this unusual circumstance was remarkable. "Much luck with my work in Germany, France. Also work translated into Italian, Swedish, Spanish and Denmark dickering for some work or other" (*Luck*, 257).

From the late 1970s onward, his foreign success allowed the author financial independence and psychological satisfaction, all the while enabling relative obscurity in America. Such circumstances were ideal for his life and for continued creative production. Bukowski shared his mixed feelings about fame with actor Sean Penn: "It's a destructor. It's the whore, the bitch, the destructor of all time. I've got it the sweetest because I'm famous in Europe and unknown here. I'm one of the most fortunate men around" (Penn, 96). Even such seemingly focused criticism of fame's seductive allure is qualified by the attractiveness and financial liberation of its attainment. During production of the Bukowski/Barbet Schroeder film *Barfly,* when Bukowski's celebrity in America was at a peak, the writer was still able to select his moments in the spotlight. He continued to evolve creatively and wrote much of his strongest work during the 1980s, a compelling argument that Bukowski had survived the "bitch" fame he always dreaded and revered.

Shakespeare Never Did This is a travelogue of the author's trips to Germany and Paris to capitalize on his European reputation. The book is ostensibly a direct account, without the mask of persona or the fictionalizing craft of a novel. However, it is revealing that the volume actually blends, without clarification, two trips into one—Bukowski's May 1978 trip to Germany, anchored by a large reading in Hamburg, and an October trip to Paris, also in 1978, to appear on the literary talk show *Apostrophes,* hosted by Bernard Pivot. Bukowski offers a deceptive and typically pragmatic reason for this artistic license: "Actually *Shakespeare Never Did This* is about TWO trips to Europe and I put them together as one. I do get them mixed up because of all the heavy drinking" (Ring, 37). Near the end of the volume, he feigns regret at his blurring excessiveness: "One hell of a writer I'd been, I hadn't written down the names of towns and places, sights, seasons, and grand feelings. All that was trash anyhow."[2]

The travelogue is an entertaining volume, although in some ways a suspicious one. Even its title seems both a recognition and an apology. The author explains that it is "kind of a business trip . . . to sell books" (*Shakespeare,* sec. 18), yet this explanation is given during a visit to Bukowski's Uncle Heinrich, a lively figure at age 80. Similarly, an exchange between Bukowski and his wife Linda on the plane back to America includes the same juxtaposition of commerce (only partially ironized) and sentimental curiosity about family and roots:

> "Well, we gave a good reading at Hamburg and we lucked it with the French press. Book sales ought to be up."
> "You talk like a business man."
> "I'm contaminated, soulless, it's over for me."

"You saw your uncle."
"Good tough boy." (*Shakespeare*, sec. 25)

These same motivations operate during the Hamburg reading. Bukowski's first words to a raucous crowd of 1,200 are revealing: " 'Hello,' I said, 'it's good to be back.' It had taken me 54 years" (*Shakespeare*, sec. 16). Among the handful of poems collected after the prose account is "German side show, 1961," recounting a battle between Spads and Fokkers—World War I fighter planes—which also suggests the hero of Bukowski's adolescent notebooks. The book is in part the story of a native son returned.

Bukowski's own fame is the central theme of the book—he continually signs autographs, speaks with the media, watches films about himself or his work, browses bookstores stocked with his books, and is recognized on the street. He grew unnerved at the artificiality of the German visit, its schedule like being "tied with ropes and drugged" (*Luck*, 251) as opposed to his customary leisure. The distance from the typewriter is epitomized by a lack of privacy. "The German gang was with us; there was a live camera and a photographer and a journalist. To live a natural life in Germany was difficult but one gave in to it because it was temporary. Back in America where I was hardly known I could have my isolation again" (*Shakespeare*, sec. 20). Despite his feelings of violation, the author clearly enjoys his celebrity and his public identification as a serious author. "As I got closer to the stage the crowd began to recognize me. 'Bukowski! Bukowski!' I was beginning to believe that I was Bukowski. . . . My poems were not intellectual but some of them were serious and mad. It was really the first time, for me, that the crowd had understood them" (*Shakespeare*, sec. 16). He is appreciative, and, as a consequence, *Shakespeare Never Did This* is a curious examination of the artist's conflicted feelings toward his late fame.

Bukowski is constantly in the spotlight in the book as he assumes a role of mentor and father figure to his "German gang" of apostles. Lovely photographs by Michael Montfort that accompany the text reiterate the constant onstage quality of the trip. This persistently public aspect initiates a paradoxical response. The author, well aware of his persona, is more extroverted than in the increasingly isolated years of his later life. The roving, drunken gang of admirers rekindles a rooming-house sentiment that he so consistently romanticized in his work: " 'Look, madam,' I told the owner's wife, 'the night is young. We'll be quiet up there. All we want to do is to drink quietly in the town of my birth' " (*Shakespeare*, sec. 19). Such a scene is typical, even archetypal, of Bukowski's depiction of his early life. Yet the differences of affluence are continually made apparent. At a tavern near Heidelberg, where Bukowski arrives with his gang, the poet admires the local patrons. "They each sat at a separate table and said nothing to each other. Their faces were very red but I could feel them thinking about the days and years of their lives; about History, about yesterday and today. They were waiting to die but they were in no particular hurry: there were many things to think about" (*Shakespeare*, sec. 14). The accompanying Montfort photograph is illustrative: individual men at tables, each thoughtful. Bukowski is alone at a table in the foreground in a similar pose, but the circle of glasses around him reminds that he is with a group just outside of the frame. In another photograph, Bukowski, robust and nicely dressed in dress shirt and jacket, is shown entering a cathedral with Linda. They are the classic tourist couple. Against the cathedral façade, in the background but unmistakable, is a bum, hat outstretched for coins. There will be no return, for the successful writer, to a life of privation and homelessness.

Bukowski the artist survives the lavish attention and upper-class lifestyle reported in the book. His humor and candid honesty are largely in place and constitute invaluable survival tools for the writer's soul. He conspicuously describes the elite society of his last night in Paris:

> We ate that night in one of those places high up and across the boulevard from the movie houses. Down below us the little automobiles raced, and the later the night got the faster they ran and the more of them there were. Paris drank and ate all night; unlike Americans they never thought of the next day. Or so it felt to me. And, as usual, the French waiter was kind and efficient. . . . Little is remembered of the night, we drank and ate and drank and drank. It seemed as if everybody were living well, as if existence were just a joke . . . (*Shakespeare*, sec. 24)

This passage effectively compresses the dilemma of the book: Bukowski is literally elevated above the bustle of the common society. Nearby are the movie houses that become increasingly involved with his celebrity. A Hemingway-like syntax highlights the author's self-consciousness. The author is meditative, nostalgic, alternating truncated sentences and stream of consciousness in a scene set in, of all cities, Paris. In the center of modernism, notions of sociability, elitism, indulgence, and celebration without consequence are enacted. The scene is tinged with awareness and implicit self-criticism and ends on a foreboding note: "as if existence were just a joke."

The artist is rescued partly by his need for material. For Bukowski, whose hardest physical years are long behind him, the higher elevation represents something new, a view from the top rather than the bottom, and he greets it with a characteristic blend of appreciation, disgust, enjoyment, and cynicism. In 1974, Bukowski voiced beginning concerns with the intentionally limited view of his earlier lifestyle, while suggesting the importance of a fuller perspective that includes all classes: "I went to every town in order to learn that town from the bottom. . . . I used to think that real men (people you could put up with for over ten minutes) were at the bottom, instead of the top. The real men weren't at the top, middle or bottom. There's no location. They're just very scarce; there aren't many of them" (Wennersten, 39 – 40). He justifies his earlier approach by imagining a situation strikingly similar to the one illustrated in the travelogue: "You come into a town from the top— you know, fancy hotel, fancy dinners, fancy drinks, money in your pocket—and you're not seeing that town at all. True, I denied myself a full view" (Wennersten, 39). One remarkable aspect of the Paris evening, as Bukowski dines with admirers and filmmakers, is the simultaneous recognition of his limited earlier view and clear skepticism toward his current position.

Bukowski's evocation of "real men" seems prophetic when considering *Shakespeare Never Did This*. Equal with the author's acceptance of literary fame is his recognition of supporters and friends. The volume is an unabashed paean to Carl Weissner and Barbet Schroeder. "I got drunkest of all and kept telling Carl and Barbet over and over again what great men they were, what warm and real men they were, my only male friends . . . the luck of knowing you is a sun which always shines . . . Which was and is true" (*Shakespeare*, sec. 12). Despite these sentiments being cloaked in a drunken delivery, they are typical of the narrator's gushing appreciation. Bukowski seems surprised and pleased by his affection for his companions: "And then there was Carl and Waltraut, I liked them both much, it startled me because I had so much difficulty with people. There weren't many for me. There was that crazy Barbet and there was Linda Lee and my daughter, and outside of that it dropped off and down, people could just as well be flies or pebbles. Well, no, pebbles weren't so bad at that" (*Shakespeare*, sec. 22).

The book is also in part an appreciation of Linda Lee, Bukowski's future wife. Her constant and complementary presence is crucial. "The girl enjoyed everything that bored me and everything that I enjoyed bored her. We were perfect mates" (*Shakespeare*, sec. 8). The three centers of the author's affections are also those central to enabling his later period of artistic acclaim: Linda Lee with her domesticating influence, Weissner with his paramount effort in generating the author's German reputation and income, and Schroeder with his subsequent, obsessive dedication to the *Barfly* project. In all cases, the admiration seems reciprocal and mutually beneficial. These relationships were crucial to Bukowski's late success and his survival as a professional writer. He is affectionate toward those who help him; otherwise, even recent relationships disappear. "We began drinking and talking over old times, like the time he had come to Los Angeles. . . . It was three years back. He asked me about various people. 'No, they're not there.' 'No, they're not there either.' 'No, she's gone. We split. I don't see her any more' " (*Shakespeare*, sec. 19). His life has changed rapidly and irrevocably, and new friends are appropriate to new status.

Shakespeare Never Did This is enlightening in how the author portrays himself, its organization more artful than any mishmash of drunken memories. Bukowski's iconoclastic appearance on French television begins the book's episodic structure, although this event actually took place during the second trip. The Paris adventure frames the visit to Germany. Only a side trip to Nice, to visit Linda's mother and uncle (the latter a rich antithesis to Uncle Bernard), shows Bukowski out of the glare of camera lights and not swarmed by admirers. Interestingly, he seems bored and uninterested during this section, ending it with a simple dismissal: "Nice had been unrewarding . . ." (*Shakespeare*, sec. 11).[3] As the narrative proceeds, Bukowski grows increasingly restless, anxious for the routine and anonymity of L.A. He offers a caveat: "Too many teachers became teachers, became gurus; they forgot their typewriters" (*Shakespeare*, sec. 15).

The travelogue concludes with a wonderfully burlesque scene that satirizes the entire book's preoccupation with celebrity. Bukowski is vaguely recognized in the airport upon his return to America: "That old guy carrying the suitcases . . . it's that genius guy . . . he writes stories and poems, novels . . ." (*Shakespeare*, sec. 25). He is back in the country of his own language, where fan recognition is comparable to insult. The woman has heard of the writer and recognizes his trademark face, but she has almost certainly not read his work. In the absurd and appropriate finale, Bukowski's attempt to acknowledge her comment with a wave sends his suitcase crashing down an escalator, where it strikes an elderly woman. He creeps away, hoping to avoid a lawsuit. The scene is a brilliant self-effacing recognition. To attempt to play the literary celebrity at home can be comically disastrous. Bukowski and Linda Lee escape to a taxi, and the author indicates the inevitable direction of his next decade, any lesson of the suitcase aside: " 'Hollywood, my good man,' and he understood exactly what I had told him" (*Shakespeare*, sec. 25).

Barfly

> Barbet just showed up at my door one day. Said he wanted to make a film about my life. . . . I was very reluctant, because I don't like film. I don't like actors, I don't like directors, I don't like Hollywood. I just don't like it. He laid a little cash on the table—not a great deal, but some. So I typed it out. That was seven years ago.
>
> I started writing dirty stories and I ended up writing a fucking screenplay.[4]

Bukowski's summary of his long involvement with the *Barfly* movie project is informative. The writer portrays himself as hesitant, yet professional. Against his own advice (offered in *Shakespeare Never Did This*), Bukowski accepted an advance for the project, perhaps in keeping with his skepticism and his limited respect for the film genre. He relates writing the screenplay and, in an understated manner, ends with a perspective on his career. That he "ended up" writing a screenplay is actually comparable to the commercialism of his short stories for men's magazines rather than a new compromise. The curiously self-reflexive piece of writing that is *Barfly* also "ends up," in a sense, the arc of Bukowski's career—from days of obscurity, recalled a last time, to an apex of his popularity in America during his lifetime.

Bukowski wrote to Carl Weissner in the spring of 1979 that "I did it. I finally finished the screenplay. Took me three months. So far I'm calling it *The Rats of Thirst*" (*Luck*, 262). The film seems to have been written concurrently with *Shakespeare Never Did This* and finished shortly afterward, although *Barfly* was not finally released as a film until 1987. While the author was recovering from his celebrity trips to Europe and reflecting in writing on their effects, he was also reapproaching the materials of his early life for a commercial treatment. He felt that the movie, if produced, "will be entertaining but maybe offensive to certain types who can't understand laughter through violence" (*Luck*, 264). Concerning the material of his earlier life, Bukowski reflected in a 1987 interview: "When I lived in Philadelphia, I was a barfly. I was about 24, 25, 26, it gets kinda mixed up. . . . This is a mixture of two areas, L.A.

and Philadelphia. Which may be cheating, but it's supposed to be fictional anyway, right?" (Hodenfield, 58–59). The author himself brings up the curious idea of "cheating," then dismisses any notion of truth necessarily equaling historical accuracy. As he had in reference to *Shakespeare Never Did This*, Bukowski attempts to dismiss his compression and reorganization as alcoholic forgetfulness, perhaps a ploy on the author's part to emphasize persona over dedicated craftsmanship.

As its author notes, the *Barfly* screenplay is extremely violent, yet the work is filled with black humor and ends on a note of celebration—of survival, of conflict, and of an uncompromised rejection of societal values. To one accustomed to Bukowski's work, some scenes in the film seem vaguely familiar. The older, successful writer recalls not only his early years but previous treatments of the period. Chinaski's poetic voice-overs are taken partly from early poems, heightening the nostalgic effect. The setting is also typical. Henry defines the bar community as "a self-sufficient delusion."[5] Near the story's conclusion, he adds, "We're basically strangers to each other. We've passed in the night and met again in a bar. Be realistic: there's no reality to any of this," and finally, "*Another round of drinks for everybody!*" (*Barfly*, 123). The community of the bar, with its arbitrary and contradictory relationships, is absurd, yet the bar persists as the closest thing to a home for its patrons. The bartender Jim feels an affection for Henry that he cannot fully articulate. Even Eddy, the night bartender who represents Henry's archetypal foil, is a needed adversary. The two sustain one another, paradoxically, by their daily beatings. As Henry says of his screaming neighbors, whose invective seeps through the walls: "It's hatred, the only thing that lasts" (*Barfly*, 83).

Barfly is inclusive in its Bukowskian themes: the importance of luck (Henry receives checks and is once forced to take cash, bounties that enable him to buy drinks and otherwise survive) and the balm of classical music are two. Drinking is obviously central to the film, the primary passion and talent of its characters. Alcohol is an escape from, and alternative to, the "normal" society occasionally glimpsed outside of the dark, self-contained bar world. Several times, the screenplay emphasizes the opening of the bar door and by implication the "day" world outside. It is this open world that is ironically imprisoning, a world of jobs, police, and societal expectations of "being." Drunkenness and madness, however relative the latter term, are preferable to physical and spiritual imprisonment. In one telling scene, Henry recognizes the anesthetizing and cleansing effect of alcohol on body and spirit. "He smiles. Holding a fifth of Scotch in one hand, he looks into the mirror and feeling with his free hand locates the gash in his skull. He lifts the bottle and pours some of the contents over the wound. Some of the Scotch runs down the side of his face. . . . He licks his fingers, smiling gently" (*Barfly*, 76). Yet when the publisher Tully labels his life a "limited world" (*Barfly*, 108), Henry agrees concerning its delusional quality.

Bukowski claimed not to idealize violent drunkenness. He preferred an emphasis on directness, honest perception of self, and a belief in knowledge gained through experience:

> YOU CAN'T WRITE WITHOUT LIVING AND WRITING ALL THE TIME IS NOT LIVING. Nor does drinking create a writer or brawling create a writer, and although I've done plenty of both, it's merely a fallacy and a sick romanticism to assume that these actions will make a better writer of one. Of course, there are times when you have to fight and times when you have to drink, but these times are really anti-creative and there's nothing you can do about them.[6]

This comment defends the screenplay's central activities even as it undercuts their relevance to creativity. *Barfly* also arguably "cheats" by its inclusion of poetry; by the author's own account, his barfly years fall within the decade during which he wrote almost nothing.

Making the film's protagonist a writer may have been due to commercial pressures to give the story a sympathetic, redemptive center. "This guy Henry I wrote about—he wasn't a writer. He was just drinking. I wasn't writing then—when I was his age, all I did was drink. They said, 'We need something to show that he's more than just, you know. That he's a writer. Show us something, a piece of paper.' OK."[7] Although the moments of Henry scribbling poems are effective and lend the movie its "art film" pathos, a rough comedy about drunks exists independent of the writing scenes. Nevertheless, Henry emerges as a complete and convincing creation, and much of his luck and durability seems linked to Bukowski's own enthusiasm for the creative process: "Writing keeps you alive because it eases the monsters in the brain by moving them to paper. The listing of horrors seems regenerative, and often comes out in the writing as a form of joy or humor. The typewriter often sings soothing songs to the sadness of the heart. It's wondrous" (Dougherty, 98).

One issue that *Barfly* questions through its violence is masculinity. Eddie, the night bartender, represents everything antithetical to Chinaski's aesthetic: "Obviousness. Unoriginal macho energy. Ladies' man."[8]

In the fascinating "Description of Characters" that precedes the printed screenplay, Bukowski describes Eddie as "a man's man, black hair jutting from his chest, his shirt open two or three buttons down. He's really a sickening prick but you don't want to admit it to anybody because he's what a man is supposed to be, and if you don't like that, you know, then there's something wrong with you" (*Barfly*, 9). Complementing Eddie is Henry's next-door neighbor Louie, seen only once but heard continually as he bullies his wife with banal platitudes of virility.[9] "*You're dealing with a real man now. I'm tough and I'm good and I'm hard.*" The woman, neither convinced nor impressed, matches scream for scream her part in their drama: "*I know a part of you that never gets good and hard!*" (*Barfly*, 82).

In contrast to Eddie and Louie, Henry is described by the bar patrons as a "fag" and a "eunuch" (*Barfly*, 41). When he participates in the ritual of the fight, his aloofness from Eddie's brand of machismo separates him from public sympathy. "What are you doing with a woman, Henry?" (*Barfly*, 65), Lilly asks balefully. A prostitute on the street offers a similar opinion: "Your boyfriend is a goddamned fag! What are you going to do with *him* when you get home?" (*Barfly*, 103). This comment is echoed later in the evening. Hurt after a perceived slight, Tully tells Henry "you were a lousy lover. Get out" (*Barfly*, 112). Even Henry seems to take for granted the social standards that leave him, by their reckoning, emasculated.

LADY
Everything here seems to read none. Hobbies, none. Religion, none. Education, none. Even where it asks your sex you have written "none" . . .

HENRY
(*smiling*)
Well, hardly none. Okay, put down "male." (*Barfly*, 69)

What begins as the tired joke response to a job application is transformed by Henry's reluctant second sentence into a critique of restrictive gender roles. The interview ends.

Barfly's denial of traditional masculine roles is integral to Henry's philosophy of retreat and nonacceptance. He attempts to act in accordance with this idea. "Sometimes, I just get tired thinking of all the things I don't want to be, of all the things I don't want to do—like go to India, get my teeth cleaned, save the whale. All that. I don't understand it."

Jim's response indicates an important difference between the two men: "You're not supposed to think about it. I think the whole trick is not to think about it" (*Barfly*, 70). Of course, such an answer implies its own impossibility. The long, slow parade of hours must be endured. Henry later explains to Tully that "I'm not pretending to *be* anything, that's the point" (*Barfly*, 106). This attitude involves a choice, an ideology that could be paraphrased as perhaps "nonbeing and somethingness." In this context, even casual remarks initiate Henry's unwillingness to accept limiting definitions of life and self. The seemingly mundane question of "Who are you?" receives a studied, albeit humorous, answer: "The eternal question and the eternal answer: I don't know" (*Barfly*, 67). When Lilly asks if Henry is "gonna buy one or be one?" his response is significant: "Give her a beer" (*Barfly*, 63). In other words, he refuses to "be" one, whatever the role.[10]

Two elements further define Henry's position of nonbeing: an appreciation of the animal over the human and unexpected moments of sudden gracefulness. A recognition of animals—their coherence, directness, spontaneity, and "natural" honesty—is a frequent subject in Bukowski's later work and is obviously linked to Jeffers's inhumanism. Henry's response to a vicious dog in a car, "at the ecstatic and eternal peak of murder" (*Barfly*, 18), typifies the Bukowskian attitude. Henry speaks, "*softly and with reverence*," a single word: "Beautiful" (*Barfly*, 19). A later image of the protagonist squatting by a fire hydrant as he washes blood from his face further equates man with beast (*Barfly*, 44). His wariness toward human beings is summarized during a subsequent conversation with Wanda. Henry doesn't hate people; he just tends "to feel better when they're not around" (*Barfly*, 47). Considering the battered condition of his body, this sentiment is comically understated. Wanda's description of Henry's beaten face as "beautiful" (*Barfly*, 49) identifies her as one of the film's enlightened characters and again associates him with the animal/primitive. Wanda, as Henry's soul mate, is a far more trustworthy commentator on the film's values than any of the bar regulars. She spends a night with Eddie but afterward recognizes the inadequacy of the male stereotype: "You're right, he's not much. I made an error, an unhappy error" (*Barfly*, 72). It is an error she vows not to make a second time, and Henry's comment before the final fight with Eddie, that "his kind is no problem" (*Barfly*, 120), seems an announcement of personal victory. In the film's last line, another barfly admonishes Eddie: "Are you gonna fight him again? Ha ha—that's a laugh!" (*Barfly*, 125).

Henry's physical roughness contains an occasional fluidity. "He moves slowly for a young man, rather still-shouldered, but at times his movements show a sudden swiftness and grace. It is as if he were saving himself for some magic moment, some magic time. Meanwhile, he drinks and drinks and drinks" (*Barfly*, 7). Henry's periodic grace and Wanda's characteristic "style" (*Barfly*, 8) mark them as survivors. Sometimes the surviving spirit flashes from beneath physical and social constraints. Henry's propriety when Wanda gets out of the bath (*Barfly*, 84), his politeness in serving Tully beer in a glass (*Barfly*, 94, not in film), these simple acts suggest the possibility of another kind of life, a gentler one beneath the bruising barfly reality. The politeness of a drunk who shakes so badly that the liquor will not reach his lips (*Barfly*, 64–66) and a sudden, prideful gesture "of magical grace" by a bum who is asked if he has a light—"Well, indeed, I *do* have *that!*" (*Barfly*, 91)—offer further examples of *Barfly*'s fleeting transcendence. "See, the angels are everywhere" (*Barfly*, 92), Wanda reminds Henry. Their flights are rare but essential.

Hollywood

Hollywood was generally well received by the critics at its publication in 1989. The book was recognized as a "hilarious *roman a clef.*"[11] Another reviewer wrote that through recollection of the writing and production of the film *Barfly*, "Bukowski takes you right into the reel Hollywood in media res."[12] Toby Moore commented that the novelist had "created a raw, teasing fiction based on his experience of writing a screenplay. . . . But what emerges is a parable for the disappointment, dottiness, decadence and deceit that somehow end up on screen."[13] Perhaps by virtue of survival, Bukowski had begun to garner modest critical acclaim, even if his work continued to be largely ignored by academia. For the reader anticipating the reemergence of the "old" Chinaski, however, *Hollywood* is a surprise. Participating in the filming of his early, bravado days gives Bukowski/Chinaski an opportunity to reflect on a youth and lifestyle that are irretrievable. As the protagonist watches his younger self portrayed by a Hollywood actor, his current self systematically hires a tax accountant, purchases a home, and buys a new BMW as a tax write-off. The novel traces this arc and the narrator's acceptance of a different life. "There were cameras flashing. Big time. I had left the park bench behind."[14]

Chronologically, *Hollywood* finds Henry Chinaski roughly after the conclusion of *Women*, in a monogamous and relatively sedate relationship with Sarah and with literary fame encroaching on his solitude. From the novel's first lines, the character stresses that he is crossing enemy lines and "heading for Marina del Rey. Strange territory" (*Holly-wood*, 9). The beginning is in a sense reminiscent of the opening of Ray-mond Chandler's *The Big Sleep*, with Marlowe entering the palatial home of the rich. Wry humor and an expectation of corruption are Chinaski's armor. "Somehow, most of them had apparently escaped the daily grind of living. . . . Such were the rewards of the Chosen in the land of the free. After a fashion, those people looked silly to me. And, of course, I wasn't even in their thoughts" (*Hollywood*, 9). His welcome into this pro-tected world of money, power, and artistic patronage elicits a typically ironic suspicion: "It was all really excellent. Life was good. All you had to do in their little world was be a writer or an artist or a ballet dancer and you could just sit around, inhaling and exhaling, drinking wine, pretending you knew what the hell" (*Hollywood*, 31). However, Chi-naski's enthusiasm for his new role is obvious, qualifications aside. By the novel's end, the distanced "they" becomes the more immediate, more comfortable, and more indeterminate "we." "Who wants to be a gardener or a taxi driver? Who wants to be a tax accountant? Weren't we all artists? Weren't our minds better than that? Better to suffer this way rather than the other. At least it looks better" (*Hollywood*, 231).

Contrasted with Hollywood society is the black ghetto in which the film's producer, Jon Pinchot/Barbet Schroeder, temporarily resides. As Chinaski steers his Volkswagen through a street cluttered with trash (he is later unwilling to risk driving his BMW in the area), he notices two young blacks staring at him with "pure, perfect hate. I could feel it. Poor blacks hated. Poor whites hated. . . . I knew politics would never solve it and there wasn't enough time left to get lucky" (*Hollywood*, 84). His further culpability is evidenced in his admission of "white flight" from the old East Hollywood neighborhoods now crowded with Latin Americans. "Sometimes I would nod or wave to them. They never responded. . . . I had noticed that each time I had moved in Los Angeles over the years, each move had always been to the North and to the West" (*Hollywood*, 62–63).

Within the tensions of such social inequities, Chinaski continually considers the state of his own artistic soul. Although *Hollywood* is a breezy and entertaining study of the vicissitudes, neurotic egos, decep-tions, and desperation of Hollywood players, the novel is, more signifi-cantly for Bukowski readers, the last chapter in the story of Henry Chi-naski. As in earlier novels, time is compressed. The story relates nearly

10 years, from Bukowski's first involvement with the screenplay in the late 1970s to *Barfly*'s eventual release in 1987, yet—as happens most notably in *Post Office* and *Women*—the duration of events seems much shorter, perhaps 1 or 2 years. This technique allows the author to isolate his themes. On the first page, Sarah suggests that Chinaski "stop worrying about [his] soul," and he later agrees that "I worry too much about my god damned soul" (*Hollywood*, 9, 43). A man who wrote stories for men's magazines for money is perhaps ideal for Hollywood screenwriting. In a discerning review of *Hollywood*, Molly Haskell wrote:

> The difference between Mr. Bukowski and other literary avengers is that he is neither a martyr nor a fallen angel. In "Hollywood," he surveys the absurdities of the passing scene with the complicitous eye of a cast member in the theater of the grotesque, and has no delusions that he can fall any lower in life than a short drop off a barstool. Of course, the image of himself as a drunk who sleeps till noon and practices craft, not art, is itself a theatrical feint, the hipster's mask for his softness, the ballet dancer pretending to be a boxer, the writer cunningly demoting himself as someone who hits the "typer."[15]

Many of the characteristics that formed foundations of the former Chinaski are conspicuously absent from *Hollywood*: the hard booze, the floozies, the flophouses. As the reader watches the older man, the professional writer, these missing elements seem increasingly superfluous. Chinaski asks himself, "Are you becoming what you've always hated?" and then continues to drink, "celebrating something" (*Hollywood*, 45).

Although an oddness, an unrest, creeps into the novel near its conclusion, still Chinaski seems intact for one primary reason: he is working consistently and well. He may take an advance to write the screenplay, but the old man does so with confidence in his abilities to produce a solid product. His durability is linked to the fact, as Sarah announces, that he is "just a natural-ass writer" (*Hollywood*, 66). The writing ritual is enacted throughout the novel, as is a crucial humor toward self and the absurdity of circumstances.

> Within an hour I was 45 thousand dollars richer. 30 years of starvation and rejection were starting to kick in.
> I walked back to the typer, poured a good tall drink, belted that, poured another. I found 3/4's of a stale cigar, lit it. Shostakovich's Fifth was on the radio. I hit the typer: (*Hollywood*, 38)

The creative act is preeminent in Bukowski, the central index of survival. Chinaski also considers the potentially problematic rehashing of old material for *Barfly*: "Somehow, the telling of old stories, again and again, seems to bring them closer to what they were supposed to be" (*Hollywood*, 33).

Such a purifying process is linked to writing and storytelling found throughout the novel. Chinaski occasionally tells or retells a story himself, to reapproach its truth, but he frequently leaves the talking to others, listens, and saves himself for the keyboard. That the protagonist is coming to the end of his life story is indicated not only by his age but by the exhaustion of his material. The screenplay dealt with "the only part of my life I hadn't written much about" (*Hollywood*, 82), he informs us, suggesting that its reexamination could prove valuable. *Hollywood* charts this scrutiny of youth even as the novel shows the character collecting new material for a last literary chapter about Hollywood and its people: "We were in this strange Beverly Hills hotel where you walked on peacocks. A magic world. I liked it because I hadn't seen anything like it before. It was senseless and perfect and safe" (*Hollywood*, 34). In its layers of artifice and reality, in its nostalgic scrutiny of the past and its "accumulation" of the present, *Hollywood* is a carefully constructed novel and a moving one.

Bukowski's novels are most effective when written from a historical distance (*Factotum, Ham on Rye*), and less consistent when employing material from his recent past (*Post Office, Women*). The wonder of *Hollywood* is that it does both, using current experience as a lens for viewing older material. The mix is unique. Chinaski has a last story to tell, and it is the story of the telling of his story. The low recognition of writers in Hollywood is suitable for this last stand: "The writer was where he belonged: in some dark corner, watching" (*Hollywood*, 156). Of course, the author receives his share of media attention. Photographs published in *Barfly* show Bukowski mugging with stars and barflies with equal ease. For the "natural-ass writer," it is all material, and for Bukowski/Chinaski, it is, as always, absurd. "Back at the house I went upstairs and did work on the screenplay but strangely or maybe not so strangely my past life hardly seemed as strange or wild or as mad as what was occurring now" (*Hollywood*, 87).

The curious effect of blending Bukowski's former and current lives is heightened by the use for film sets of two actual locations known by Chinaski as a young man—one a rooming house where he had lived, the other a field where corn is grown. The unlikely recurrence of these locations makes the narrator even more acutely nostalgic during filming, as does the performance of Jack Bledsoe/Mickey Rourke. "He had it. He had it the way it was, whether it meant anything or not, he had it the way it was" (*Hollywood*, 148). Seeing his youth reincarnated sends Chinaski deep into memory. "Shit, it was the young Chinaski! It was me! I felt a tender aching within me. Youth, you son of a bitch, where did you go? I wanted to be a young drunk again. . . . But I was just the old guy in the corner, sucking on a beer" (*Hollywood*, 148). This out-of-body oddness, mixed with a sadness accumulated through passing time, grows stronger as the novel proceeds. Each visit by Chinaski to the set elicits a similar response: "I watched and I have to tell you I grew weak watching that old dream. I wanted to be one of them, going at it again. Stupid or not, I felt like punching the alley wall. Born to die" (*Hollywood*, 187). His viewing of the filming is analogous to the creative recollection of writing the screenplay. The considerable difference, however, is the narrator's separation from the actual filming. Standing at the side, away from the camera, he is perhaps the writer collecting material, but the film consistently increases the distance between the old man and the dream of his youth. This is a technique Bukowski employs extensively in *Hollywood,* to a melancholy effect.

Mickey Rourke's eccentric performance, viewed both during the filming and subsequently on screen, exacerbates the confusion between the author's younger and older personalities. Pauline Kael, in her review of the film, noted an intriguing discrepancy: "Bukowski is writing about himself . . . when he was a scrappy young man. . . . But Mickey Rourke, who plays the role, imitates the tortoise movements of the battle-scarred survivor Bukowski, the writer-philosopher, the sage. Looking at the world through puffy, slitted eyes and smiling to himself, Rourke is a facsimile of Bukowski as he is now, and the effect is weirdly romantic."[16] She notes, as did several critics, Rourke's "soft, slow rhythms that are like a gently honeyed version of W. C. Fields' drawl" (Kael, 138). Locklin agrees, presumably in reference to the writer during his later years, that "this is precisely how Bukowski sounds."[17] This "confusion" in Rourke's performance is appropriate to *Hollywood*'s theme of dichotomy—the Chinaski of *The Dance of Jim Beam* both is and is not the Chinaski who witnesses the film's production. Nevertheless, Rourke gives a courageous performance, perhaps the definitive performance of his career. His thoughts on his work in the film are concomitant to Bukowski's aesthetic approach. Rourke explains: "I was drawing off the fact that I really didn't care if I stunk or not. That gave me a certain freedom to go all the way with the character. To me, that was growth in itself: It may have been a little self-destructive, but it gave me the sense that I really didn't have anything to prove."[18] The words could virtually be Bukowski's own in reference to the necessity of freedom and risk in artistic production.

Rourke's ambivalence toward Hollywood and success also show him to be the correct intellectual and spiritual choice to play Chinaski: "Look, I've sold chestnuts in Central Park. I'm not afraid to go back there and do it again. It's better to do that and keep your mind and your soul than it is to lose them to these cocksuckers. I feel [the film industry] takes a lot of good out of you. I was more at peace with myself before I was successful—and that's very confusing to me" (Rochlin, 60). Chinaski recognizes something right in Jack Bledsoe, and it is clear in *Hollywood* that they develop a mutual, although unarticulated, fondness for one another that transcends their participation in the film. Bledsoe's eccentric, sometimes childish behavior is accepted by the protagonist with minimal criticism. Instead, he speculates on the difficulty of the acting profession: "You know, when you spend many hours, many years pretending to be a person who you aren't, well, that can do something to you" (*Hollywood*, 192). That Chinaski is thinking as much about himself and the burden of his own persona is supported by the paragraph's conclusion: "Maybe it would be hard to remember who you were yourself, especially if you had to make up your own lines" (*Hollywood*, 193).

The writer, not the actor, must continually write his own script. And throughout *Hollywood* Chinaski seems uncharacteristically exposed—others tell the stories, others broker deals, others make the movie. Even before filming begins, the Buk myth is shown to be a comic but potentially dangerous burden. After being recognized in a biker bar by aggressive fans, the protagonist has the surprising impulse to throw his "arms around them, consoling and embracing them like some Dostoyevsky, but I knew that would finally lead nowhere except to ridicule and humiliation, for myself and for them" (*Hollywood*, 49). Instead, Chinaski and Sarah barely escape without violence. Moments later, in the car, he is thoughtful, making a seemingly unrelated leap to "Dennis Body. . . . He was my only friend in grammar school. I wonder whatever happened to him" (*Hollywood*, 49). Among the fragments of a discarded and no longer functional persona, he cannot find the Chinaski who existed before the crafted public self was formed. *Hollywood* involves a narrator trying to keep track of who he is, a man involved and determined to get the story of his youth on screen, yet increasingly detached and even naive. "Who are all these people, Sarah? What do they want here?" (*Hollywood*, 225). That Bukowski's persona is out of sync and out of his depth in the novel suggests the persistence of a creative exploration. Like Hemingway or like the novel's character Victor Norman/ Norman Mailer, the macho mythification of Bukowski and his career finally become insupportable, and *Hollywood* is a subtle yet courageous exploration of Chinaski's life as it is winding down and masks are discarded.

One aspect that makes Bledsoe's portrayal of Chinaski surprising is the actor's abstinence from alcohol. Drinking, as part of the Bukowski myth, is also reexamined in the novel. A harsh critic reported that "when all the Hollywood types Chinaski encounters . . . fit the same drunken-outcast-but-artistic-genius mold, Bukowski seems to have exhausted his resourcefulness."[19] Such a comment suggests a careless reading. Chinaski continually meets nondrinkers and reformed alcoholics—Jack Bledsoe; Mack Austin/Dennis Hopper; Helga, the wife of a lawyer for Firepower Productions; film critic Rick Talbot, all are conspicuous soda drinkers and teetotalers. Moreover, he repeatedly finds himself in situations where drinking is inappropriate. Two scenes in particular are memorable, one at the premiere of a "life-affirming" film about bums who are reformed drunks. The screening devolves into an Alcoholics Anonymous meeting. Chinaski and Sarah finish their wine and hurry for the car. On location for his own film, he recognizes a former ballroom that is now a rehabilitation center for alcoholics. A beautiful irony emerges—a crucial scene in an unrepentant film about drunks is filmed in the shadow of the rehab center. No drinking is allowed on the set. Chinaski hides his beer in his jacket.

Hollywood makes it increasingly clear that Chinaski's alcoholism is another feature of his personality that seems anachronistic in a new world of safer, blander, and more speciously healthy choices. The narrator, of course, clings to his old vice/virtue. "It took at least twenty years to become a bonafide alcoholic. I was on my 45th year and didn't regret any of it" (*Hollywood*, 75). Locklin argues that Bukowski "abhors the public life and it drives him to triple his drinking" and that *Barfly* is "the only unapologetic film about alcohol ever made in Hollywood" ("Bukowski/*Barfly*," 44, 47). Supporting Bukowski's own argument, Locklin further notes that after a childhood of "the twin scourges" of an abusive father and disfiguring boils, booze represented for the author "not destruction but salvation, an alternative to suicide . . . or homicide"

("Bukowski/*Barfly*," 54). Chinaski explains that "I'm not happy around people and after I drink enough they seem to vanish" (*Hollywood*, 182). Haskell wrote perceptively of *Hollywood* that "a haze of alcohol always descends in time to rescue Chinaski from having to listen too closely to what goes on below the surface of his own or other people's lives. It is also, one comes to realize, a protection from his own acute vision. Anyone who sees life this clearly needs something to cloud the lens" (Haskell, 11).

On an existential level, Chinaski's alcoholism addresses the novel's motifs of waste, of the world's slippage, and of the oppressiveness of vacant time. When the narrator is told that his answer to everything is drink, he responds tellingly: "No, that's my answer to nothing" (*Hollywood*, 92). At the end of the novel, after he and his wife have seen the film a last time, they summarize his screenwriting effort:

> "As a historian of drink I don't have a peer."
> "That's because none of them have lived as long as you."
> (*Hollywood*, 237)

Chinaski is out of kilter with the contemporary world, and *Hollywood* constitutes, if not an apology, at least an explanation and reconsideration of his commitment to drink. As Henry asserts in *Barfly*, in a sentiment perhaps more akin to the older author: "Endurance is more important than truth" (*Barfly*, 96).

Chinaski does endure, and at last recognition catches up with artistic achievement. "I had the bottle *and* the typer," he observes simply (*Hollywood*, 88). The regenerative ritual is intact. The racetrack also persists, its daily characters and systems a trusted index of spiritual health. The precision and meticulousness of Bukowski's several betting theories are an antidote to the corrupting influence of fame. "Now some of the boys are going to think the movie is going to kill me off, but they've always hoped something would. . . . Actually, 2 of the things that keep me clear are my drinking and my gambling" (quoted in Locklin, "Bukowski/*Barfly*," 57). At the track, Chinaski is dogmatic, empirical, and private, and his rules are consistently presented as philosophical profundities. "Excessive greed can create errors because very heavy outlays affect your thinking processes. Two more things. Never bet the horse with the highest speed rating off his last race and never bet a big closer" (*Hollywood*, 177). This is advice for the horse player and for the artist. Keep the system simple, precise, and controlled. Don't overrate past speed—who was the competition?—and bet on those in front, who lead at least for a while.

The Chinaski depicted in *Hollywood* is a calmer, quieter, and more domesticated version of his earlier self. He is a conscientious husband. "Sarah was still asleep. I turned on my right side, toward the window, because sometimes I snored and I wanted to direct the sound away from her" (*Hollywood*, 35). Physical craziness is decades behind him. The novel lacks literary groupies and any hint of unfaithfulness. The protagonist becomes fully encroached in the San Pedro home where he will make his last stand at the "typer." Chapters repeatedly end with Chinaski and Sarah returning to their home and its soothing domestic responsibilities. "Drinking could wait. Hollywood could wait. The cats could not wait. I agreed" (*Hollywood*, 149). Obviously this is a radical shift from Bukowski's characteristic chapter ending: a single man returning alone to a dark room. The couple's life is pleasant, even a bit bland.

Hollywood significantly inverts the Bukowski/Chinaski myth in another manner: not only has Chinaski's lifestyle changed, but against the raucous backdrop of Hollywood money, celebrity, and artificiality, he now represents stability. "One of my successes in life was that in spite of all the crazy things I had done, I was perfectly normal" (*Hollywood*, 151). The persona, in short, has been utterly deconstructed. This Chinaski does not drink hard liquor, uses a seat belt, watches television, and appreciates flowers and peacefulness. He has survived the excesses of youth and has survived fame, and he is writing well and enjoying his security. When he now returns from the track, he returns to a home, a wife, and cats. "Did you notice the roses?" Sarah hardly needs to ask.

> "Yes, they look great. Those reds and whites and yellows. Yellow is my favorite color. I feel like eating yellow."
> Sarah walked with the hose over to the faucet, shut off the water and we walked into the house together. Life was not too bad, sometimes. (*Hollywood*, 179)

Chinaski's request for a white stretch limousine ride to the film's premiere is not a compromise, but a celebration, the climax of his absurd and improbable success. *Hollywood* is a novel about looking back and regret, but it is also an appreciation of the present and of simple happiness. The film involvement ends, but the Chinaskis' life together continues beyond the book, for a while: "The real hero is this 67-year old man on the sidelines, whose brain and liver have survived 40 years of strenuous—if intermittent—alcoholism. He talks a tough game, but there's a streak of fellow feeling. . . . His wife, Sarah, is more than a supporting player: she gets her share of good lines and . . . comes off as an unlikely combination of drinking companion, drinking conscience, straight talker, and nursemaid" (Haskell, 11). Bukowski's first novel ends with these self-referential lines: "In the morning I was still alive. Maybe I'll write a novel, I thought. And then I did" (*Post*, 196). *Hollywood*'s conclusion is eerily similar:

> "What will you do?" . . .
> "Oh, hell, I'll write a novel about writing the screenplay and making the movie." . . .
> "What are you going to call it?"
> "*Hollywood*."
> "*Hollywood*?"
> "Yes . . ."
> And here it is. (*Hollywood*, 239)

After 20 years, five novels, and a lifetime of pain, humor, artistic commitment, and endurance recalled and chronicled, Henry Chinaski's story ends.

Pulp

Charles Bukowski completed one more novel. The detective spoof *Pulp* appeared in print only weeks after the author's death in 1994. He was dedicated to completing the project: "And I got leukemia, you know, and I came out of the hospital, and I was supposed to go back, and I didn't know whether I was gonna die or not, and so I finished it. To make sure, you know, before I die."[20] Even on the verge of death, Bukowski was writing and challenging himself. *Pulp* abandons the persona of Henry Chinaski (except for the joke of one offhand reference). For the first time in any of his novels, the author in his seventies wrote a work of purely imagined fiction. "I guess I got tired of writing about myself, about what happened to me. So I wrote this entirely fictional thing about this fifty-five year old detective." He adds that the novel is "going to ruin my reputation. Lot of bad stuff in it. I hope I've done it on purpose" (Freyermuth, 88).

Pulp is fast and raunchy, mostly dialogue, and full of gags and punch lines. Gundolf Freyermuth notes that Bukowski "had instinctively interwoven two outstanding Los-Angeles-myths: the *Noir*-myth of the California hard-boiled detective and his own legend, the Bukowski-myth" (90). Through the trappings of trash detective fiction, *Pulp* satirizes male violence and specifically the macho writer's life. Both detective and writer are occupied by two primary pursuits which lead to existential speculation: waiting and watching. Despite the inaccurate comments of some reviewers, *Pulp* parodies not the chivalric, romantic fictions of Raymond Chandler, but the sadistic luridness of Mickey Spillane. Bukowski's protagonist, Nick Belane (Belane/Spillane), is ultraviolent and links his violence with orgasm. He is limited mentally. Like Spillane's Mike Hammer, Belane himself is the primary source of aggression. John Cawelti observes that Spillane leaves "the basic formulaic framework as simple and uncomplicated as possible. Instead of adding human complexity to the skeleton, he heightens the pattern of the formula through violence, quasi-pornography, and other devices of emotional intensification."[21] Continuing, Cawelti reveals an important difference between Spillane's novels and *Pulp:* "When Spillane does a seduction scene, not a hint of irony or pathos enters in, except unintentionally. In its place is a voyeuristic fascination" (184). *Pulp* is full of ironic "winks" on the part of its author, and Belane's distaste for humanity undercuts his voyeuristic proclivity.[22]

As Belane's fixation with death and his facile musings intensify, the novel's existential theme comes into focus. As one reviewer commented, "apropos of nothing, business suddenly picks up."[23] Suddenly working on three cases, all seemingly unrelated, Belane struggles to make connections: "I am working on a tie-in, a link."[24] Yet his mental deficiencies and the largeness of the equation frustrate him. "I had to think about all of it. Somehow, it was all tying together: space, death, Sparrow, stiffs, Celine, Cindy, Bass. But I couldn't quite fit the pieces together. Not yet. My temples began to throb. I had to get out of there" (*Pulp*, 81). The novel is a series of comic false starts, vacillating confidence, and debilitating ennui. Belane's assurance that he is moving toward "something big" (*Pulp*, 57) is soon countered by the tired realization that "nothing was moving. . . . I put my feet up on the desk and leaned back in the chair and closed my eyes" (*Pulp*, 66). The novel teases with notions of interconnectedness and randomness, in this way vaguely reminiscent of the existential "anti"-detective novels of Paul Auster's New York Trilogy and of Thomas Pynchon's *The Crying of Lot 49.*

Even as Belane's cases begin to overlap, still the connections suggest both fatefulness and arbitrariness. The detective questions his own sanity: "None of it really made sense. Was I out of it? And where was I going and why?" (*Pulp*, 101). In a more lighthearted mood, he summarizes his situation: "Business was good, it was just without direction" (*Pulp*, 106). What might otherwise seem like haphazard plotting advances *Pulp*'s theme of connectedness:

> "He been in lately?"
> "Not since you were here. You trailing this bird?"
> "You might say so."
> Then, just like that, he walked in. Celine. (*Pulp*, 51)

Not only does Celine appear virtually on cue, but the colloquialism "this bird" recalls Belane's search for the Red Sparrow, a maguffin increasingly central in the novel. Moreover, the conversation takes place in Red's bookstore, further suggesting an implicit link between Celine and the Sparrow. The color red is mentioned throughout the novel, seemingly gratuitously, and even the book's garish red cover is unavoidable. Does the Red Sparrow represent death? Literary immortality? Either way, Celine would be implicated. A connection seems certain, yet ambiguous and evasive. This is Bukowski's approach in his most systematically plotted and least episodic novel. Belane must, like every creature, suffer the arbitrariness of whatever power determines his plot.

During the writing of *Pulp*, which took over two years to complete, Bukowski commented that the work "goes slowly because I get this detective into terrible jams and have to work him out" (*Beat*, 17). This recalls Kurt Vonnegut's *Breakfast of Champions* and the machinations of its author/character. Belane's paranoia is demonstrated by his ability to make perhaps meaningless connections, but connections that cannot be discounted in a grotesque, disjointed world. He seems especially observant and suspicious of numbers: "I got in my car and drove 5 miles west. Just to do it. Then I parked and looked around. I was parked in front of a bar. *Hades*, said the neon sign. I got out of the car, went in. There were 5 people in there. 5 miles, 5 people. Everything was coming up 5s" (*Pulp*, 179). At another bar he enters by chance, Belane stands in the doorway and preposterously solicits clues: "Has anybody here seen Cindy, Celine or the Red Sparrow?" (*Pulp*, 43). The ineptness of his method and the absurdity of the question in such a context delineate the book's philosophy. Belane, in brown derby and driving a Volkswagen Bug that suggests his place in the universal hierarchy, trusts in chance, inaction, occasional explosions of violence, and, most of all, randomness. As a tough guy, he is a clown. There is nothing else to do.

Much of the humor of *Pulp* is achieved by the distance between Belane's macho stance, with its code of action and discovery, and the purposelessness and apathy that pervade his life. Bukowski hilariously juxtaposes chapters ending with affirmation and zealous promises of action against those beginning with failure. "But I had things to do. I was Nicky Belane, private detective" (*Pulp*, 25), asserts the narrator, only to begin the next chapter with a disclaimer: "Unfortunately, I ended up at the racetrack that afternoon and that night I got drunk" (*Pulp*, 26). Little is solved or accomplished, and the novel implies that Belane's inaction may be the appropriate response to a decaying world paralyzed by death. "I had work to do. I was the best dick in L.A. *and* Hollywood. I hit the button and waited for the fucking elevator to come on up"; such a surge of ambition is consistently frustrated, usually by the detective's own (in)actions. The entire next chapter reads: "Skip the rest of the day and night here, no action, it's not worth talking about" (*Pulp*, 37). When Belane has a rare instinctive impulse—"I felt like I had better get over to the office. I felt like somebody was waiting for me"—it is incorrect. "I was wrong. There was nobody in the office. I went around and sat behind my desk" (*Pulp*, 102). The verbs used often suggest Belane's drifting. He continually "finds himself" or "ends up" somewhere other than expected, and no particular reason or significance is offered for his altered plans. When he reaches a decision, purposeful-ness is undercut by the triviality of the subject: "There wasn't even any smog that day. I moved forward with a purpose. I had decided on lunch: shrimp and fries. My feet looked good moving along the pavement" (*Pulp*, 61). This distance between voice and act is used to tremendous comic effect in the novel. Belane's confidence and self-love are impervi-ous to his ineptitude.

The novel's position that meaningful action is impossible is linked to frequent waiting, the latter both an existential fixation on death and an indication of the writer's patience. "Man was born to die. What did it mean? Hanging around and waiting. Waiting for the 'A train.' Waiting for a pair of big breasts on some August night in a Vegas hotel room. Waiting for the mouse to sing. Waiting for the snake to grow wings. Hanging around" (*Pulp*, 16). Belane's introspective mode and surreal imagination identify him as a facile poet of the tough streets, a poet who has low expectations and low opinions of human beings. "What god-damned things we were. We had to eat. And eat and eat again. We were all disgusting, doomed to our dirty little tasks. Eating and farting and scratching and smiling and celebrating holidays. . . . I pulled the covers up to my neck and waited" (*Pulp*, 89).

Belane's continual disgust is appropriate to his search for the character Louis-Ferdinand Celine. On one level, *Pulp* is a parodic homage to *Journey to the End of the Night*, a book Bukowski greatly admired. Céline's narrator confides, "I had no great opinion of myself and no ambition, all I wanted was a chance to breathe and eat a little better. I put my nameplate over the door and waited."[25] For Belane, the waiting is not so much for answers as for the passage of time and tedium. When connections arrive, they hold little significance. "I was feeling odd. Like nothing mattered, you know. Lady Death. Death. Or Celine. The game had worn me down. I'd lost my kick. Existence was not only absurd, it was plain hard work. Think of how many times you put on your underwear in a lifetime. It was appalling, it was disgusting, it was stupid" (*Pulp*, 108). The narrator's attitude in *Journey to the End of the Night* is remarkably similar. He is not as ironic as Belane but is nevertheless disgusted with waiting and routine.

> The worst part is wondering how you'll find the strength tomorrow to go on doing what you did today and have been doing for much too long, where you'll find the strength for all that stupid running around, those thousand projects that come to nothing, those attempts to escape crushing necessity. . . . Not much music left inside us for life to dance to. Our youth has gone to the ends of the earth to die in the silence of the truth. And where, I ask you, can a man escape to, when he hasn't enough madness left inside him? The truth is an endless death agony. The truth is death. (Céline, 183)

Bukowski's model for the ruined earth is a mottled and smog-choked Los Angeles at the end of the century. The character Celine is an appropriate adversary for Belane during their last days. The Frenchman's cynicism, self-scrutiny, and depth of thought distinguish him as equally anachronistic in the superficiality of Hollywood and Musso's.

The protagonist's ruminations and desultory experiences are always connected with death. "You know, I see a box boy at the supermarket, he's packing my groceries, then I see him sticking himself into his own grave along with the toilet paper, the beer and the chicken breasts" (*Pulp*, 70). Goals and enjoyment are impeded, ridiculous. "Survival seemed the only necessity. That didn't seem enough. Not with Lady Death waiting. It drove me crazy when I thought about it" (*Pulp*, 127). Death overwhelms life in *Pulp,* and a recurring joke is Belane's sexual attraction to "her." Both as an abstraction and as a sexy character, death supplies the connection between cases. After all, the novel posits, death links everything. The protagonist glumly comments on the mortuary business: "Damn good business to get into—no slack periods" (*Pulp*, 93).

Céline's novel also charts an unshakable presence of death that, once identified, cripples the ability to live fully. The searcher for the truth finds it in the shadows behind him. "I was up to my neck in the truth; death dogged my every step, so to speak. . . . Once you've been through it, you'll know what you're talking about till the end of your days" (Céline, 53). The narrator's ambiguous statement addresses the plight of the detective—one mystery involves all others, and its answer is, as Belane knows, Lady Death. The contemplation of this enigma perhaps gives some small meaning to human endeavor and again suggests the writer at work: "Often the best parts of life were when you weren't doing anything at all, just mulling it over, chewing on it. I mean, say that you figure that everything is senseless, then it can't be quite senseless because you are aware that it's senseless and your awareness of senselessness almost gives it sense. You know what I mean?" (*Pulp*, 152–53). From this comically garbled syntax, a simple truth struggles to emerge, one imparting modest value to human consciousness. Nevertheless, Belane is limited intellectually. He strives to unravel the "mystery" and gets nowhere. His head hurts. He stares at blank faces and is more effective at violence than philosophy.

Pulp hints that Belane may already be dead. Oblique comments fill the novel: "I was alive. Maybe" (*Pulp*, 19). The code name "Mr. Slow Death" (*Pulp*, 28), that Belane uses with his bookie, indicates a somnambulant stumble through life nearly indistinguishable from what will end it. His moniker identifies him as a fated companion for Lady Death. He feels that he is "three quarters dead" (*Pulp*, 170) and even sees a double of himself at the mortuary. "The casket was lined in velvet and I was smiling a waxy smile" (*Pulp*, 96). These references are related to *Pulp*'s central concern of identity. Is Celine the real Céline? Is Lady Death who she says she is, and who are the space aliens in human form? What, most importantly, is the Red Sparrow? For his part, Belane is fragmented and unsure even of his own name. "Was Celine Celine or was he somebody else? Sometimes I felt that I didn't even know who *I* was. All right, I'm Nicky Belane. But check this. Somebody could yell out, 'Hey, Harry! Harry Martel!' and I'd most likely answer, 'Yeah, what is it?' I mean, I could be anybody, what does it matter? What's in a name?" (Pulp, 14). This peculiar passage early in the novel initiates a series of misidentifications. Belane is regularly called by other names, and his frequent assertions of self and role seem as much a personal reminder of identity as they are ironic assertions of his ineffectiveness. "I had another hit of *sake*. I was coming around. . . . I was Nick Belane, super dick" (*Pulp*, 104). He seems increasingly uncertain of such a title, and this uncertainty extends to others. At a meeting between Celine and Lady Death that Belane engineers, he is hesitant. "I really don't know how to introduce you two because I'm not sure who either of you are" (*Pulp*, 109).

Finally, *Pulp*'s bawdy humor drains away. The novel's final pages reflect the tired, shocked attitude of the protagonist as his fate and the mystery of the Red Sparrow rush toward him. One reviewer noted that the several cases "dovetail into an existential nightmare."[26] Another wrote that the novel's most Bukowskian feature "is its gleefully escalating bleakness."[27] The enigmatic figure of the Red Sparrow lurks beneath the surface action of *Pulp*. At first, the sparrow seems little more than one of the novel's many in-jokes, this one concerning Bukowski's long relationship with John Martin (depicted as John Barton), Martin's faith in the writer, and Bukowski's impact on the creation and growth of Black Sparrow Press. However, the Red Sparrow soon represents more than personal authorial references and more than a plotting device to link the disparate elements of the novel. During the last quarter of *Pulp*, Belane dedicates himself exclusively, with a sense of increasing urgency and importance, to locating the Red Sparrow.

Several "red" herrings are misrepresented as the true bird, one in a horrific dream sequence that foreshadows the novel's grim conclusion. A man in a bar presents a dead pigeon to Belane and identifies it as the Red Sparrow. The nightmare ends with the bartender's gruesome and unexplained consumption of the bird. "He had the pigeon in his hands and was eating it, gnawing at it. His mouth was full of feathers and blood. He winked at me" (*Pulp*, 69). This scene makes explicit the link between red and blood and offers a glimpse of the novel's ominous subtext. Belane later considers dreams in relation to his own possible madness. His attempt to reject a symbolic interpretation of the subconscious aligns him with Bukowski's aesthetic. "Sometimes things are just what they seem to be and that's all there is to it. The best interpreter of the dream is the dreamer" (*Pulp*, 103). This thought is cloaked in another of the character's comic meditations, yet it is troubling when introduced into a novel containing aliens, personified death, and the lingering enigma of the Red Sparrow.

Nearly everyone in *Pulp* seems to have heard rumors of the bird and that Belane is searching for it, but no one knows where or what it is. He is presented with other fraudulent manifestations, first a catnip toy— suggesting another ingestion—and later a painted canary. During his search, the detective is more focused on the sparrow than any previous enterprise and connects the bird to questions involving identity and fate. "Maybe if I could find the Red Sparrow, the Red Sparrow would sing me the answer. Was I crazy? Was all this happening?" (*Pulp*, 131). He shows a childlike tenderness and affection toward the dyed sparrow foisted on him by a loan shark. "I walked over to the cage and looked at my red canary. Some of the dye was wearing off, some of the natural yellow was beginning to show through. It was a nice bird. It looked at me and I looked back. Then it made a little bird sound: 'cheep!' and somehow that made me feel good" (*Pulp*, 194). This simple relationship involves several of the novel's themes. The bird is nonhuman and therefore attractive, and it is linked with, and anticipatory of, the Red Sparrow. Its fading dye reiterates notions of uncertain identity and exploitation. The canary's call of "cheep" may even echo Belane's low hourly rate of $6.00. Moments later, he refers to his apartment of five years as "a nest, only nothing was hatching" (Pulp, 194). In a few simple strokes, Bukowski makes Belane's loneliness palpable.

Not surprisingly, one character does know the identity and location of the Red Sparrow. The bird and Lady Death appear together in the novel's abrupt conclusion. Even after an absurd life, Belane is not certain whether he wants the arbitrary death coming to him, but it arrives rapidly and without discussion. "This whole thing is a bad senseless dream" (*Pulp*, 200), he comments before the loan shark's thugs gun him down. In the moments preceding the narrator's death, the last mystery is revealed:

> Then I seemed to be hearing music, music like I'd never heard before. And then it happened. Something was taking shape, appearing before me. It was red, red, and like the music, a red I have never seen before. And there it was:
> THE RED SPARROW.
> Gigantic, glowing, beautiful. Never a sparrow so large, so real, never one so magnificent. (*Pulp*, 201)

As Belane's own "red" drains from his chest, Lady Death explicates a last few details of the plot, then concludes, "I'm leaving you with the Red Sparrow" (*Pulp*, 202).

Last, the bird represents Bukowski's own cessation. George Stade wrote that as *Pulp* progresses, "the fun thins out, the death-haunted atmosphere thickens and there is a sense of time running out." Belane moves "inexorably toward the Red Sparrow, in the way a man might move in fear and longing to embrace his own death. Belane gets 'enveloped' by the Sparrow in the way a dead writer gets absorbed by his words" (Stade, 51). Given the novel's cynicism, it is appropriate that the Red Sparrow, representative of vitality and awesome creative forces, consumes Belane. Like dye wearing off of a canary, red becomes yellow.

> This can't be true, I thought. This isn't the way it is supposed to happen. No, this isn't the way it is supposed to happen.
> Then, as I watched, the Sparrow slowly opened its beak. A huge void appeared. And within the beak was a vast yellow vortex, more dynamic than the sun, unbelievable.
> This isn't the way it happens, I thought again. (*Pulp*, 202)

Returned to the animal, then to the primordial, man is left with no solution but the final arrival of the enigma itself, no truth but the passage into death. "As parody, *Pulp* does not cut very deep. As a farewell to readers, as a gesture of rapprochement with death, as Bukowski's sendup and send-off of himself, the bio-parable cuts as deep as you would want" (Stade, 51). The author's knowledge of his imminent death and his dedication to completing *Pulp* add pathos to Belane's story. Bukowski's last novel is not his best, but it is a gift to his many readers. "The beak opened wide, the Sparrow's head moved closer and the blaze and the blare of yellow swept over and enveloped me" (*Pulp*, 202). Yellow was Charles Bukowski's favorite color.

Notes and References

Preface

1. John Martin elaborates: "The release of *Barfly* did have a huge impact on Hank's sales starting in 1987 but the real boost in his popularity began in 1994 right after his death. His obituary was carried on the front page in almost every newspaper in western Europe and Scandinavia, and in over 100 domestic newspapers. At the time of his death we had approximately 70,000 copies of his books in stock and within a month they were all sold and had to be reprinted. Since that time (1994) we have sold more Bukowski books each year than ever before."

2. *Buk: The Life and Times of Charles Bukowski*, a one-man stage play based on the writings of Bukowski, was completed by Paul Peditto in 1992. *Hank* was written by Bukowski's longtime protégé Neeli Cherkovski. Graduate studies of Bukowski include "Henry Chinaski Goes to Hell: A Journey through the Wasteland of Modern American Society," a master's thesis by Jimmie Cain, University of Mississippi, 1982; "The Grotesque Tradition in the Short Stories of Charles Bukowski," a master's thesis by James Michael Cooke, University of North Texas, 1988; and "Charles Bukowski vs. American Ways," a doctoral dissertation by David Charlson, University of Kansas, 1995.

3. *Poetry* (July 1994). *Prairie Schooner* (Summer 1994).

4. Manohla Dargis, "Goodbye, Barfly," *Village Voice,* 19 April 1994, 65.

5. Michael Andrews, "Charles Bukowski," *ONTHEBUS* 5 (Spring 1990): 164; hereafter cited in text.

6. Charles Bukowski, *You Get So Alone at Times That It Just Makes Sense* (Santa Rosa: Black Sparrow Press, 1986), 134; hereafter cited in text as *Alone*.

Chapter One

1. Robert Wennersten, "Paying for Horses: An Interview with Charles Bukowski," *London Magazine,* December 1974–January 1975, 50; hereafter cited in text.

2. Steve Richmond, *Spinning Off Bukowski* (Northville, Mich.: Sun Dog Press, 1996), 26.

3. Kevin Ring, "Charles Bukowski: Outsider Looking In," *Beat Scene* 20 (1994): 37; hereafter cited in text.

4. "The Bukowski Letters," *Letter eX: Chicago's Poetry Newsmagazine* 93 (April–May 1994): 8.

5. Gerald Locklin, "Setting Free the Buk," *Review of Contemporary Fiction* 5.3 (Fall 1985): 28; hereafter cited in text as Locklin, "Setting Free the Buk."

6. "Pen and Drink," *Sure, the Charles Bukowski Newsletter* 4 (1992): 31.

7. Kevin Ring, "Charles Bukowski: *Pulp*," *Beat Scene* 20 (1994): 40.

8. Jay Dougherty, "Charles Bukowski and the Outlaw Spirit," *Gargoyle* 35 (1988): 102; hereafter cited in text.

9. Charles Bukowski, "Charles Bukowski," interview by William Packard, in *The Poet's Craft: Interviews from the New York Quarterly,* ed. William Packard (New York: Paragon House, 1987), 321; hereafter cited in text as *NYQ.* Interview reprinted from *NYQ* 27.

10. Sean Penn, "Tough Guys Write Poetry," *Interview,* September 1987, 96; hereafter cited in text.

11. For Bukowski's interesting account of meeting Carver, see "Pen and Drink," 27–28.

12. Doren Robbins, "Drinking Wine in the Slaughterhouse with Septuagenarian Stew: For Bukowski at 71," *ONTHEBUS* 10 and 11 (1992): 282–83; hereafter cited in text.

13. Norman Mailer, "Hemingway and Miller," *Pieces and Pontifications* (Boston: Little, Brown, 1982), 86–93; quoted from 88, 91, 93. Hereafter cited in text.

14. Russell Harrison, "The Letters of Charles Bukowski," *Sure, the Charles Bukowski Newsletter* 8–9 (1993): 19.

15. Paul Ciotti, "Bukowski," *Los Angeles Times Magazine,* 22 March 1987, 12; hereafter cited in text.

16. Jack Grapes, "This Thing upon Me," *Poetry East* 34 (Fall 1992): 8; hereafter cited in text.

17. Russell Harrison, *Against the American Dream: Essays on Charles Bukowski* (Santa Rosa: Black Sparrow Press, 1994), 42; hereafter cited in text.

18. Charles Bukowski, "The Bukowski Letters," *Beat Scene* 20 (1994): 17; hereafter cited in text as *Beat.*

19. Myrna Oliver, "Charles Bukowski Dies; Poet of L.A.'s Low-Life," *Los Angeles Times,* 10 March 1994, A24.

Chapter Two

1. Neeli Cherkovski, *Hank: The Life of Charles Bukowski* (New York: Random House, 1991), 209; hereafter cited in text as Cherkovski, *Hank.*

2. Jack Byrne, "Bukowski's Chinaski: Playing Post Office," *Review of Contemporary Fiction* 5.3 (Fall 1985): 43.

3. Charles Bukowski, *Post Office* (Los Angeles: Black Sparrow Press, 1970), 19; hereafter cited in text as *Post.*

4. For all of Chinaski's proclaimed distaste for the city and crowds, the persistent implication in Bukowski's work is that an urban landscape and its odd and damned occupants are necessary for his work.

5. Loss Glazier, "Mirror of Ourselves: Notes on Bukowski's *Post Office*," *Review of Contemporary Fiction* 5.3 (Fall 1985): 39; hereafter cited in text.

6. Knut Hamsun, *Hunger* (1890; reprint, New York: Noonday Press, 1967), 181; hereafter cited in text.

7. Robert Bly, "The Art of *Hunger*," introduction to *Hunger,* by Knut Hamsun (New York: Noonday Press, 1967), xiii–xxiii; quoted xxiii, xx.

8. Isaac Bashevis Singer, "Knut Hamsun, Artist of Skepticism," introduction to *Hunger,* by Knut Hamsun (New York: Noonday Press, 1967), v–xii; quoted vii.

9. Charles Bukowski, "Preface," introduction to *Ask the Dust,* by John Fante (Santa Barbara: Black Sparrow Press, 1980), 5–7; quoted 6; hereafter cited in text as "Preface."

10. John Fante, *Ask the Dust* (1939; reprint, Santa Barbara: Black Sparrow Press, 1980), 18; hereafter cited in text.

11. Charles Bukowski, *Factotum* (Santa Barbara: Black Sparrow Press, 1975), 64; hereafter cited in text as *Factotum*.

12. The decade when Bukowski ceased to write, roughly from his mid-twenties to his mid-thirties, is the only large period of his life left unchronicled by a novel. When assembled chronologically according to biography, *Ham on Rye*, *Factotum*, *Post Office*, *Women*, and *Hollywood* account for most of the author's life. Regarding the "lost decade," however, the *Barfly* screenplay is the only lengthy document, and even there Chinaski composes verse. However much the act of writing may recede into the background, there is no Chinaski novel where it is not present. Writing is integral to the personality of Bukowski's persona.

13. Charles Bukowski, *Women* (Santa Barbara: Black Sparrow Press, 1978), 82; hereafter cited in text as *Women*.

14. Jimmie Cain, "*Women*: The Siren Calls of Boredom," *Review of Contemporary Fiction* 5.3 (Fall 1985): 9.

15. It is difficult to understand an unqualified comment such as Neeli Cherkovski's that *Women* contains "no hint of misogyny . . ." (Cherkovski, *Hank: The Life of Charles Bukowski,* 264).

16. Charles Bukowski, *Ham on Rye* (Santa Barbara: Black Sparrow Press, 1982), 9; hereafter cited in text as *Ham*.

17. Ernest Fontana, "Bukowski's *Ham on Rye* and the Los Angeles Novel," *Review of Contemporary Fiction* 5.3 (Fall 1985): 5; hereafter cited in text.

18. Chinaski's sports fantasies abruptly end after his graduation from high school. He abandons such adolescent daydreams of herohood as he moves into adult life and begins writing seriously.

19. Consider this passage from *Ham on Rye*: "I really felt like puking when I thought that I had started off as my father's juice" (54). Such a sentence could, with little alteration, be uttered by Billy Pilgrim in *Slaughterhouse-Five*. Bukowski's stylistic similarity to Vonnegut also appears in other novels, particularly *Post Office*.

20. " 'Don't you love your mother, dear boy?' 'No. . . . I don't love anybody,' Krebs said. It wasn't any good. He couldn't tell her, he couldn't make

her see it. It was silly to have said it" (Ernest Hemingway, "Soldier's Home," in *Complete Short Stories of Ernest Hemingway* [New York: Scribners, 1987], 116); "I have noticed that doctors who fail in the practice of medicine have a tendency to seek one another's company and aid in consultation. . . . These were three such doctors" (Ernest Hemingway, *A Farewell to Arms* [New York: Scribner's, 1929], 95).

21.   James Thurber, *My Life and Hard Times* (1933; reprint, New York: Harper & Row, 1973), xv–xvii; hereafter cited in text.

22.   Thurber even specifically notes that such a person, the humorist writer, will "walk into the wrong apartments" (xv), a scene that occurs with Chinaski in both *Factotum* and *Barfly*.

Chapter Three

1.   Julian Smith, "Charles Bukowski and the Avant-Garde," *Review of Contemporary Fiction* 5.3 (Fall 1985): 56; hereafter cited in text.

2.   Charles Bukowski, *Screams from the Balcony: Selected Letters 1960–1970,* ed. Seamus Cooney (Santa Rosa: Black Sparrow Press, 1993), 338; hereafter cited in text as *Screams.*

3.   Charles Bukowski, *Notes of a Dirty Old Man* (San Francisco: City Lights Books, 1973), 7; hereafter cited in text as *Notes.*

4.   Steve Richmond, untitled essay, *Second Coming* 2.3 (1974): 6.

5.   Compare this to a later, similar assertion in Bukowski's work: "You also told Mr. Pelvington that only two men were needed on the loading dock instead of ten, and that it would cut down on the theft if each employee was given one live lobster to take home each night in a specially constructed cage that could be carried on buses and streetcars" (*Factotum*, 195).

6.   Jerry Kamstra, "Buk," *Second Coming* 2.3 (1974): 12.

7.   Charles Bukowski, *Tales of Ordinary Madness* (San Francisco: City Lights Books, issued as single volume 1983), 204; hereafter cited in text as *Tales.*

8.   Translated in Harrison, 252.

9.   Charles Bukowski, *The Most Beautiful Woman in Town* (San Francisco: City Lights Books, issued as single volume 1983), 230; hereafter cited in text as *Beautiful.*

10.   Ernest Hemingway, *A Moveable Feast* (New York: Scribners, 1964), 207–8.

11.   David Mamet, "Gems from a Gambler's Bookshelf," *Make-Believe Town* (Boston: Little, Brown, 1996), 7–20; quoted 19.

12.   David Glover, "A Day at the Races: Gambling and Luck in Bukowski's Fiction," *Review of Contemporary Fiction* 5.3 (Fall 1985): 33.

13.   Stephen Kessler, "Notes on a Dirty Old Man," *Review of Contemporary Fiction* 5.3 (Fall 1985): 63.

14.   The exceptions are three longer stories, composites of short scenes, that end the book. Two of these were published as independent chapbooks by

Douglas Blazek, editor of *Ole*. The three are the loosest and apparently most autobiographical stories in *South of No North* and its least effective.

15. Charles Bukowski, *South of No North* (Los Angeles: Black Sparrow Press, 1973), 28; hereafter cited in text as *South*.

16. Norman Weinstein, "*South of No North*: Bukowski in Deadly Earnest," *Review of Contemporary Fiction* 5.3 (Fall 1985): 52; hereafter cited in text.

17. Ernest Hemingway, "The Short, Happy Life of Francis Macomber," in *Complete Short Stories of Ernest Hemingway* (New York: Scribners, 1987), 5–28; quoted 18.

18. Charles Bukowski, *Hot Water Music* (Santa Barbara: Black Sparrow Press, 1983), 105; hereafter cited in text as *Music*.

19. Jack Byrne, "Book Reviews," *Review of Contemporary Fiction* 11.1 (Spring 1991): 314.

20. Lois E. Nesbitt, "Fiction," *New York Times Book Review*, 25 November 1990, 19.

21. Lawrence Rungren, "Literature," *Library Journal*, 15 June 1990, 112.

22. Charles Bukowski, *Septuagenarian Stew: Stories and Poems* (Santa Rosa: Black Sparrow Press, 1990), 87; hereafter cited in text as *Stew*.

23. "Poetry," *Publishers Weekly*, 11 May 1990, 255.

24. Ernest Hemingway, "Fifty Grand," in *Complete Short Stories of Ernest Hemingway* (New York: Scribners, 1987), 231–49; quoted 249.

Chapter Four

1. Lee Fulton, "See Bukowski Run," *Small Press Review* 16 (May 1973): 27; hereafter cited in text.

2. Bob Graalman, "Charles Bukowski," *Dictionary of Literary Biography vol. 5: American Poets since World War II* (Detroit: Gale, 1980), 113.

3. Charles Bukowski, *The Bukowski/Purdy Letters: 1964–1974*, ed. Seamus Cooney (Ontario: Paget Press, 1983), 66; hereafter cited in text as *Purdy*.

4. Although the collection of four volumes selects from an 18-year period, it is still shorter in pages than any single book of Bukowski's verse from the mid-1970s onward except for *Play the Piano Drunk like a Percussion Instrument Until the Fingers Begin to Bleed a Bit*, another collection containing some earlier poems. The tendency of the contemporary reader is, justifiably, to take *Burning in Water, Drowning in Flame* as a single, representative volume of the poet's earlier work. Nevertheless, the density and texture of many of these poems make it clear that much more time was necessary for the composition of this volume than a thicker collection of Bukowski's later poems.

5. Walt Whitman, "One's Self I Sing," lines 1–3.

6. Neeli Cherkovski, *Whitman's Wild Children* (Venice, Calif.: Lapis Press, 1988), 14; hereafter cited in text as Cherkovski, *Whitman's Wild Children*.

7. Charles Bukowski, *Burning in Water, Drowning in Flames: Selected Poems 1955–1973* (Santa Barbara: Black Sparrow Press, 1974), 190; hereafter cited in text as *Burning*.

8. Charles Bukowski, "He Beats His Women," *Second Coming* 2.3 (1974): 68; hereafter cited in text as "His Women."

9. Jimmie Cain, "Bukowski's Imagist Roots," *West Georgia College Review* 19 (1987): 15.

10. Robinson Jeffers, *Collected Poems of Robinson Jeffers: Volume Two 1928–1938,* ed. Tim Hunt (Stanford, Calif.: Stanford University Press, 1989), 526; hereafter cited in text as Jeffers, *Collected Poems*.

11. Bukowski refers to Jeffers as his "god" in the brief, unnumbered preface to *Longshot Pomes for Broke Players* (1962) and in a 1960 letter to Jory Sherman (*Screams*, 13).

12. Robinson Jeffers, *Selected Letters of Robinson Jeffers,* ed. Ann N. Ridgeway, 5th printing (New York: Random House, 1968), 16; hereafter cited in text as Jeffers, *Selected Letters*.

13. Hugh Fox, *Charles Bukowski: A Critical and Bibliographical Study* (Somerville, Mass.: Abyss Publications, 1969), 37; hereafter cited in text.

14. Robinson Jeffers, *Collected Poems of Robinson Jeffers: Volume Three 1939–1962,* ed. Tim Hunt (Stanford, Calif.: Stanford University Press, 1991), 204.

15. Pablo Neruda, "The Lamb and the Pinecone" interview of Neruda by Bly, in *Neruda and Vallejo: Selected Poems,* ed. Robert Bly (Boston: Beacon Press, 1993), pgs. 156–164, quoted 157; hereafter cited in text as Bly, *Neruda and Vallejo*.

16. Robert Bly, "Refusing to Be Theocritus," *Neruda and Vallejo: Selected Poems* (Boston: Beacon Press, 1993), 3–15, quoted 6; hereafter cited in text.

17. John William Corrington, foreword to *It Catches My Heart in Its Hands,* by Charles Bukowski (New Orleans: Loujon Press, 1963), 5–10, quoted 5.

18. Robert Peters, "Gab Poetry, or Duck vs. Nightingale Music: Charles Bukowski," in *Where the Bee Sucks: Workers, Drones and Queens of Contemporary American Poetry* (Santa Maria, Calif.: Asylum Arts, 1994), 61; hereafter cited in text.

19. Jim Schwada, "Charles Bukowski's *Man the Humping Guns: The Roominghouse Madrigals,*" *Sure, the Charles Bukowski Newsletter* 7 (1993): 22.

20. Charles Bukowski, *The Roominghouse Madrigals: Early Selected Poems 1946–1966* (Santa Rosa: Black Sparrow Press, 1988), 5; hereafter in text as *Madrigals*.

21. Its final lines are included as a voice-over in the screenplay *Barfly*.

22. Charles Bukowski, *The Days Run Away like Wild Horses over the Hills* (Los Angeles: Black Sparrow Press, 1969), 13; hereafter cited in text as *Days*.

23. Charles Bukowski, *Mockingbird Wish Me Luck* (Los Angeles: Black Sparrow Press, 1972), 14; hereafter cited in text as *Mockingbird*.

24. Charles Bukowski, *Play the Piano Drunk like a Percussion Instrument Until the Fingers Begin to Bleed a Bit* (Santa Barbara: Black Sparrow Press, 1979), 59–60; hereafter cited in text as *Piano*.

Chapter Five

1. Of course, this distinction must be taken as partly arbitrary. In style and content, *Love Is a Dog from Hell* is distinct from much of Bukowski's work in the 1980s and is more in line with his approach during the previous decade.

2. Charles Bukowski, *Living on Luck: Selected Letters 1960s–1970s,* ed. Seamus Cooney (Santa Rosa: Black Sparrow Press, 1995), 234; hereafter cited in text as *Luck.*

3. Roger Mitchell, "Poetry," *Library Journal,* 15 February 1978, 465.

4. Any reader skeptical as to how closely many of these poems parallel the author's emotional turmoil should read Bukowski's fragmented, wildly shifting, and finally touching notes to Pamela Brandes from 1976. The older man's appeal to "Scarlet" (also fictionalized in *Women*) is answered by a deafening, unequivocal silence. See *Luck,* 216–18.

5. Charles Bukowski, *Love Is a Dog from Hell: Poems 1974–1977* (Santa Barbara: Black Sparrow Press, 1977), 13; hereafter cited in text as *Love.*

6. Again, this finds various parallels in the Bukowski letters collected in *Living on Luck.* The author readily engages in letter swapping with a number of women. Particularly interesting are a series of letters written to Patricia Connell in 1972. Bukowski is charming, avuncular, amusing, explicit, alternately tentative and probing, and obviously interested sexually. The letters end abruptly, indicating that the two finally had their long-anticipated meeting. A telling silence ensues.

7. Glen Esterly, "Buk: The Pock-Marked Poetry of Charles Bukowski," *Rolling Stone,* 17 June 1976, 34; hereafter cited in text.

8. The tournefortia is defined as "a large tropical tree, ideally suited to the Southern California climate, that produces small delicate flowers and a kind of fleshy fruit" (Charles Bukowski, *Dangling in the Tournefortia* [Santa Barbara: Black Sparrow Press, 1981], 6); hereafter cited in text as *Dangling.*

9. Gerald Locklin, *"Dangling in the Tournefortia," American Book Review* 4.5 (July–August 1982): 6; hereafter cited in text as Locklin, *Tournefortia.*

10. Gerald Locklin, "Bukowski's *War All the Time* and *Horses Don't Bet on People and Neither Do I," Review of Contemporary Fiction* 5.3 (Fall 1985): 36; hereafter cited in text as Locklin, *War All the Time.*

11. Charles Bukowski, *War All the Time* (Santa Barbara: Black Sparrow Press, 1984), 37; hereafter cited in text as *War.*

12. Thorstein Veblen, *The Theory of the Leisure Class* (1899; reprint, New York: Augustus M. Kelley, 1965), 36, 42; hereafter cited in text.

13. Raymond Carver, *Ultramarine* (New York: Random House, 1986), 59.

14. Jules Smith, "A Singular Self," *Times Literary Supplement,* 7 September 1990, 956.

15. Sherwood Anderson, *Winesburg, Ohio* (New York: Random House, 1919), 3.

16. Rochelle Ratner, "Poetry," *Library Journal,* 15 April 1992, 96.

17. Jules Smith, "Bad Times Again," *Times Literary Supplement,* 18 December 1992, 19; hereafter cited in text as Smith, "Bad Times Again."

18. Charles Bukowski, *The Last Night of the Earth Poems* (Santa Rosa: Black Sparrow Press, 1992), 148; hereafter cited in text as *Night.*

19. e. e. cummings, *Selected Poems 1923–1958* (London: Faber and Faber, 1960), 4.

20. The tranquil, meditative quality of Bukowski's writing evenings is indicated by several poems during his later years written to the Buddha on his desk—a grinning, elusive, accepting figure analogous to the poet.

21. Robert Sandarg, "The Classical Buk," *Sure, the Charles Bukowski Newsletter* 3 (December 1991): 22.

22. And, it should be noted, an artistic act not in competition with Bukowski's own literary pursuits.

Chapter Six

1. Jay Dougherty, "Translating Bukowski and the Beats," *Gargoyle* 35 (1988): 78.

2. Charles Bukowski, *Shakespeare Never Did This* (1979; reprint, Santa Rosa: Black Sparrow Press, 1995), sec. 23; hereafter cited in text as *Shakespeare* and according to the book's 25 sections (pages are otherwise unnumbered).

3. "Nice" is also wordplay regarding Bukowski's effort to be "nice" to Linda's kind but unperceptive mother, Serena.

4. Chris Hodenfield, "Gin-Soaked Boy: Charles Bukowski Interviewed," *Film Comment,* July–August 1987, 56.

5. Charles Bukowski, *The Movie: "Barfly"* (Santa Rosa: Black Sparrow Press, 1987), 108; hereafter cited in text as *Barfly.*

6. Charles Bukowski, "Upon the Mathematics of the Breath and the Way," in *All's Normal Here: A Charles Bukowski Primer,* ed. Loss Pequeño Glazier (Fremont, Calif.: Ruddy Duck Press, 1985), 84.

7. Tom McDonough, "Down and (Far) Out," *American Film,* November 1987, 29.

8. *Barfly,* directed by Barbet Schroeder, Cannon Films, 1987, quote in film only.

9. The blending of hatred and love that Louie represents is demonstrated by his wife's willing participation in their brutal performances, and also by his last mention in the screenplay. After being inadvertently stabbed by Henry during a fight, Louie is carried out of his room "smoking a cigarette" (*Barfly,* 115), his intercourse of violence fulfilled.

10. That the additional line "I'm going to *be* one" is added to the film before "Give her a beer" merely emphasizes this point. Rourke's delivery is obviously ironic.

11. William Gargan, "Book Reviews: Fiction," *Library Journal,* 15 May 1989, 87.

12. Jack Byrne, "Book Reviews," *Review of Contemporary Fiction* 10.1 (Spring 1990): 302.

13. Toby Moore, "Unreal City," *Times Literary Supplement,* 11–17 August 1989, 877.

14. Charles Bukowski, *Hollywood* (Santa Rosa: Black Sparrow Press, 1989), 219; hereafter cited in text as *Hollywood.*

15. Molly Haskell, "So Much Genius! So Little Money!" *New York Times Book Review,* 11 June 1987, 11; hereafter cited in text.

16. Pauline Kael, "The Current Cinema: Cons," *New Yorker,* 2 November 1987, 137; hereafter cited in text.

17. Gerald Locklin, "In the Presence of Greatness: The Bukowski/ *Barfly* Narrative," (1989; reprinted in *Charles Bukowski: A Sure Bet* [Sudbury, Mass.: Water Row Books, 1996], 46); hereafter cited in text as Locklin, "Bukowski/*Barfly.*"

18. Margy Rochlin, "Acting Out," *American Film,* November 1987, 59; hereafter cited in text.

19. "Paperbacks: Fiction Originals," *Publishers Weekly,* 21 April 1989, 84.

20. Gundolf S. Freyermuth, "Portrait of a Dirty Old Man Dying" (1996, unpublished in English), 89; hereafter cited in text. Published in Germany as *"Das war's": Letzte Worte mit Charles Bukowski* (Hamburg: Rasch and Röhring Verlag, 1996). With photographs by Michael Montfort.

21. John G. Cawelti, *Adventure, Mystery, and Romance* (Chicago: University of Chicago Press, 1976), 184; hereafter cited in text.

22. "Disgusting" is one of *Pulp*'s most repeated words, used by Belane and others.

23. George Stade, "Death Comes for the Detective," *New York Times Book Review,* 5 June 1994, 51; hereafter cited in text.

24. Charles Bukowski, *Pulp* (Santa Rosa: Black Sparrow Press, 1994), 79; hereafter cited in text as *Pulp.*

25. Louis-Ferdinand Céline, *Journey to the End of the Night,* trans. Ralph Manheim (1932; reprint, London: John Calder, 1988), 215; hereafter cited in text. *Pulp* spells the author's name *Celine,* without an accent mark.

26. Ron Antonucci, "Book Review: Fiction," *Library Journal,* 1 June 1994, 154.

27. "Books Briefly Noted: Fiction," *New Yorker,* 15 August 1994, 78.

Selected Bibliography

PRIMARY WORKS

Poems

At Terror Street and Agony Way. Los Angeles: Black Sparrow Press, 1968.
Bone Palace Ballet. Santa Rosa, Calif.: Black Sparrow Press, 1997.
Burning in Water, Drowning in Flame: Selected Poems 1955–1973. Santa Barbara: Black Sparrow Press, 1974. In addition to new poems, contains poems from *It Catches My Heart in Its Hands*, *Crucifix in a Deathhand*, and *At Terror Street and Agony Way*.
Cold Dogs in the Courtyard. Chicago: Literary Times-Cyfoeth, 1965.
Crucifix in a Deathhand. New Orleans: Loujon Press, 1965.
Dangling in the Tournefortia. Santa Barbara: Black Sparrow Press, 1981.
The Days Run Away like Wild Horses over the Hills. Los Angeles, Black Sparrow Press, 1969.
Flower, Fist and Bestial Wail. Eureka, Calif.: Hearse Press, 1960.
The Genius of the Crowd. Cleveland: 7 Flowers Press, 1966.
It Catches My Heart in Its Hands. New Orleans: Loujon Press, 1963.
The Last Night of the Earth Poems. Santa Rosa: Black Sparrow Press, 1992.
Longshot Pomes for Broke Players. New York: 7 Poets Press, 1962.
Love Is a Dog from Hell: Poems 1974–1977. Santa Barbara: Black Sparrow Press, 1977.
Mockingbird Wish Me Luck. Los Angeles: Black Sparrow Press, 1972.
Play the Piano Drunk like a Percussion Instrument Until the Fingers Begin to Bleed a Bit. Santa Barbara: Black Sparrow Press, 1979.
Poems Written before Jumping out of an 8 Story Window. Glendale, Calif.: Poetry X/Change/Litmus, 1968.
The Roominghouse Madrigals: Early Selected Poems 1946–1966. Santa Rosa: Black Sparrow Press, 1988.
Run with the Hunted. Chicago: Midwest Press, 1962.
War All the Time: Poems 1981–1984. Santa Barbara: Black Sparrow Press, 1984.
You Get So Alone at Times That It Just Makes Sense. Santa Rosa: Black Sparrow Press, 1986.

Poems and Short Stories

Betting on the Muse: Poems and Stories. Santa Rosa: Black Sparrow Press, 1996.
Septuagenarian Stew: Stories and Poems. Santa Rosa: Black Sparrow Press, 1990.

Short Stories

All the Assholes in the World and Mine. Bensenville, Ill.: Ole Press, 1966.
Confessions of a Man Insane Enough to Live with Beasts. Bensenville, Ill.: Ole Press, 1965.
The Day It Snowed in L.A. Santa Barbara, Calif.: Paget Press, 1986.
Erections, Ejaculations, Exhibitions and General Tales of Ordinary Madness. San Francisco: City Lights Books, 1972; reprinted in 1983 as two books: *The Most Beautiful Woman in the Town* and *Tales of Ordinary Madness.*
Hot Water Music. Santa Barbara: Black Sparrow Press, 1983.
South of No North. Los Angeles: Black Sparrow Press, 1973.

Novels

Factotum. Santa Barbara: Black Sparrow Press, 1975.
Ham on Rye. Santa Barbara: Black Sparrow Press, 1982.
Hollywood. Santa Rosa: Black Sparrow Press, 1989.
Post Office. Los Angeles: Black Sparrow Press, 1971.
Pulp. Santa Rosa: Black Sparrow Press, 1994.
Women. Santa Barbara: Black Sparrow Press, 1978.

Screenplay

The Movie: "Barfly." Santa Rosa: Black Sparrow Press, 1987. Photographs by Michael Montfort and Andrew Cooper. Published in earlier form, Toronto: Paget Press, 1984.

Letters

The Bukowski/Purdy Letters: 1964–1974. Edited by Seamus Cooney. Sutton West, Ontario: Paget Press, 1983. A fascinating decade of correspondence between Bukowski and Canadian poet Al Purdy.
Screams from the Balcony: Selected Letters 1960–1970. Edited by Seamus Cooney. Santa Rosa: Black Sparrow Press, 1993.
Living on Luck: Selected Letters 1960s–1970s. Edited by Seamus Cooney. Santa Rosa: Black Sparrow Press, 1995.

Nonfiction and Journalism

Notes of a Dirty Old Man. North Hollywood: Essex House, 1969; reprint, San Francisco: City Lights Books, 1973.
Shakespeare Never Did This. San Francisco: City Lights Books, 1979; reprint, with additional text, Santa Rosa: Black Sparrow Press, 1995. Photographs by Michael Montfort.

Collected Writings

Run with the Hunted: A Charles Bukowski Reader. Edited by John Martin. New York: HarperCollins Publishers, 1993.

Audio and Video Recordings

Bukowski at Bellevue. Santa Rosa: Black Sparrow Press, 1998. Video recording of very early reading from 1970.

Bukowski Reads His Poetry. Santa Rosa: Black Sparrow Graphic Arts, 1995. Compact disc 1001 features Bukowski reading some of his best-known poems.

The Charles Bukowski Tapes. Directed by Barbet Schroeder. Lagoon Video. These interviews, conducted and filmed by Barbet Schroeder in the mid-1980s, were shown on French television in these three- to five-minute segments. The double video, which runs for four hours, is divided into 52 topics ranging from "The Masses Are Always Wrong" to "Elizabeth Taylor."

Hostage. Rhino Records, 1994. Compact disc reissue of Freeway 1058, 1985. Live reading at Redondo Beach, Calif., April 1980.

Run with the Hunted. Caedmon Audio, 1993. Cassette of 1992 recording by Bukowski released in conjunction with the HarperCollins anthology.

Essays

"He Beats His Women." *Second Coming* 2.3 (1974): 67–69.

"Preface." Introduction to *Ask the Dust,* by John Fante, 5–7. Santa Barbara: Black Sparrow Press, 1980.

"Upon the Mathematics of the Breath and the Way." In *All's Normal Here: A Charles Bukowski Primer,* edited by Loss Pequeño Glazier. Fremont, Calif.: Ruddy Duck Press, 1985.

Papers

There is a collection of Bukowski's papers at the University of California, Santa Barbara.

SECONDARY SOURCES

Andrews, Michael. "Charles Bukowski." *ONTHEBUS* 5, no. 2.1 (Spring 1990): 162–76. Although the exact date of this interview is uncertain, this is a lively and lengthy discussion between Andrews, Bukowski, and the author's wife Linda.

Antonucci, Ron. "Book Reviews: Fiction." *Library Journal,* 1 June 1994, 154. A single-paragraph review of *Pulp*.

"*Bas Ventre* by Theatre la Chamaille." *Drama Review* 28.1 (Spring 1984): 62–76. Reproduction of the script of *Bas Ventre* in a "French Theatre" issue of the *Drama Review*. The performance piece was a composite of writings by Bukowski, Baudelaire, Beckett, Burroughs, Joyce, and Chekhov. With production photographs.

"Books Briefly Noted: Fiction." *New Yorker,* 15 August 1994, 78. A single-paragraph review of *Pulp*.

Bukowski, Charles. "The Bukowski Letters." *Letter eX: Chicago's Poetry News-magazine* 93 (April–May 1994): 6–8. A series of interesting and often lengthy avuncular letters written by Bukowski from 1990–1992 to Paul Peditto, author of the stage show *Buk: The Life and Times of Charles Bukowski*.

———. "The Bukowski Letters." *Beat Scene* 20 (1994): 14–18. Letters written from 1990 to 1993 to Kevin Ring, editor of *Beat Scene*. Among the topics are Bukowski's thoughts on the Beats and on the writing of *Pulp*.

Byrne, Jack. "Bukowski's Chinaski: Playing Post Office." *Review of Contemporary Fiction* 5.3 (Fall 1985): 43–51. An overview of Bukowski's history and reception and the labor theme in *Post Office*. Extensive quotes from primary and secondary sources.

———. "Book Reviews." *Review of Contemporary Fiction* 10.1 (Spring 1990): 301–3. Byrne's positive review of *Hollywood* includes a long quotation from the novel and explains parallels between *Barfly* and the fictionalized *The Dance of Jim Beam*.

———. "Book Reviews." *Review of Contemporary Fiction* 11.1 (Spring 1991): 314. A praising, lengthy paragraph review of *Septuagenarian Stew*.

Cain, Jimmie. "Bukowski's Imagist Roots." *West Georgia College Review* 19 (1987): 10–17. Cain traces the imagist influence, especially that of William Carlos Williams, on Bukowski.

———. "*Women*: The Siren Calls of Boredom." *Review of Contemporary Fiction* 5.3 (Fall 1985): 9–14. This essay considers the development of the Chinaski persona through the character's relationships with women.

Canby, Vincent. "Alienation as Somber Poetic Spectacle in 'Cold Moon.' " *New York Times,* 22 April 1992, B3. Canby gives a generally positive review to Patrick Bouchitey's *Cold Moon*, a French film based on the Bukowski short stories "The Copulating Mermaid of Venice" and "Trouble with the Battery." Canby briefly compares Bouchitey's more grim and solemn film with *Barfly*.

"Charles Bukowski." In *The Poet's Craft: Interviews from the New York Quarterly,* edited by William Packard, 318–23. New York: Paragon House, 1987. Interview reprinted from *NYQ*. Bukowski discusses such topics as revision and his persona.

Cherkovski, Neeli. *Whitman's Wild Children*. Venice, Calif.: Lapis Press, 1988. Even by Bukowski's own account, this study of various contemporary poets is superior to the disappointing biography *Hank*. The book's first chapter (30+ pages) is a reminiscence of Cherkovski's history with Bukowski and an introduction to the poet's primary themes.

———. *Hank: The Life of Charles Bukowski*. New York: Random House, 1991. An uneven but informative full-length biography of Bukowski, set in the context of his relationship with longtime follower Cherkovski.

Christy, Jim, and Claude Powell. *The Buk Book: Musings on Charles Bukowski*. Toronto: ECW Press, 1997. A small book/pamphlet of biographical anecdotes regarding Bukowski. Christy's text is lively, but loose and dot-ted with inaccuracies. More notable are the 20+ photographs of Bukowski taken by Powell in the early 1970s.

Ciotti, Paul. "Bukowski." *Los Angeles Times Magazine,* 22 March 1987, 12. A long and interesting magazine feature based on interviews with Bukowski, John Martin, and others. Includes photographs and two reproduced poems.

Combs, Richard. "Off the Page." *Times Literary Supplement,* 11 March 1988, 281. A review of *Barfly* that briefly compares it to Norman Mailer's film *Tough Guys Don't Dance.*

Conroy, Jack. "A Skidrow Poet." *American Book Collector* (February 1996): 5. An early, praising review of *Crucifix in a Deathhand* and *Cold Dogs in the Courtyard,* with special mention of *Crucifix*'s elaborate printing.

Corrington, John William. Foreword to *It Catches My Heart In Its Hands,* by Charles Bukowski, 5–10. New Orleans: Loujon Press, 1963.

Cytrynbaum, Pamela. "Rhythm, Dance, Quickness." *New York Times Book Review,* 11 June 1987, 11. This brief sidebar article to Molly Haskell's "So Much Genius! So Little Money!" quotes Bukowski on Hollywood and writing.

Dargis, Manohla. "Goodbye, Barfly." *Village Voice,* 19 April 1994, 65. A reflection on Bukowski's death and Dargis's experience with the deceased author's works.

Dorbin, Sanford. *A Bibliography of Charles Bukowski.* Los Angeles: Black Sparrow Press, 1969. A fairly comprehensive listing of Bukowski primary and secondary works up to 1969.

Dougherty, Jay. "Charles Bukowski and the Outlaw Spirit." *Gargoyle* 35 (1988): 92–103. An interview with Bukowski in which he discusses, among other topics, craft, academicians, and John Martin's role in shaping the poetry collections. With photographs and reproductions of letter typescripts.

——. "Translating Bukowski and the Beats." *Gargoyle* 35 (1988): 66–86. A long, informative interview with Carl Weissner, Bukowski's German translator and European agent. Weissner considers his relationship with Bukowski, the craft of translation, and Bukowski's reception in Germany. Includes photographs and reproductions of typescript letters from Bukowski to Weissner.

Dougherty, Margot. "Boozehound Poet Charles Bukowski Writes a Hymn to Himself in *Barfly,* and Hollywood Starts Singing Too." *People,* 16 November 1987, 79–80. A summary of Bukowski's history and lore with quotes from the author concerning his late success.

Esterly, Glenn. "Buk: The Pock-Marked Poetry of Charles Bukowski." *Rolling Stone,* 17 June 1976, 28–34. One of the first lengthy articles in a national magazine to consider Bukowski's life and work. Includes photographs and excerpts from poems.

Fontana, Ernest. "Bukowski's *Ham on Rye* and the Los Angeles Novel." *Review of Contemporary Fiction* 5.3 (Fall 1985): 4–8. Places Bukowski's fourth novel in the tradition of Los Angeles literature.

Fox, Hugh. *Charles Bukowski: A Critical and Bibliographical Study*. Somerville, Mass.: Abyss Publications, 1969. An early account of Bukowski's poetry. Even in 1969, Fox demonstrates the difficulty of a complete bibliographical index to Bukowski's huge number of periodical publications. Limited, numbered edition of 300.

———. "The Living Underground: Charles Bukowski." *North American Review* (Fall 1969): 57–58. A brief essay contrasting the surrealistic and poseur sides of Bukowski's poetry and also recounting early visits with the poet.

Freyermuth, Gundolf S. "Portrait of a Dirty Old Man Dying." Unpublished manuscript. 1996. Freyermuth, a journalist and novelist, spent several hours with Bukowski the day before his 73rd and last birthday. Freyermuth has developed this interview into an insightful study that is particularly valuable for its overview of Bukowski's critical and popular reputation in Germany. Among the topics Bukowski discusses are his failing health and the recently completed *Pulp*. An excerpt of Freyermuth's manuscript was published in the March 1996 issue of *Buzz*. Published in its entirety in Germany, with photographs by Michael Montfort, under the title *"Das war's": Letzte Worte mit Charles Bukowski* (Hamburg: Rasch and Röhring Verlag, 1996).

Fulton, Lee. "See Bukowski Run." *Small Press Review* 4.4, no. 16 (May 1973): 2+. A seven-page critical overview of Bukowski in a special issue, edited by Tony Quagliano, devoted to Bukowski.

Gargan, William. "Book Reviews: Fiction." *Library Journal,* 15 May 1989, 87. A single-paragraph review that highly recommends *Hollywood*.

Glazier, Loss. "Mirror of Ourselves: Notes on Bukowski's *Post Office*." *Review of Contemporary Fiction* 5.3 (Fall 1985): 39–42. This article and review traces Bukowski's use of biographical materials in *Post Office* and discusses briefly the durability of the Chinaski character as antihero.

Glover, David. "A Day at the Races: Gambling and Luck in Bukowski's Fiction." *Review of Contemporary Fiction* 5.3 (Fall 1985): 32–33. A brief article on the importance of luck and gambling in Bukowski's fiction, particularly *Post Office*.

Graalman, Bob. "Charles Bukowski." In *Dictionary of Literary Biography vol. 5: American Poets since World War II*. Detroit: Gale, 1980. An intelligent introductory essay on Bukowski, including primary bibliography, photograph, and reproduction of "The Lady in Red" typescript.

Grapes, Jack. "This Thing upon Me." *Poetry East* 34 (Fall 1992): 7–23. Using recollections of his father and memories of his first readings of Bukowski, Grapes praises *It Catches My Heart In Its Hands* and Bukowski in general.

Harrison, Russell. "The Letters of Charles Bukowski." *Sure, the Charles Bukowski Newsletter* 8–9 (1993): 17–29. An insightful essay on Bukowski's early letters and how their unguarded aspect is revelatory of the author's aesthetic and his self-doubts.

———. *Against the American Dream: Essays on Charles Bukowski*. Santa Rosa: Black Sparrow Press, 1994. This is the first scholarly, full-length study of

Bukowski and is valuable reading. Harrison pursues in detail the working-class consciousness in Bukowski's poetry, focusing especially on the author's work during the 1980s.

Haskell, Molly. "So Much Genius! So Little Money!" *New York Times Book Review,* 11 June 1987, 11. A lengthy, well-written, and laudatory review of *Hollywood* by the film critic.

Hodenfield, Chris. "Gin-Soaked Boy: Charles Bukowski Interviewed." *Film Comment,* July–August 1987, 53. An excellent six-page interview, largely concerning Bukowski's views on films and the background and making of *Barfly.*

Joyce, William. *Miller, Bukowski, and Their Enemies: Essays on Contemporary Culture.* Greensboro, N.C.: Avisson Press, 1996. Joyce's book contains a loosely written but interesting 25-page essay on Bukowski that covers such topics as Bukowski and W. C. Fields, Bukowski as outsider, and Joyce's disappointment over the biography *Hank.*

Kael, Pauline. "The Current Cinema: Night Life." *New Yorker,* 21 March 1983, 118–21. A positive review of Marco Ferreri's *Tales of Ordinary Madness,* based on the life and works of Bukowski. Kael is especially enthusiastic about Ben Gazzara's performance in the lead role of "Charles Serking."

———. "The Current Cinema: Cons." *New Yorker,* 2 November 1987, 137–40. Kael's thoughtful but finally negative review of *Barfly* discusses why the critic prefers Marco Ferreri's 1981 film adaptation of Bukowski's *Tales of Ordinary Madness.*

Kaganoff, Penny. "Poetry." *Publishers Weekly,* 11 May 1990, 254–55. A single-paragraph review of *Septuagenarian Stew.*

Kamstra, Jerry. "Buk." *Second Coming* 2.3 (1974): 12–13. Kamstra's unqualified praise for Bukowski makes special note of his move into short fiction.

Kessler, Stephen. "Notes on a Dirty Old Man." *Review of Contemporary Fiction* 5.3 (Fall 1985): 60–63. Kessler recounts meeting Bukowski and then offers brief comments on several subjects, including the author's use of the mundane.

Locklin, Gerald. "*Dangling in the Tournefortia.*" *American Book Review* 4.5 (July–August 1982): 6. Locklin considers the reviewed collection a return to top form for Bukowski.

———. "Bukowski's *War All the Time* and *Horses Don't Bet on People and Neither Do I.*" *Review of Contemporary Fiction* 5.3 (Fall 1985): 34–36. A review of two Bukowski collections and comments on the poet's changing style during the 1980s.

———. "Setting Free the Buk." *Review of Contemporary Fiction* 5.3 (Fall 1985): 27–31. An essay of thoughts and fragments, most centrally about the unprecedented freedom that Bukowski has enjoyed in his writing and its importance.

———. *Charles Bukowski: A Sure Bet.* Sudbury, Mass.: Water Row Books, 1996. A slim but handy volume that collects bits and pieces that poet Gerald

Locklin wrote about his friend Bukowski, ranging from their first meeting in 1970 to the concluding essay, "The Funeral of Charles Bukowski." In addition to reprints of the reviews and essays cited in this manuscript, also collected are additional short reminiscences, reviews, and poems.

———. "In the Presence of Greatness: The Bukowski/*Barfly* Narrative." In *Charles Bukowski: A Sure Bet*. Sudbury, Mass.: Water Row Press, 1996. This 1989 essay, reprinted from Locklin's book *The Gold Coast*, is an account of his experience at the *Barfly* screening and subsequent party. Written in Locklin's easy, colloquial style, it serves as a different point of view from the comparable scenes related in *Hollywood*.

McDonough, Tom. "Down and (Far) Out." *American Film,* November 1987, 26–30. This magazine article, heavily illustrated with photographs, focuses on Bukowski and quotes him extensively regarding the circumstances and characters behind *Barfly*.

Mitchell, Roger. "Poetry." *Library Journal,* 15 February 1978, 465. A one-paragraph review of *Love Is a Dog from Hell*.

Moore, Toby. "Unreal City." *Times Literary Supplement,* 11–17 August 1989, 877. Moore contrasts the novels *Hollywood* and *Sister Hollywood* (by C. K. Stead) and writes favorably of both works.

Nesbitt, Lois E. "Fiction." *New York Times Book Review,* 25 November 1990, 19. A one-paragraph review of *Septuagenarian Stew*.

Norse, Harold. "To Know You Has Been Grace." *Small Press Review* (May 1973): 7–8. Norse reflects on his personal relationship with Bukowski, viewing the man critically but praising his work.

O'Brien, John, ed. *Review of Contemporary Fiction* 5.3 (Fall 1985): Charles Bukowski/Michel Butor Number. Contains 13 brief articles on Bukowski. The issue is indispensable for anyone interested in the critical/scholarly reception of Bukowski's fiction.

Oliver, Myrna. "Charles Bukowski Dies; Poet of L.A.'s Low-Life." *Los Angeles Times,* 10 March 1994: 1A+. This lengthy page-one obituary of Bukowski collects information and quotes from several sources.

Packard, William. "Notes on the Bukowski." *Small Press Review* (May 1973): 9–20. An early essay divided into 20 sections, with interesting comments concerning Bukowski's persona and the risky payoff of the "intuitive" style of Bukowski and Kenneth Patchen.

"Paperbacks: Fiction Originals." *Publishers Weekly,* 21 April 1989, 84. A single-paragraph review of *Hollywood*.

"Pen and Drink." *Sure, the Charles Bukowski Newsletter* 4 (1992): 22–32. Reprinted from the *Weekend Guardian,* 14–15 December 1991, this uncredited article is apparently based on an interview with Bukowski and quotes liberally regarding, among other subjects, *Pulp* and Bukowski's meeting of Raymond Carver.

Penn, Sean. "Tough Guys Write Poetry." *Interview,* September 1987, 94–100. A detailed interview conducted by actor Sean Penn, organizing

Bukowski's comments under thematic headings. Includes photographs and three reprinted poems.

"Penniless Poet to Laureate of Lowlife." *U.S. News and World Report,* 9 January 1989, 52. An article on the history and success of Black Sparrow Press with much of the credit given to Bukowski. Quotes from John Martin.

Peters, Robert. "Gab Poetry, or Duck vs. Nightingale Music: Charles Bukowski." In *Where the Bee Sucks: Workers, Drones and Queens of Contemporary American Poetry.* Santa Maria, Calif.: Asylum Arts, 1994. As the above titles suggest, Peters's collection of essays on contemporary American poets is irreverent, proudly subjective, and a guilty pleasure to read. His subjects—or targets—include both serious and popular poets, from John Ashbery to Leonard Nimoy. His essay on Bukowski quotes extensively and especially praises Bukowski's early poems.

Quagliano, Tony. "The Natural Shape of the Loner." *Small Press Review* (May 1973): 3–6. An introductory and laudatory essay on Bukowski, touching upon the author's use of idiomatic speech and his resistance to politics.

Ratner, Rochelle. "Poetry." *Library Journal,* 15 April 1992, 96. A single-paragraph review of *The Last Night of the Earth Poems.*

Rexroth, Kenneth. "There's Poetry in a Ragged Hitch-Hiker." *New York Times Book Review,* 5 July 1964, 5. In his review of new books of poetry by four authors, Rexroth devotes two of the four columns to Bukowski and a positive critique of *It Catches My Heart In Its Hands.*

Richmond, Steve. Untitled essay. *Second Coming* 2.3 (1974): 4–8. Gushing and sometimes obscure praise for Bukowski by his early disciple Richmond. An interesting piece to compare in tone to the much more qualified sentiment in Richmond's later *Spinning Off Bukowski.*

———. *Spinning Off Bukowski.* Northville, Mich.: Sun Dog Press, 1996. An eccentric but interesting portrait of Bukowski as he was beginning to acquire underground fame and notoriety as a poet. Richmond also explores his own ambivalent feelings about Bukowski's new relationships as he rose to success.

Ring, Kevin. "Charles Bukowski: Outsider Looking In." *Beat Scene* 20 (1994): 35–37. A 1990 interview with Bukowski reprinted from *Beat Scene* 11.

———. "Charles Bukowski: *Pulp.*" *Beat Scene* 20 (1994): 40. A sympathetic review of *Pulp* lodged among the bits and pieces of the *Beat Scene* Bukowski tribute issue.

Robbins, Doren. "Drinking Wine in the Slaughterhouse with Septuagenarian Stew: For Bukowski at 71." *ONTHEBUS* 4.2–5.1 (1992): 282–85. A brief but worthwhile article that quotes three poems, discusses what Robbins considers to be Bukowski's central themes, and notes the difficulty of placing him in the canon.

Rochlin, Margy. "Acting Out." *American Film,* November 1987, 30. A provocative interview with Mickey Rourke including the history of his involvement with *Barfly* and his thoughts on portraying Henry Chinaski. A companion article to Tom McDonough's "Down and (Far) Out" in the same issue.

Rungren, Lawrence. "Literature." *Library Journal,* 15 June 1990, 112–13. A single-paragraph review of *Septuagenarian Stew.*

Sandarg, Robert. "The Classical Buk." *Sure, the Charles Bukowski Newsletter* 3 (December 1991): 22–32. Sandarg compiles and organizes the frequent Bukowski references to classical music, noting the author's particular fondness for the nineteenth-century romantics.

Schwada, Jim. "Charles Bukowski's *Man the Humping Guns: The Roominghouse Madrigals.*" *Sure, the Charles Bukowski Newsletter* 7 (1993): 21–23. A positive review of Bukowski's collected early poems.

Sherman, Jory. *Bukowski: Friendship, Fame and Bestial Myth.* Augusta, Ga.: Blue Horse Publications, 1981. A slim, peculiar volume. Sherman traces his erratic relationship with Bukowski during the 1960s and 1970s. Includes letters from Bukowski and a few photographs.

Smith, Jules. "A Singular Self." *Times Literary Supplement,* 7 September 1990, 956. Smith praises *Septuagenarian Stew* and discusses, among other topics, Bukowski's use of narrative.

———. "Bad Times Again." *Times Literary Supplement,* 18 December 1992, 19. A perceptive review of *The Last Night of the Earth Poems* and Bukowski's death fixation in his late poems.

Smith, Julian. "Charles Bukowski and the Avant-Garde." *Review of Contemporary Fiction* 5.3 (Fall 1985): 56–59. Smith considers Bukowski's work as a comic and intentional rewriting of Hemingway and thereby identifies Bukowski as postmodern.

Stade, George. "Death Comes for the Detective." *New York Times Book Review,* 5 June 1994, 50–51. A lengthy, insightful, and sympathetic review of *Pulp.*

Travers, Pete. "Movie Reviews." *People,* 2 November 1987, 14. A review of *Barfly* that discusses in particular the strength of the screenplay.

Young, Elizabeth. "Bum Steered." *New Statesman and Society,* 17 June 1994, 37–38. A positive review of the anthology *Run with the Hunted: A Charles Bukowski Reader* and a brief mention of *Pulp.*

Weinstein, Norman. "*South of No North*: Bukowski in Deadly Ernest." *Review of Contemporary Fiction* 5.3 (Fall 1985): 52–55. Weinstein discusses Hemingway's presence, both stylistically and as a character, in Bukowski's collection of stories.

Wennersten, Robert. "Paying for Horses: An Interview with Charles Bukowski." *London Magazine,* December 1974–January 1975, 35–54. An excellent and in-depth interview covering a range of topics, conducted as Bukowski was beginning to gain wide recognition.

Winans, A. D. *The Charles Bukowski/Second Coming Years.* Warwickshire, England: Beat Scene Press, 1996. A roughly written reminiscence of Bukowski's 17-year relationship with Winans and Second Coming Press.

Special Issues

In most cases, individual reviews, brief essays, and memoirs contained in the issues below (for example, from *Sure, the Charles Bukowski Newsletter*) are not listed as individual entries in the secondary bibliography unless quoted in the text.

All's Normal Here: A Charles Bukowski Primer. Edited by Loss Pequeño Glazier. Fremont, Calif.: Ruddy Duck Press, 1985. This 100-page typescript issue, which constituted *Oro Madre* 4.1–4, is dedicated entirely to Bukowski and his admirers. Includes tribute essays, poems, and letters by others, and drawings and poems by Bukowski.

Atom Mind 4.14 (Summer 1994). Edited by Gregory Smith. Contains a 16-page appreciation of Bukowski, with tributes by Ana Christy, Steve Richmond, Ron Offen, A. D. Winans, and others, the most memorable being Harold Norse's bitter "Laughter in Hell: Charles Bukowski Is Dead."

Beat Scene 20 (1994). Edited by Kevin Ring. A special memorial issue of this British magazine, dedicated entirely to Bukowski. Includes short articles, tributes, reproduced letters, poems, and an interview.

A Bukowski Sampler. Edited by Douglas Blazek. East Haven, Conn.: Quixote Books, 1983. This special issue of *Quixote* (11.9) is, as its title indicates, made up almost entirely of reprinted poems. Contains a few brief prose excerpts, including Bukowski's essay "A Rambling Essay on Poetics and the Bleeding Life Written While Drinking a Six-Pack (Tall)." Also offers the introductory essay "St. Bukwoski" [*sic*] by Morris Edelson, and brief pieces by Blazek and William Wantling.

Charles Bukowski and Alpha Beat Press: 1988–1994. Edited by Ana Christy and Dave Christy. New Hope, Pa.: Alpha Beat Press, 1994. This inexpensively produced volume is a memorial tribute that reprints the Bukowski poems that appeared in *Alpha Beat Soup* and *Bouillabaisse*. Includes reproductions of some brief notes from Bukowski, a few eulogies, and three photographs of Bukowski by Ulvis Alberts.

Das ist Alles: Charles Bukowski Recollected. Edited by Joan Jobe Smith. Long Beach, Calif.: Pearl Editions, 1995. One of the most diverse of the many small-press tributes that have appeared since Bukowski's death. Ten poems by Bukowski that appeared in *Pearl* are reproduced, and photographs and Bukowski sketches dot the issue, but this edition is primarily a tribute in poetry, by Gerald Locklin, Ann Menebroker, Marvin Malone, Billy Collins, and many others.

The New Censorship. Edited by Ivan Suvanjieff. This monthly small-press review (in which Bukowski is listed as a contributing editor) produced three issues dedicated entirely to Bukowski poems and drawings: 2.3 (June 1991), 3.1 (April 1992), and 4.2 (May 1993).

New York Quarterly. Edited by William Packard. *NYQ* has been among Bukowski's most consistent and reliable sources of periodical publication, for years featuring several poems in each handsome issue. The admiration between author and journal was mutual.

ONTHEBUS. Edited by Jack Grapes. Grapes's thick Los Angeles–based literary review has in recent years extensively included various Bukowski items and special sections, including a series of 1962 letters from Bukowski to Jon Webb (6 and 7, 1990–1991), two selections of 1991 journal entries (10 and 11, 1992; 12, 1993), and many poems.

Second Coming 2.3 (1974). Edited by A. D. Winans. A special issue dedicated entirely to Charles Bukowski. Laudatory recollections and thoughts by Gerald Locklin, Hugh Fox, Linda King, Harold Norse, and others. Includes several Bukowski poems and the author's essay "He Beats His Women."

Small Press Review 4.4, no. 16 (May 1993). Edited by Tony Quagliano. A special issue devoted to Bukowski, with articles by Quagliano, Harold Norse, William Packard, Len Fulton, and others.

Sure, the Charles Bukowski Newsletter. Edited by Edward L. Smith. A small-press periodical fanzine founded in 1991 and now published annually from Ojai, California. The magazine includes reviews, brief articles, creative pastiches, photographs, and illustrations by Bukowski and others. Since the first 24-page issue in May 1991, the journal has grown in size and attractiveness. *Sure* #10, published in 1994, was 100 pages and perfect-bound. In addition to various pieces mourning Bukowski's death, it included essays such as "The Long Labor and Painful Birth of *Flower, Fist and Bestial Wail*," by David Barker, and "Bukowski and Celine," by Robert Sandarg.

Wormwood Review. Edited by Marvin Malone. From issue 7 (1962), until editor Marvin Malone's recent death, small-press publication *Wormwood Review* consistently published and supported Bukowski's poetry.

Index

The Author

Gay Brewer is a native of Louisville, Kentucky. He received a Ph.D. from Ohio State University in 1992 and is currently an assistant professor in the English Department at Middle Tennessee State University, where he edits *Poems & Plays*. His previous criticism includes *David Mamet and Film: Illusion/Disillusion in a Wounded Land* (McFarland, 1993), *Laughing like Hell: The Harrowing Satires of Jim Thompson* (Borgo, 1996), and articles in *Contemporary Literature*, *American Drama*, and *Literature/Film Quarterly*. His creative work includes the collection of poems *Presently a Beast* (Coreopsis, 1996) and more than 300 poems in literary journals. He has received writing fellowships at the Fundación Valparaíso (Spain) and Hawthornden Castle (Scotland).

The Editor

Frank Day is a professor of English and head of the English Department at Clemson University. He is the author of *Sir William Empson: An Annotated Bibliography* (1984) and *Arthur Koestler: A Guide to Research* (1985). He was a Fulbright lecturer in American literature in Romania (1980–1981) and in Bangladesh (1986–1987).